International Series in Operations Research & Management Science

Volume 342

The book series **International Series in Operations Research and Management Science** encompasses the various areas of operations research and management science. Both theoretical and applied books are included. It describes current advances anywhere in the world that are at the cutting edge of the field. The series is aimed especially at researchers, advanced graduate students, and sophisticated practitioners.

The series features three types of books:

- Advanced expository books that extend and unify our understanding of particular areas.
- Research monographs that make substantial contributions to knowledge.
- Handbooks that define the new state of the art in particular areas. Each handbook will be edited by a leading authority in the area who will organize a team of experts on various aspects of the topic to write individual chapters. A handbook may emphasize expository surveys or completely new advances (either research or applications) or a combination of both.

The series emphasizes the following four areas:

Mathematical Programming: Including linear programming, integer programming, nonlinear programming, interior point methods, game theory, network optimization models, combinatorics, equilibrium programming, complementarity theory, multiobjective optimization, dynamic programming, stochastic programming, complexity theory, etc.

Applied Probability: Including queuing theory, simulation, renewal theory, Brownian motion and diffusion processes, decision analysis, Markov decision processes, reliability theory, forecasting, other stochastic processes motivated by applications, etc.

Production and Operations Management: Including inventory theory, production scheduling, capacity planning, facility location, supply chain management, distribution systems, materials requirements planning, just-in-time systems, flexible manufacturing systems, design of production lines, logistical planning, strategic issues, etc.

Applications of Operations Research and Management Science: Including telecommunications, health care, capital budgeting and finance, economics, marketing, public policy, military operations research, humanitarian relief and disaster mitigation, service operations, transportation systems, etc.

This book series is indexed in Scopus.

Marcus Matthias Keupp
Editor

Cyberdefense

The Next Generation

Springer

Editor
Marcus Matthias Keupp
Department Head,
Department of Defense Economics
Military Academy at the Swiss Federal
Institute of Technology
Zurich, Switzerland

ISSN 0884-8289 ISSN 2214-7934 (electronic)
International Series in Operations Research & Management Science
ISBN 978-3-031-30190-2 ISBN 978-3-031-30191-9 (eBook)
https://doi.org/10.1007/978-3-031-30191-9

This Springer imprint is published by the registered company Springer Nature Switzerland AG
The registered company address is: Gewerbestrasse 11, 6330 Cham, Switzerland

Preface

Ignis aurum probat, miseria fortes viros.
—Seneca, De providentia, 5, 9

Those who must defend a computer network against cyber attacks certainly have no carefree life. Despite decades of investment in novel software and hardware solutions, countless consultancy studies and op-eds from management writers, attackers still have the advantage, and firms and government organizations regularly are victims of cyber attacks.

Economists remind them that productive processes should use resources effectively (to attain the desired goal) and efficiently (to prevent waste), but contemporary cyberdefense realizes none of these goals. If defence was effective, we should expect a declining incidence rate of cyber attacks—instead, both the number of attacks and the average damage they cause keep growing. And if defense was efficient, why would firms require management advice and procure hardware and software which may already be outdated at the time it is deployed? And how would they navigate a technology landscape that evolves faster than their bureaucratic budgeting processes?

Contemporary cyberdefense is too slow, it lacks foresight, and it is often ineffective. The authors in this volume present novel methods, models and interdisciplinary perspectives that I hope will help defenders to tackle these problems. Many authors have provided generally applicable models and code, so the analyses in this volume can be reproduced irrespective of particular contexts. While the book has strong foundations in operations research, applied mathematics and statistics, its viewpoint is deeply rooted in the economics of information security: Cyber defense is too important an issue to leave it to the technicians. The book therefore spans different domains in an attempt to create interdisciplinary expertise.

My sincere thanks go to Fabian Muhly, Sébastien Gillard, Valerie Gürmann and Philipp Fischer, all of whom helped to organize the publication process and to finalize the volume. I also thank my executive editors at Springer Nature, Christian Rauscher and Nikos Chtouris, who always supported the work and positioned it in the renowned

International Series in Operations Research and Management Science. In particular, I thank series editor Camille C. Price for all her support and encouragement.

I hope this book can inspire defenders as they build the next generation cyberdefense we so desperately need today. This task is heavy, so their future lives will not be easy either. But attacks cannot be thwarted unless those who are attacked stand their ground and strike back. And so the defenders may find solace in Seneca's immortal words: It is in adversity where the strong prove themselves.

Zurich, Switzerland
September 2023

Marcus Matthias Keupp

Contents

Editor and Contributors

About the Editor

Marcus Matthias Keupp is the editor of this volume. He chairs the Department of Defense Economics at the Military Academy of the Swiss Federal Institute of Technology (ETH) Zurich. He was educated at the University of Mannheim (Germany) and Warwick Business School (UK) and obtained his Ph.D. and habilitation from the University of St. Gallen (Switzerland). He has authored, co-authored, and edited twelve books and more than 30 peer-reviewed journal articles and received numerous awards for his academic achievements.

Contributors

Cédric Aeschlimann Department of Defense Economics, Military Academy at the Swiss Federal Institute of Technology Zurich, Birmensdorf
Switzerland;
Department of Defense Economics, Military Academy at ETH Zurich, Birmensdorf ZH, Switzerland

Chuadhry Mujeeb Ahmed Computer and Information Sciences Department, University of Strathclyde, Glasgow, UK

David Baschung D-MTEC, Swiss Federal Institute of Technology Zurich, Zurich, Switzerland

William Blonay Cyber-Defence Campus, armasuisse Science and Technology, Thun, Switzerland

Kilian Cuche Swiss Armed Forces Command Support Organization, Berne, Switzerland

Ljiljana Dolamic Cyber-Defence Campus, armasuisse Science and Technology, Thun, Switzerland

Philipp Fischer Department of Computer Science, Swiss Federal Institute of Technology Zurich, Zurich, Switzerland

Sébastien Gillard Department of Defense Economics, Military Academy at the Swiss Federal Institute of Technology Zurich, Zurich, Switzerland;
Department of Defense Economics, Military Academy at ETH Zurich, Birmensdorf ZH, Switzerland;
Information Science Institute, Geneva School of Economics and Management, University of Geneva, Geneva, Switzerland

Marcus M. Keupp Department of Defense Economics, Military Academy at the Swiss Federal Institute of Technology Zurich, Birmensdorf, Switzerland

Thomas Maillart Information Science Institute, Geneva School of Economics and Management, University of Geneva, Geneva, Switzerland

Loïc Maréchal Department of Information Systems, HEC lausanne, University of Lausanne, Lausanne, Switzerland

Aditya P. Mathur iTrust Center for Research in Cyber Security, Singapore University of Technology and Design, Singapore, Singapore

Alain Mermoud Cyber-Defence Campus, armasuisse Science and Technology, Thun, Switzerland

Jean-Claude Metzger Hemotune AG, Zurich, Switzerland

Anita Mezzetti Credit Suisse, Zurich, Switzerland;
Swiss Federal Institute of Technology Lausanne, Section of Financial Engineering, Lausanne, Switzerland

Santiago Anton Moreno Section of Applied Mathematics, Swiss Federal Institute of Technology Lausanne, Lausanne, Switzerland

Fabian Muhly Department of Defense Economics, Military Academy at the Swiss Federal Institute of Technology Zurich, Birmensdorf, Switzerland

Sara Pangrazzi Institute of International Law and Comparative Constitutional Law, University of Zurich, Zurich, Switzerland

Dimitri Percia David Institute of Entrepreneurship and Management, University of Applied Sciences Valais, Sierre, Switzerland

Siddhant Shrivastava iTrust Center for Research in Cyber Security, Singapore University of Technology and Design, Singapore, Singapore

KuiZhen Su Singapore University of Technology and Design, Singapore, Singapore

Michael Tsesmelis Cyber-Defence Campus, armasuisse Science and Technology, Thun, Switzerland

Jianying Zhou Singapore University of Technology and Design, Singapore, Singapore

Chapter 1
Introduction and Overview

Marcus M. Keupp

1.1 Next Generation Cyberdefense

Cyber attackers are intentionally violating one or more security objectives an organization has defined for its IT infrastructure or computer networks [31]. By doing so, they inflict significant costs on organizations, businesses, and individuals [7, 10, 15]. While global cybersecurity expenditure grew by 28% from 2015 to 2018, the average cost of cybercrime incidents increased by 73% within the same period [1, 39]. Ransom paid by private firms to hackers is at a historic height. The average cost per data breach for companies was 3.86 million US$ [18]. But cyberattacks also target government organizations and individuals with public exposure, so that state-sponsored hacks, cyber espionage, and cyber sabotage exhibit likewise growth rates [17, 27, 29]. The absolute amount of cyberattacks against private or public organizations has increased by 67% since 2014 and by 11% since 2018 [1]. Investments meant to produce cyberdefense seem to lag attacks, and their effectiveness appears to be limited.

Academic work has trouble finding answers to this problem. In fact, public and private organizations fail so regularly at defending their systems that this failure has become a research object of its own [12]. Over the past three decades, many contributions have proposed technical measures to counter cyberattacks (for an overview, see [38]). However, the success of such technology-based approaches to cyberdefense has been limited, not the least because they ignore the weakest link in the cyberdefense chain—human beings and their fallacies [2, 3, 7]. While numerous models for cyberdefense investment strategies have been developed (e.g., [13, 22, 33]), their significance in the real world is limited due to imperfect information, misaligned incentives, moral hazard, and subjective bias [3, 5, 30].

M. M. Keupp (✉)
Military Academy at the Swiss Federal Institute of Technology Zurich, Birmensdorf, Switzerland
e-mail: mkeupp@ethz.ch

M. M. Keupp (ed.), *Cyberdefense*, International Series in Operations
Research & Management Science 342,
https://doi.org/10.1007/978-3-031-30191-9_1

Why then, one might ask, are organizations so bad at pre-empting, detecting and defending cyberattacks? It appears that contemporary cyberdefense is too slow, lacks technological foresight, and often proves to be ineffective. This book is an attempt to provide answers and applicable analytical tools for all three problems.

1.2 Structure and Overview

1.2.1 Speed

Many cyberattacks are not only successful, but they also go unnoticed for a significant period of time. In 2019, it took companies an average of 230 days to identify security breaches induced by malicious attacks. The average lifecycle of a breach from identification to containment was 280 days [18]. Attackers still have the initiative—the technology landscape is large, and there are many backdoors and zero-day vulnerabilities that can be exploited. Even if all of them would be technologically known, pre-emptively defending all of them by an all-hazard approach may prove to be prohibitively expensive. It is true that many organizations use digital forensics to clarify what has happened once an attack has been finally neutralized, but they are in fact analyzing lost chess games when they do so—players may improve their skills by learning from past mistakes, but they still have to suffer the bitter taste of defeat. A more productive approach should focus on shortening the cyber kill chain as much as possible, and provide fast responses that deny attackers the ability to continue with their attack. Speed is certainly of the essence, so the contributions in the first part of this volume intend to assist defenders with this task.

In Chap. 2, *Gillard et al.* start out with an agent-based model. They investigate how autonomous agents improve their response patterns as they react instantly to exogenous attacks. Moreover, they highlight the role of cooperation and incentive alignment among defenders using a game-theoretic approach, and they show that cooperative defense is both fast and effective.

In industrial control systems, attacks constitute rare events in a stream of permissible commands, and although Pareto or Poisson distributions could be used to model this imbalance, the sheer rareness of exploits makes it hard to attain good accuracy. In Chap. 3, *Su et al.* propose an alternative path. They study how unsupervised clustering algorithms can respond fast to attacks against industrial control systems. They compare the performance of four different algorithms and discuss the implications of their findings for the security of cyber-physical systems.

Both chapters demonstrate how threats can be dynamically captured and dealt with. Note that none of them requires big data analytics, so they should be particularly interesting for operators of SCADA systems which have both security requirements that differ from those of commercial computer networks and low computational capabilities [31].

In Chap. 4, *Fischer and Gillard* discuss novel security information sharing platforms that have recently emerged as an alternative to ISACs. Using a hierarchical simulation model that is informed by real user data from such platforms, they discuss the trade-offs between the value of information units and the speed with which they are shared.

1.2.2 Foresight

As organizations face budget constraints, they must maximize the efficiency of any investment they make in cyber security processes, products, or services [33]. Prior research has produced quantitative models that propose to optimize such investment, and also many recommendations that instruct firms about how to invest in particular technologies or systems (e.g., [16, 34, 41]). However, these models are deeply rooted in microeconomic and behavioral assumptions that need not apply to actual investment problems. Firms must protect their systems today against future attacks. Therefore, investments often lag actual threats since vendors must first commercialize defense technology to market maturity, particularly so if the technology in question is only just emerging. The media report about attacks that have been discovered, but knowledge of past incidents is not necessarily a predictor for future threat vectors. Hence, firms must forecast technological trajectories and prioritize investments accordingly.

Just as contemporary economists attempt to replace static ex-ante predictions with 'nowcasting' (e.g., [4, 24]), firms must learn to preempt rather than react to technological developments if they want to neutralize the attacker's advantage. While traditional forecasting methods and big data analytics are costly in terms of resources and computing power, the contributions in the second half of this book offer parsimonious yet efficient solutions that work with open source data.

In Chap. 5, *Percia David et al.* propose a reproducible, automated, scalable, and free method for bibliometric analysis that requires little computing power and informs managers about the maturity and likely future development of technological domains. They also show how timelines of expert sentiment about these domains can be generated. They illustrate their approach with an analysis of the `arXiv` repository and suggest how even larger databases can inform investment decisions about future cybersecurity technologies.

In Chap. 6, *Mezzetti et al.* propose a novel recursive algorithm that analyzes publicly available data and ranks the relative influence that companies and technologies have in a technology landscape. The results provide investors with an optimal ranking of technologies and thus help them to make more informed decisions about companies and technologies.

In Chap. 7, *Tsesmelis et al.* develop a lean recommender system which predicts emerging technology by a sequential blend of machine learning and network analytics. They illustrate the capabilities of this system with a large-scale patent data analysis and discuss how it can help organizations make more informed decisions.

Since patent data are public and freely available, organizations can obtain objective advice at very little cost.

In Chap. 8, *Aeschlimann et al.* map the landscape of cyberdefense capabilities among public, private and academic organizations in Switzerland. They also study the extent to which these organizations exchange capabilities with each other, and they produce a map of their informal networks. The results suggest that the ecosystem under study is a scale-free network that hosts many but unevenly distributed capabilities. Further, inter-organizational cooperation is limited although opportunities to cooperate exist.

While this contribution focuses on the question of where cyberdefense capabilities are located right now, in the subsequent Chap. 9, *Moreno et al.* show how job offers can be analyzed to predict future capability requirements. Their link prediction approach features a parsimonious algorithm which crawls publicly available job offer databases and predicts which capabilities firms will require up to six months in the future. They compare the efficiency of this method across several unsupervised learning algorithms as well as against a supervised learning method.

1.2.3 Effectiveness

Any investment in cyberdefense is wasted unless it provides organizations with effective protection against attacks. However, all too often effectiveness is confused with ticking off boxes in bureaucratic checklists. Formal certifications and regulatory requirements certify the proper implementation of risk management processes, but not the existence of effective defense [8, 19, 35]). Moreover, 'stress tests' are often limited to penetration testing exercises [9, 36] or bug bounty programs [25]. Moreover, formal performance indicators often fail to capture the effectiveness of cyber defense systems first [14, 32]. The third part of the book therefore explores how organizations realize effective defense.

First, they need to understand how and why attackers act. Therefore, in Chap. 10, *Fischer et al.* discuss the selection problem attackers face when they attempt to exfiltrate information from a computer network: They must identify valuable information units among many irrelevant ones. The authors model such attacks as a repeated urn draw under different distributional patterns and use prospect theory to model risk aversion and overconfidence among attackers. Their findings are particularly relevant to 'silent' attacks and computer network exploitation operations which prefer to gather intelligence over blocking or damaging a system, and they propose a number of measures the defenders can take to thwart attacks.

However, human fallacies also exist among defenders. In Chap. 11, *Baschung et al.* discuss the extent to which there is a principal-agent problem between the individual career goals of corporate security officers and the effectiveness of their investment decisions. The authors develop a recursive model which simulates the complex relationships between investment dynamics, CSO reputation and inter-firm migration, and cyberdefense effectiveness. Using data from real cybersecurity breaches, they find that a positive (negative) dynamic should exist between high (low) CSO reputation and effective corporate protection.

In Chap. 12, *Muhly* discusses how serious gaming can confront defenders with their own overconfidence and thus improve their resilience to social engineering (which is still one of the major threat vectors by which attackers execute cyberattacks). He reports the results of a randomized experiment that modeled a phishing attack and investigates the extent to which serious gaming can be applied as an immunization treatment. The results suggest that participation in serious gaming reduces the probability to be victimized by social engineering attacks. Overconfident and indifferent users are more likely to fall for such attacks, whereas a more pessimistic stance is negatively associated with failure.

In Chap. 13, *Shrivastava and Mathur* propose how virtualized environments can help operators of industrial control systems to detect and respond to anomalies more effectively. However, they also note that effectiveness requires radical architectural adaptations and a departure from IT security models of the past. They argue how and why zero trust architectures and autonomous mechanisms can not only make industrial control systems safer, but also empower machines to respond faster and more accurately to threats and attacks. Ultimately, such developments may enable industrial plants to defend themselves in a fully automated way.

In Chap. 14, *Gillard and Aeschlimann* expand this path. They discuss automated and scalable procedures that can identify and recombine related indicators of compromise which decentral users provide. In particular, these methods allow system operators to identify incidents which may have been running unnoticed but in fact constitute the root of many other anomalies. The authors simulate these procedures and show how users can control them to generate more accurate threat information which increases the effectiveness of their cyberdefense activities.

In the final Chap. 15, *Pangrazzi and Muhly* remind organizations and governments alike that they need not wait for a global cyberdefense regime to emerge until they can effectively defend their systems. The norms that exist in international law today provide users with powerful tools that can contribute to a more effective national cyber defense as well as to international collaboration—provided nation-states master the transformation of these norms into national contexts. The authors highlight four areas where this transformation would yield productive results.

1.3 Outlook: From Defense to Counter-Attack

The era which left cyberdefense to the technicians is over. What Keupp [21] said about the architectural challenges of next generation critical infrastructures also applies to cyberdefense: Technical knowledge alone does not provide an effective defense. Efforts to systematically advance cyber risk management must draw on not only computer science but also fields such as behavioral studies, economics, law, and management science. In particular, interaction with legal scholars is key here [12, 36]. Without such collaboration, legislators will continue to develop reactive measures that run the risk of rapid obsolescence as newer technologies are more widely adopted, and technicians may fail to understand how international law provides them with institutions that can shape effective defense on a global scale. All in all, this volume firmly subscribes to these perspectives and reiterates earlier initiatives which have called for more interdisciplinary work (e.g., [11, 20, 37, 40]) and for the introduction of economic perspectives into IT security [3, 7].

But there is more to next generation cyberdefense than interdisciplinary cooperation. To date, defense is still seen from a passive perspective: With some desperation, defenders take attacks as a natural evil one has to live with and defended against in the best possible way. It is about time to forego this passive stance.

The next challenge is to push for attribution—defenders must begin to identify the technical and physical locations of attackers and hence master attribution, with an eventual view to neutralizing the technical infrastructure from which attacks are carried out. Again, this 'strike back capability' will require interdisciplinary skills: automated defense algorithms could be trained to not only defend, but also to detect where the attack is coming from, economic perspectives can help calculate if the attack is worth the cost of striking back, and legal perspectives can help judge if retaliation conforms to international law.

The Tallinn manuals have tried to develop a perspective in cyberspace that is akin to article 51 of the United Nations charter—a nation that is unlawfully attacked has not only the right to defend itself, but it can use all force necessary to neutralize the aggression, reestablish the status quo, and preserve the integrity of its territory and statehood. This perspective, long established in the international law of warfare and the fundament of the post-WWII peace order, should be expanded to the cyberspace. Defense is therefore not limited to responding to attacks—it can even include striking the aggressor's territory as long as a state of war exists. Once this principle is adapted for the cyberspace, there is no more need to simply tolerate attacks.

Finally, states or state-sponsored parties have begun to use offensive cyber operations to realize military or political goals. For example, `stuxnet` disabled Iranian centrifuges which were enriching uranium, probably the first offensive cyber operation in military history [23]. Russia tried to influence the 2016 U.S. presidential elections by cyber and information operations [28], and China has been using cyber intelligence activities to realize commercial advantages [26]. These attacks constitute a new level of aggression whose damage goes far beyond ordinary cybercrime. Next generation cyberdefense will have to deal with this increased intensity of violence in the cybersphere. Defenders will continue to lead a difficult life, but they have no alternative but to stand their ground in the face of adversity.

References

1. Accenture. (2019). *The cost of cybercrime: Ninth annual cost of cybercrime study*. Accenture Security with Ponemon Institute LLC, Traverse City MI: Research report.
2. Anderson, R. J. (2010). *Security engineering: A guide to building dependable distributed systems*. Wiley.
3. Anderson, R., & Moore, T. (2006). The economics of information security. *Science, 314*(5799), 610–613.
4. Barbaglia, L., Frattarolo, L., Onorante, L., Maria Pericoli, F., Ratto, M., & Tiozzo Pezzoli, L. (2022). Testing big data in a big crisis: Nowcasting under Covid-19. *International Journal of Forecasting*, forthcoming.
5. Baron, J., & Ritov, I. (2004). Omission bias, individual differences, and normality. *Organizational Behavior and Human Decision Processes, 94*(2), 74–85.
6. Beal, B. (2005). IT security: The product vendor landscape. *Network Security, 5*, 9–10.
7. Böhme, R. (2013). *The economics of information security and privacy*. Berlin, Heidelberg: Springer.
8. Böhme, R. (2012). Security audits revisited. In A. D. Keromytis (Ed.), *Financial cryptography and data security* (pp. 129–147). Berlin, Heidelberg: Springer.
9. Böhme, R., & Félegyházi, M. (2010). Optimal information security investment with penetration testing. In T. Alpcan, L. Buttyan, & J. S. Baras (Eds.), *Decision and game theory for security* (pp. 21–37). Berlin, Heidelberg: Springer.
10. Campbell, K., Gordon, L. A., Loeb, M. P., & Zhou, L. (2003). The economic cost of publicly announced information security breaches: Empirical evidence from the stock market. *Journal of Computer Security, 11*(3), 431–448.
11. Cresson Wood, C. (2004). Why information security is now multidisciplinary, multi-departmental, and multi-organizational in nature. *Computer Fraud & Security, 2004*(1), 16–17.
12. Falco, G., et al. (2019). Cyber risk research impeded by disciplinary barriers. *Science, 366*(6469), 1066–1069.
13. Gordon, L. A., Loeb, M. P., Lucyshyn, W., & Zhou, L. (2015). Externalities and the magnitude of cyber security underinvestment by private sector firms: A modification of the Gordon-Loeb model. *Journal of Information Security, 6*(1), 24–30.
14. Gordon, L. A., Loeb, M. P., & Sohail, T. (2010). Market value of voluntary disclosures concerning information security. *MIS Quarterly, 34*(3), 567–594.
15. Gordon, L. A., Loeb, M. P., Lucyshin, W., & Richardson, R. (2005). CSI/FBI computer crime and security survey. *Computer Security Journal, 21*(3), 1.
16. Herath, H., & Herath, T. (2008). Investments in information security: A real options perspective With Bayesian post-audit. *Journal of Management Information Systems, 25*(3), 337–375.
17. Hunter, L. Y., Albert, C. D., & Garrett, E. (2021). Factors that motivate state-sponsored cyberattacks. *The Cyber Defense Review, 6*(2), 111–128.
18. IBM. (2020). Cost of a data breach report. (2020). *IBM Security*. Armonk NY: IBM Corp.
19. Islam, M. S., Farah, N., & Stafford, T. F. (2018). Factors associated with security/cybersecurity audit by internal audit function: An international study. *Managerial Auditing Journal, 33*(4), 377–409.
20. Kam, H. J., Mattson, T., & Goel, S. (2020). A cross industry study of institutional pressures on organizational effort to raise information security awareness. *Information Systems Frontiers, 22*(5), 1241–1264.
21. Keupp, M. M. (2020). *The security of critical infrastructures* (pp. 1–14). Cham: Springer Nature.
22. Lelarge, M. (2012). Coordination in network security games: A monotone comparative statics approach. *IEEE Journal on Selected Areas in Communications, 30*(11), 2210–2219.
23. Lindsay, J. R. (2013). Stuxnet and the limits of cyber warfare. *Security Studies, 22*(3), 365–404.
24. Macias, P., Stelmasiak, D., & Szafranek, K. (2022). Nowcasting food inflation with a massive amount of online prices. *International Journal of Forecasting*, forthcoming.

25. Malladi, S., & Subramanian, H. C. (2020). Bug bounty programs for cybersecurity: Practices, issues, and recommendations. *IEEE Software, 37*(1), 31–39.
26. NCSC. (2018). Foreign economic espionage in cyberspace. U.S. National Counterintelligence and Security Center, Washington D.C.: Office of the Director of National Intelligence.
27. OECD. (2012). *Cybersecurity policy making at a turning point: Analysing a new generation of national cybersecurity strategies for the internet economy*. Paris: OECD Publishing.
28. Ohlin, J. D. (2016). Did Russian cyber interference in the 2016 election violate international law? *Texas Law Review, 95*, 1579.
29. Osawa, J. (2017). The escalation of state sponsored cyberattack and national cyber security affairs: Is strategic cyber deterrence the key to solving the problem? *Asia-Pacific Review, 24*(2), 113–131.
30. Patt, A., & Zeckhauser, R. (2000). Action bias and environmental decisions. *Journal of Risk and Uncertainty, 21*(1), 45–72.
31. Pliatsos, D., Sarigiannidis, S., Lagkas, T., & Sarigiannidis, A. (2020). A survey on SCADA systems: Secure protocols, incidents, threats and tactics. *IEEE Communications Surveys and Tutorials, 22*(3), 1942–1976.
32. Purser, S. A. (2004). Improving the ROI of the security management process. *Computers & Security, 23*(7), 542–546.
33. Schatz, D., & Bashroush, R. (2017). Economic valuation for information security investment: A systematic literature review. *Information Systems Frontiers, 19*(5), 1205–1228.
34. Shirtz, D., & Elovici, Y. (2011). Optimizing investment decisions in selecting information security remedies. *Information Management & Computer Security, 19*(2), 95–112.
35. Smith, T., Higgs, J., & Pinsker, R. (2019). Do auditors price breach risk in their audit fees? *Journal of Information Systems, 33*(2), 177–204.
36. Soomro, Z. A., Shah, M. H., & Ahmed, J. (2016). Information security management needs more holistic approach: A literature review. *International Journal of Information Management, 36*(2), 215–225.
37. Srivastava, S. K., Das, S., Udo, G. J., & Bagchi, K. (2020). Determinants of cybercrime originating within a nation: A cross-country study. *Journal of Global Information Technology Management, 23*(2), 112–137.
38. Tselios, C., Tsolis, G., & Athanatos, M., et al. (2020). A comprehensive technical survey of contemporary cybersecurity products and solutions. Springer lecture notes in computer scienceIn A. P. Fournaris (Ed.), *Computer security* (Vol. 11981, pp. 3–18). Cham: Springer International Publishing.
39. Wirth, A. (2019). Reviewing today's cyberthreat landscape. *Biomedical Instrumentation & Technology, 53*(3), 227–231.
40. Yeh, Q. J., & Chang, A. J. (2007). Threats and countermeasures for information system security: A cross-industry study. *Information & Management, 44*(5), 480–491.
41. Zhou, L., Loeb, M. P., Gordon, L. A., & Lucyshyn, W. (2018). Empirical evidence on the determinants of cybersecurity investments in private sector firms. *Journal of Information Security, 9*(2), 720–726.

Marcus M. Keupp is the editor of this volume. He chairs the Department of Defense Economics at the Military Academy of the Swiss Federal Institute of Technology (ETH) Zurich. He was educated at the University of Mannheim (Germany) and Warwick Business School (UK) and obtained his Ph.D. and habilitation from the University of St. Gallen (Switzerland). He has authored, co-authored, and edited twelve books and more than 30 peer-reviewed journal articles and received numerous awards for his academic achievements.

Part I
Speed

Chapter 2
Reducing Time to Response in Cyber Defense: An Agent-based Model

Sébastien Gillard, Thomas Maillart, and Marcus M. Keupp

2.1 Introduction

The speed and evolution of cybersecurity threats force organizations and governments to quickly respond and adapt in order to protect their networks and infrastructures. Still, defenders often fail to respond in due time [18, 20]. Attackers still have the initiative because it is hard, if not impossible, for any one system or human agent to entirely grasp the evolution of the complex adaptive system that is the cybersphere [28].

Many authors have highlighted the potential benefits of cooperation and collective approaches to cybersecurity, such as ISACs, CERTs, bug bounty programs, or security information sharing [7, 8, 10, 17, 24, 27]. However, these approaches are also fraught with problems, and the intended benefits of collaboration are often realized slowly or not at all [15, 22].

Using an agent-based model approach, we explore how and why defenders can cooperate swiftly and effectively to neutralize attacks. This model has its origins in biology; it can be thought of as a spatial discretization of the generalized

Supplementary Information The online version contains supplementary material available at https://doi.org/10.1007/978-3-031-30191-9_2.

S. Gillard (✉) · M. M. Keupp
Department of Defense Economics, Military Academy at the Swiss Federal Institute of Technology Zurich, Birmensdorf, Switzerland
e-mail: sebastien.gillard@vtg.admin.ch

M. M. Keupp
e-mail: mkeupp@ethz.ch

T. Maillart
Information Science Institute, Université de Genève, 40, Boulevard du Pont-d'Arve, 1211 Geneva 4, Switzerland
e-mail: thomas.maillart@unige.ch

M. M. Keupp (ed.), *Cyberdefense*, International Series in Operations Research & Management Science 342,
https://doi.org/10.1007/978-3-031-30191-9_2

Lotka-Volterra equations [5, 12, 25]. For example, agents A could be pathogens which attempt to infect cells, and agents B could be antibodies which attempt to neutralize them. We apply this thinking to a cyberdefense setting where agents A attack the cyberspace of an organization which its security agents B defend. In doing so, we follow pioneering work that has applied evolutionary game theory to cybersecurity contexts [3, 26]. Coupling this model with a game-theoretic approach and simulating the dynamics, we show that agents B can adapt to both neutralize the attack and resolve uncooperative behavior among themselves. Thus, they can thwart attacks not only effectively, but also faster than by acting in isolation.

2.2 Agent-based Model

2.2.1 Structure

We model the interaction of agents A and B and their evolution over time on a continuous square grid of side length L which excludes boundary effects by design [16, 19].[1] Table 2.1 provides an overview of the key parameters and their definition ranges.

There are $L \times L$ squares in the grid, each of which is designated by coordinates (i, j). Each square is either empty, occupied by one agent A, and/or by one agent B. Hence, if a square is occupied by an agent A, an attack against a particular element of the cybersphere is taking place. If a square is occupied by an agent B, defensive measures have been deployed to thwart or neutralize the attack against this element.

Initially, the grid is populated at random by a number N_A of agents A and a number N_B of agents B. Their respective initial locations are recorded by two matrices $\mathbf{G^A}$ with elements g_{ij}^A, and $\mathbf{G^B}$ with elements g_{ij}^B $\forall i, j \in [1, L]$. The densities $d_A = N_A/L^2$ and $d_B = N_B/L^2$ show how intensely the grid is populated by either agent. The damage that a focal agent A causes in the square it occupies is recorded in $\varepsilon_{ij} \geq 0$ $\forall i, j \in [1, L]$, and the matrix $\mathbf{E}$ collocates these individual damages. The damage per square is initialized uniformly with the location data of agents A, hence $\varepsilon_{ij} = g_{ij}^A$.

The dynamic interaction of agents A and B is analyzed by a sequential iteration of t rounds, in each of which a focal agent A is selected randomly among the N_A agents A in the grid, and its actions (if any) are recorded. Then, a focal agent B is selected randomly among the N_B agents B, and both its actions (if any) and the implications of this action for agents A (if any) are analyzed. Each particular agent evolves K times on average, and the evolution process is represented by a number of Monte

[1] Note that, for the purposes of illustration, we treat the term "grid" spatially here, but the grid should rather be thought of as a graphical abstraction of a cyberspace in which each square represents an element of this sphere that can be attacked. Hence, if a square is "occupied" by an agent A, the organization requires a particular defense capability to thwart or neutralize an attack directed against it.

Table 2.1 Key variables and parameters in our model

Variable or parameters	Range/defined in	Description
L	$\mathbb{N}_{\geq 0}$	Side length of the square grid
i, j	$[1, L]$	Location indices for squares in the grid
t	$\mathbb{N}_{\geq 0}$	Number of rounds in the simulation
k	$[0, N_{\mathrm{MCS}}]$	Number of Monte Carlo steps
$\mathbf{G^A} = (g_{ij}^{A})$	$(0, 1)(L \times L)$	Matrix of locations (g_{ij}^{A}) where agents A are present
$\mathbf{G^B} = (g_{ij}^{B})$	$(-1, 0, 1)(L \times L)$	Matrix of locations (g_{ij}^{B}) where agents B are present
d_A, d_B	$]0, 1[$	Initial density of agents A, B in the grid
N_A, N_B	$]0, L^2[$	Number of agents A, B in the grid
$\mathbf{E} = (\varepsilon_{ij})$	$\mathbb{R}_{\geq 0}^{L \times L}$	Matrix of damages ε_{ij} caused by agents A present in square (i,j)
η	$]0, 0.5]$	Growth rate of the damage ε_{ij}
Ω	$[0.5, 1[$	Minimum damage threshold for ε_{ij}; agent A is neutralized if underrun
m_x, m_y	$[-M, M]$	x- and y-coordinates of Moore neighborhood $(2M + 1)^2$ defined by Moore range M
$\mathcal{P}_R$	$]0, 0.5[$	Probability that an agent A replicates
$\mathcal{P}_M$	$]0, 0.5[$	Probability that an agent A migrates
$\mathcal{P}_N$	$[\frac{1}{8}, \frac{1}{168}]$	Probability that an agent A migrates to a site within the Moore neighborhood
C_L	$]0, 1[$	Share of agents B which initially cooperate
$\mathbf{\Lambda} = (\lambda_{ij})$	$\mathbb{R}_{\geq 0}^{L \times L}$	Matrix recording individual play payoffs λ_{ij}
$\mathbf{U} = (u_{ij})$	$\mathbb{R}_{\geq 0}^{L \times L}$	Matrix recording the payoffs including agent A damage attractiveness
$\mathcal{P}_W$	$]0, 1[$	Probability that agent B to moves to the closest possible site with equivalent payoff
$1 - \mathcal{P}_F$	$[0.5, 1[$	Probability that a focal agent B changes its strategy
δ	$\mathbb{R}_{\geq 0}$	Euclidean distance between two sites of the grid
ω	$]0, 0.5]$	Factor by which damage ε_{ij} is reduced once agent B moves into a location occupied by an agent A

Carlo steps k. After each round, the grid is updated. The simulation which displays and analyzes this setup and the subsequent dynamics was programmed in `C/C++`. Plots and visualizations were produced in `Python`.

2.2.2 *Dynamics of Agents A*

The locations of agents A are mapped in $\mathbf{G}^{\mathrm{A}}$ such that each element g_{ij}^{A} takes the value 1 if a square is occupied by an agent A, and 0 otherwise. At the beginning of each round t, a focal agent A has three options of how to proceed. First, with a probability of $\mathcal{P}_R \in]0, 0.5[$, it chooses to replicate, i.e., to increase the damage ε_{ij} caused in the square it occupies. Second, with a probability of $\mathcal{P}_M \in]0, 0.5[$, it chooses to migrate to another square and damages another element there (say, because in its current position, all opportunities to do damage have been exploited). Alternatively, with a probability of $1 - (\mathcal{P}_R + \mathcal{P}_M) \in]0, 1[$, it remains in the square it occupies and continues to do damage as in the round before. All three options are mutually exclusive, and any agent A can only choose one option per round.

If it takes no action, neither the damage caused nor the geographical position changes, so all values stored in the matrices $\mathbf{E}$ and $\mathbf{G}^{\mathrm{A}}$ are carried over unchanged into the next round. If it replicates, the location data remain unchanged (the focal agent A remains in the square it occupies), but the damage it causes in this square increases; in other words, the attack against a particular element in the system intensifies. As a result, in the next round the location data stored in matrix $\mathbf{G}^{\mathrm{A}}$ remain unchanged, whereas the elements in the matrix $\mathbf{E}$ are increased by a growth factor of η in the next round, hence $\varepsilon'_{ij} = (1 + \eta) \cdot \varepsilon_{ij}$.

We posit that any migration of an agent A is restricted to the Moore neighborhood since population diffusion requires energy and is therefore predetermined by spatial patterns [14]. Hence, a focal agent A can only migrate to a site within a $(2M + 1) \times (2M + 1)$ subgrid. Its x- and y-components $m_x, m_y \in [-M, M]$ therefore define the universe of migration possibilities, and since migration to any site in this neighborhood is equally probable, the probability of migrating to any one site is $\mathcal{P}_N = \frac{1}{(2M+1)^2-1}$.

After migration, the location matrix $\mathbf{G}^{\mathrm{A}}$ is updated. The entry for the previously occupied square is set to "empty," whereas the square the agent migrated to is set to "occupied," formally: $g_{ij} = 0$ and $g_{i+m_x, j+m_y} = 1$, where i and j are the original location coordinates, and $m_x \in [-2, -1, 0, +1, +2]$ and $m_y \in [-2, -1, 0, +1, +2]$ define the range of migration options in the Moore neighborhood for a Moore range of $M = 2$. In the damage matrix $\mathbf{E}$, a fraction of ε_{ij} is subtracted from the original location of the focal agent A and transferred to the site it migrates to. Figure 2.1 illustrates the options that agents A have. Hence, replication increases the depth of the attack—the focal agent A remains at its location but executes attacks more

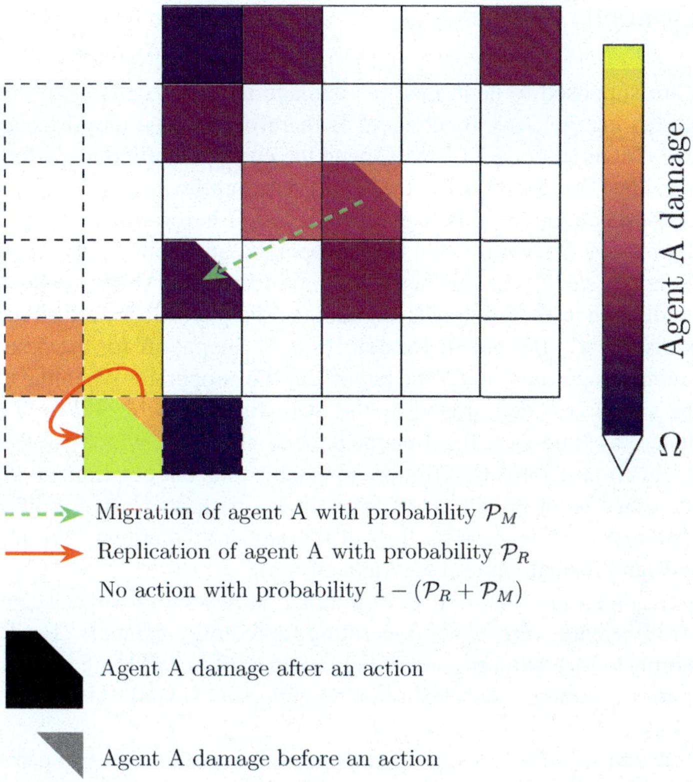

Fig. 2.1 Options for agents A in each round

intensely there—whereas migration increases its breadth: the focal agent A moves to a new location and begins a fresh attack there.[2]

We assume that any agent A can only remain active as long as a minimum damage level of $\Omega > 0$ is exceeded. Else, the agent A is considered neutralized; in this case, both its location entry g_{ij}^A in the matrix $\mathbf{G^A}$ and damage entry ε_{ij} in the matrix $\mathbf{E}$ are set to 0. This condition implies that migration is subject to the condition $\varepsilon'_{ij} \geq \Omega$, where ε'_{ij} is the fraction of the damage transferred to the new location. Else, a focal agent A that causes only little damage in its current location could theoretically self-destruct by migrating if the damage would exceed $(1 + \Omega)$.

[2] Note that, for the purposes of illustration, we treat the term "migration" spatially, but conceptually, migration means that the current attack mutates into a new type of attacks.

2.2.3 Dynamics of Agents B

Agents B are supposed to neutralize the damage agents A cause, but this counteraction requires energy. Any focal agent B therefore faces a moral hazard: It may simply hope that another agent B will spend the energy required for defense, so that it can remain idle. This incentive for free-riding is a significant problem in cooperative games. Although cooperation between any agents B is rewarded in game theory—both agents receive a reward when both cooperate, and both receive a punishment when both defect-each individual agent has an incentive to shirk a collective effort. More formally, when R (for "reward") denotes the payoff for mutual cooperation, P (for "punishment") the payoff for defection, T the payoff for the defector when the other agent cooperates, and S the payoff for the cooperator when the other agent defects, the situation is determined by the inequalities $T > R > P > S$ and $2R > T + S$. Hence, as long as a focal agent B does not know which strategy another agent B might choose, defection is more profitable than cooperation, no matter what strategy the other agent selects. Therefore, the cooperative Nash equilibrium is not reached although it offers superior payoff ("prisoner's Dilemma," see [1, 4, 9] for backgrounds and formal game-theoretic analysis).

Figure 2.2 illustrates a subset of all interaction possibilities that agents B have. The blue (red) squares represent cooperating (defecting) agents B. The focal agent B first attempts to find an empty site with better payoff in its Moore neighborhood. It then compares its strategy with that of its neighbors and changes it if a better payoff can be expected.

In each round t, we let a focal agent B play the cooperation game with its four adjacent neighbors in the locations $g^B_{i-1,j}, g^B_{i+1,j}, g^B_{i,j-1}$ and $g^B_{i,j+1}$. Initially, agents B are randomly assigned a status of either cooperator or defector. In the location matrix $\mathbf{G^B}$, entries take the value 0, 1 if a square is empty, 1 if the square is occupied and agent B cooperates, and -1 if the square is occupied and agent B defects. We assume that agents B attempt to maximize their payoff in each round t [6]. We introduce a parameter of $C_L > 0$ that measures the share of cooperating agents B, hence the remainder $(1 - C_L)$ captures the share of those which defect.

The payoff is defined by the available locations in the Moore neighborhood the focal agent B can reach when it plays the cooperation game with its neighbors. After each round t, the payoffs realized from playing are stored in the matrix $\mathbf{\Lambda}$ with elements λ_{ij}. Further, after each round, a focal agent B can adapt its playing strategy ("cooperate" or "defect"). Following [11], we posit that in any subsequent round, a focal agent B will imitate strategies which provide higher payoffs with a probability of $\mathcal{P}_F$ (Fermi rule).

Since agents B are payoff maximizers, they consider the matrix $\mathbf{\Lambda}$ after each round t and ask themselves how they might be better off beyond changing their playing strategies. Since noncooperating behavior can be overcome by migration [13, 21], a focal agent B can migrate to a square with higher payoffs if the square it is currently in provides only a low payoff (e.g., because its playing partners repeatedly defect).

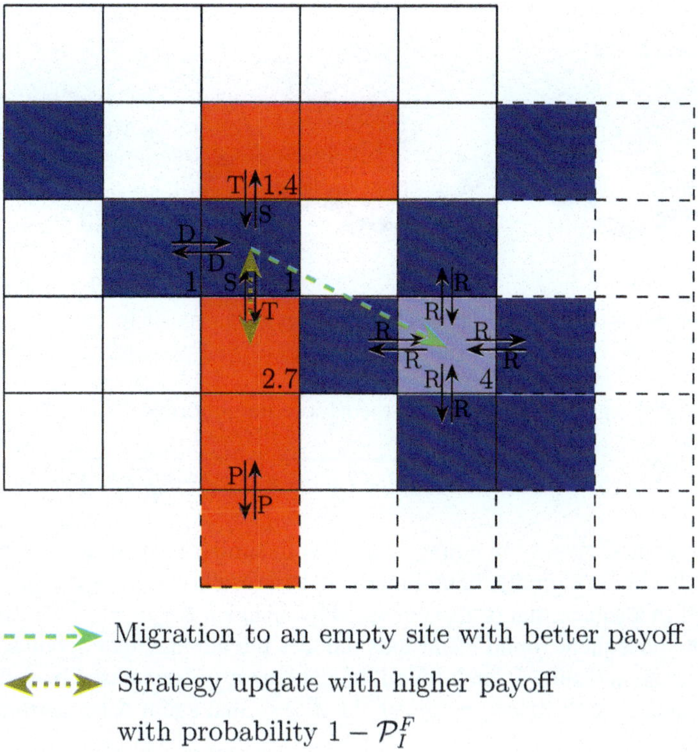

Fig. 2.2 Illustration of interaction among agents B

A focal agent B can therefore be expected to migrate if the payoff in another square is higher.

In addition, this payoff is also influenced by the damage the agents A cause. Since agents B are supposed to defend the system, they can expect to reap rewards for effective defense (e.g., bonuses, promotions, or status if they are human agents, or learning opportunities if they are machines), so the payoff increases with the level of damage they can neutralize. We double-count the rewards from this effect, so that the final payoff matrix that determines migration patterns is **U** with elements $u_{ij} = \lambda_{ij} \cdot 2\varepsilon_{ij}$. Since our model sets $\Omega \geq 0.5$, we always have $2\varepsilon_{ij} \geq 1$, so that weak agents A in any one site cannot decrease payoffs by which agents B are attracted.

Once it knows the final payoff matrix **U**, a focal agent B migrates according to a pre-set order. If the payoff of all empty squares is less than that of the current square, agent B does not migrate. If the payoff of an empty square within the Moore neighborhood is higher than the payoff of the square agent B is currently in, agent B moves to the closest of such squares. If payoffs between its current and empty squares are similar, agent B moves with a probability $\mathcal{P}_W$ to the closest empty square. Closeness is measured by the Euclidian distance $\delta_{0,m_{x,y}}$ which gives the spatial distance between

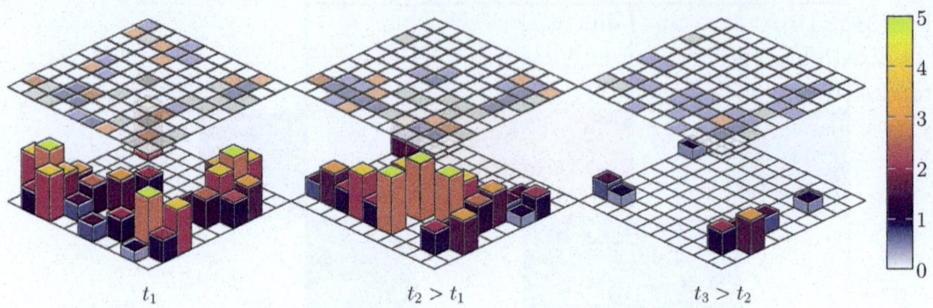

Fig. 2.3 Snapshots of interaction at three discrete times t

the center of the grid and a square in the Moore neighborhood:

$$\delta_{0,m_{x,y}} = \sqrt{(m_x - m_{x=0})^2 + (m_y - m_{y=0})^2} = \sqrt{{m_x}^2 + {m_y}^2} \qquad (2.1)$$

If the distances to several empty squares with similar payoffs are identical, agent B randomly chooses among them. Finally, if, as a result of this migration, an agent B finds itself in a square that is also occupied by an agent A ($g_{ij}^A = g_{ij}^B$), it fights agent A in each subsequent round t and thus reduces the damage that agent A causes in this square. As a result, in each round the damage ε_{ij} is decreased by a factor of ω until the damage falls below the threshold of Ω so that agent A is neutralized.

2.2.4 *Worked Example*

Figure 2.3 provides a snapshot of a small-scale demonstrator we built to illustrate our agent-based model. It depicts the state of the interaction at three discrete time steps t_1, t_2 and t_3 with $t_3 > t_2 > t_1$. In the grid of side length $L = 10$, there are $L \times L = 100$ squares. The locations of agents A are shown in the lower layer, and the damage these agents cause is shown in the third dimension. The colored legend on the right indicates the size of the damage. The upper layer shows agents B; cooperating (defecting) agents are marked in blue (red).[3]

Initially, this grid is populated at random by 25 agents A who cause an initial damage of $\varepsilon_{ij} = 1$ in the squares they occupy. There are also 25 randomly distributed agents B, of which 13 have initially chosen to cooperate while 12 have chosen to initially defect. Hence, the initial densities are $d_A = d_B = 0.25$. The initial damage ε_{ij} that each agent A causes is set to 1.

After multiple Monte Carlo steps, the situation at time step t_1 occurs. At this time, agents A have intensively migrated and replicated and cause much damage, whereas agents B are still not very cooperative (as indicated by the high share of defectors

[3] The code for this worked example is available on request from the corresponding author.

marked in red). At the same time, the damage now caused by agents A provides agents B with high potential payoffs, so that they have an incentive to cooperate and migrate. At time step t_2, agents B have migrated and show a more cooperative pattern. They have also begun to reduce the damage agents A cause, and some agents A have been neutralized, as the empty squares in the lower layer which were occupied at time step t_1 show. Finally, at time step t_3, cooperative behavior among agents B is now very widespread, and almost all agents A have been neutralized.

2.3 Illustration

To illustrate the model dynamics, we simulated the evolution of a grid with $L \times L = 50 \times 50 = 2,500$ squares randomly populated by $N_A = 625$ agents A and $N_B = 625$ agents B, so the initial densities are $d_A = d_B = 0.25$. The initial damage that agents A cause in the squares they occupy is set to $\varepsilon_{ij} = 1$, so the total initial damage is $\sum_{\varepsilon_{ij}>0} \cdot \varepsilon_{ij} = d_A \cdot L^2 = 625$.

The simulation is run over 250,000 Monte Carlo time steps (2,500 rounds during each of which each agent A and B receive 100 updates respectively). We set the Moore ranges for agents A and B as $M_A = M_B = 2$, so the Moore neighborhoods are given by the subgrids of $(2M_A + 1)^2 = 2(M_B + 1)^2 = 25$ in the center of which the focal agent resides. Hence, each agent has 24 squares to migrate to, and so the probability it moves to any of these is $\mathcal{P}_N = \frac{1}{24}$.

If a focal agent A migrates, the damage in its original square is reduced by 1, and a fraction of the damage it causes is transferred to the new location, so $\varepsilon'_{ij} = \varepsilon_{ij} - 1$ and $\varepsilon'_{i+m_x,j+m_y} = \varepsilon_{i+m_x,j+m_y} + 1$, for $m_x, m_y \in [-2, -1, 0, 1, 2]$. However, migration is subject to the condition $\varepsilon_{ij} \geq 1 + \Omega$, and we set the threshold below which any agent A is considered neutralized at $\Omega = 0.9$.

We let a focal agent A replicate with (varying) probability $\mathcal{P}_R = \{0.2, 0.3, 0.5\}$, migrate with (fixed) probability $\mathcal{P}_M = 0.2$ and remain in its location with a probability of $1 - (\mathcal{P}_R + \mathcal{P}_M)$. If it replicates in its current location, the damage it causes there grows at the rate of $\eta = \{0.1, 0.2, 0.3\}$.

We set the initial inclination to cooperate among the agents B at $C_L = 0.5$, so that at the start of the simulation, a number of $C_L \cdot N_B \approx 313$ agents B cooperate, while the remaining $(1 - C_L) \cdot N_B \approx 312$ agents B defect. We set the payoffs for the cooperation game the agents B play among themselves at $R = 1$, $P = 0.1$, $T = 1.3$, and $S = 0$. Any agent B can migrate within its Moore neighborhood with probability $\mathcal{P}_W = 0.5$ if any empty square has the highest payoff in this neighborhood, or if any empty square has a higher or equivalent payoff than the square the focal agent B is currently located at, else, it remains in its original square. After each decision to (not) migrate, it plays the cooperation game again, but chooses the inverse to the strategy played before. If the payoff it obtains now is higher, it changes its strategy with a probability $\mathcal{P}_F \approx 1$ (Fermi rule).

Once an agent B migrates to a field that is occupied by an agent A, the damage this agent A causes is reduced by $\omega = \{0.1, 0.2, 0.5\}$, so the remaining damage is

$\varepsilon'_{ij} = \varepsilon_{ij} \cdot \omega$, and once the condition $\varepsilon'_{ij} < \Omega$ holds, agent A is considered neutralized and the square is set to empty again.

Since the complete grid is too complex for a single plot, we illustrate the results in a subgrid of side length $L = 20$ as shown in Fig. 2.4. The left-hand side panels A, C, and E show the initial situation at the beginning of the simulation, and panels B, D, and F show the final situation after 250,000 Monte Carlo steps. Note that in each of the panels, the right-hand bar is in log-scale. It documents the maximum damage found during the simulation.[4]

Panels A and B depict the development of the attack if agents B sit idly and do not defend. In this case, agents A quickly migrate and replicate until they fill the complete grid. At this stage, attackers would completely control a real cybersphere. Panels C and D show the development once agents B react. Both the number and the spatial movement of the attackers as well as the damage they cause are reduced quickly. Panels E and F show how the behavior of the defenders evolves. Whereas at the beginning of the simulation, cooperative (blue) and uncooperative (red) defenders equally populate the subgrid, by the end of the simulation, cooperative behavior clearly prevails.

Figure 2.4 provides the steady states at the beginning and the end of the simulation, but it does not analyze the evolution between these states. We therefore computed, at each time step, the matrix $\mathbf{E}$ which records the damage caused by the agents A. Thus, we obtained a timeline of how the damage developed. At the end of the simulation, we normalized the results with the maximum damage $\max_t(\sum_i \sum_j \varepsilon_{ij})$ to obtain $\varepsilon\% = \frac{\sum_i \sum_j \varepsilon_{ij}}{\max_t(\sum_i \sum_j \varepsilon_{ij})}$. Panel A in Fig. 2.5 plots these values by time step.

Further, we computed, at each time step, the matrix $\mathbf{G^B}$ which stores the information about the location of all agents B. We then computed the extent to which agents B are inclined to cooperate during each time step, $C_L = \frac{\sum_i \sum_j \mathbb{1}_{\{g^B_{ij}=1\}}}{N_B}$, where $\mathbf{1}_{\{g^B_{ij}=1\}}$ is the indicator function which takes the value 1 if $g^B_{ij} = 1$ and 0 otherwise. Panel B in Fig. 2.5 plots these values by time step.

The comparison of both panels over time suggests that the growth of the damage that agents A cause initially attracts individual agents B which do neutralize some of the damage, but they do not necessarily cooperate with other agents B. As a result, the damage is reduced, but not eradicated, and the attack continues. Only once it reaches a much stronger growth level, more and more agents B begin to change their behavior and cooperate to neutralize the attack. While this relation is a first indication that cooperative behavior does not only neutralize an attack, but also speeds up the defense, more evidence is required to corroborate this claim.

Given that the matrix $\mathbf{E}$ records all damages per square and agent, and given we calculated this matrix per time step, we can pinpoint the beginning of an attack to the very time step t during which any one element $\varepsilon_{ij} = 0$ is altered to $\varepsilon'_{ij} = 1$ (which indicates that an agent A has newly occupied a particular square). As long as the inequality $\varepsilon_{ij} \geq \Omega$ holds, this agent continues to do damage until the time step t' when the condition $\varepsilon_{ij} = 0$ applies again. We therefore set the difference $\Delta_\varepsilon = t' - t$

[4] The full set of results is available on request from the corresponding author.

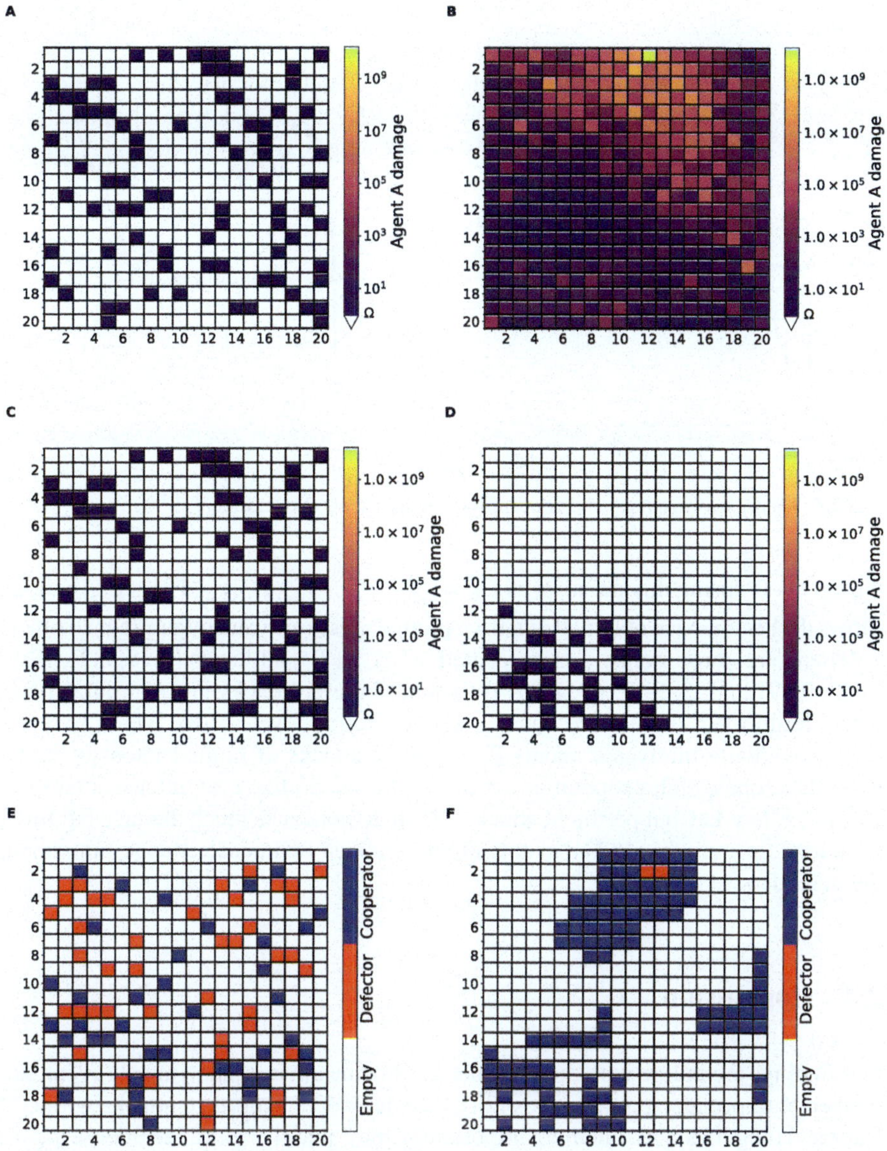

Fig. 2.4 Simulation results for a 20 × 20 subgrid

as the duration of the attack. Further, we define the average cooperation level among

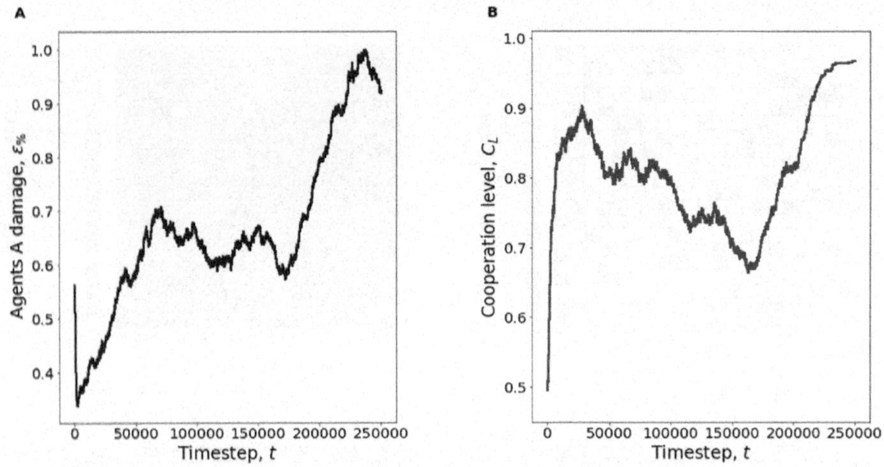

Fig. 2.5 Damage by agents A and cooperation among agents B over time

the agents B during this duration as $\overline{C_L} = \frac{1}{t'-t} \cdot \frac{1}{N_B} \cdot \sum_t^{t'} \sum_i \sum_j \mathbf{1}_{\{g_{ij}^B=1\}}$. Figure 2.6 shows the heatmap we obtained when we plotted these two values against each other.[5]

There are three dense zones located at $\Delta_\varepsilon = 0$ and $\overline{C_L} \in [0.18, 0.2]$, $\overline{C_L} \in [0.43, 0.59]$ and $\overline{C_L} \in [0.63, 1.00]$. In each of these, attacks are neutralized fast. In the leftmost of these three zones, the cooperation level is low, which indicates that individually motivated agents B neutralize attacks of limited intensity. In the two other zones, high cooperation levels quickly neutralize even intense attacks. In particular, low-key but pertinent attacks which do not cause much damage but linger for a long time are fought and eventually neutralized by intense cooperation among the defenders.

2.4 Conclusion

Our findings are in line with the idea that in a hostile environment, agents eventually cooperate to produce public goods [23]. The defenders neutralize attacks with both short and long lifespans, but more importantly, they quickly neutralize intense attacks when they collaborate. Our results therefore confirm the finding that in cooperative games supposed to produce a public good or collaborative result, self-interested agents who want to maximize their individual payoffs may produce beneficial macro-properties of the entire system [2].

In particular, our model emphasizes the role of migration as a mechanism that can overcome uncooperative behavior. Defenders who are frustrated by a lack of

[5] In order to add contrast to the map, we subdivided the area provided by the simulation data into smaller zones and transformed the density of each zone to logarithmic values.

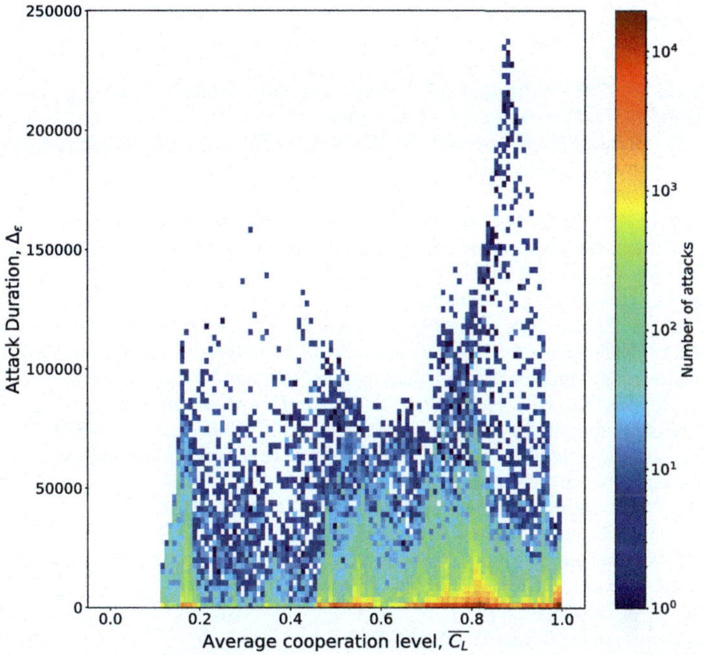

Fig. 2.6 Speed of defense by cooperation level

cooperation among themselves may simply migrate to other locations. Thus, the defectors remain among themselves and realize little payoff, whereas the defenders can jointly organize a defense which is both effective and fast. Therefore, defenders who are interested in maximizing their individual payoffs need not abide by an uncooperative climate. When many defenders migrate in this way, a self-organizing system emerges. We therefore believe that models which were originally conceived to analyze complex adaptation processes in nature can be productively applied to cyberdefense, and we suggest that such interdisciplinary perspectives enrich the technical discussion about cyberdefense.

Still, the model could be extended in a number of ways. First, it assumes that the defenders know about the locations the attackers have occupied. This assumption need not apply in more complex settings where defenders do not or not yet know about the full extent and nature of the attack. Future research may introduce a delay or information asymmetry factor that captures deferred responses or migration patterns. Second, we assume that $\omega > 0$, i.e., we posit that the defenders are actually capable to at least partially neutralize the damage the attackers cause. However, just like bacteria can be immune to certain antibiotics, some attackers may be technologically advanced to a degree where the technological capabilities of the defenders are insufficient to reduce the damage. Future research should therefore introduce an immunity factor by which superior attack skills or inferior neutralization capabilities could be captured.

References

1. Andreoni, J. (1988). Why free ride?: Strategies and learning in public goods experiments. *Journal of Public Economics, 37*(3), 291–304.
2. Behar, H., Brenner, N., & Louzoun, Y. (2014). Coexistence of productive and non-productive populations by fluctuation-driven spatio-temporal patterns. *Theoretical Population Biology, 96*, 20–29.
3. Boudko, S., & Abie, H. (2018). An evolutionary game for integrity attacks and defences for advanced metering infrastructure. In *Proceedings of the 12th European Conference on Software Architecture: Companion Proceedings*, pp. 1–7.
4. Brandt, H., Hauert, C., & Sigmund, K. (2003). Punishment and reputation in spatial public goods games. *Proceedings of the Royal Society B, 270*(1519), 1099–1104.
5. Brigatti, E., Núñez-López, M., & Oliva, M. (2011). Analysis of a spatial Lotka-Volterra model with a finite range predator-prey interaction. *The European Physical Journal B, 81*(3), 321–326.
6. Burton-Chellew, M., Nax, H., & West, S. (2015). Payoff-based learning explains the decline in cooperation in public goods games. *Proceedings of the Royal Society B, 282*, 20142678.
7. ENISA. (2010). *Incentives and Barriers to Information Sharing*. Heraklion: European Union Agency for Network and Information Security.
8. ENISA. (2017). *Information Sharing and Analysis Centres (ISACs) Cooperative models*. Heraklion: European Union Agency For Network and Information Security.
9. Fehr, E., & Gächter, S. (2000). Cooperation and punishment in public goods experiments. *American Economic Review, 90*(4), 980–994.
10. Gal-Or, E., & Ghose, A. (2005). The economic incentives for sharing security information. *Information Systems Research, 16*, 186–208.
11. Grujić, J., Röhl, T., Semmann, D., Milinski, M., & Traulsen, A. (2012). Consistent strategy updating in spatial and non-spatial behavioral experiments does not promote cooperation in social networks. *PLOS One, 7*(11), e47718.
12. Helbing, D. (2012). *Social self-organization*. Berlin, Heidelberg: Springer.
13. Helbing, D., & Yu, W. (2008). Migration as a mechanism to promote cooperation. *Advances in Complex Systems, 11*(4), 641–652.
14. Huang, T., Zhang, H., Hu, Z., Pan, G., Ma, S., Zhang, X., & Gao, Z. (2019). Predator-prey pattern formation driven by population diffusion based on Moore neighborhood structure. *Advances in Difference Equations, 2019*, 399.
15. Laube, S., & Böhme, R. (2017). Strategic aspects of cyber risk information sharing. *ACM Computing Surveys, 50*(5), article no 77.
16. Louzoun, Y. (2003). Proliferation and competition in discrete biological systems. *Bulletin of Mathematical Biology, 3*, 375–396.
17. Maillart, T., Zhao, M., Grossklags, J., & Chuang, J. (2017). Given enough eyeballs, all bugs are shallow? Revisiting Eric Raymond with bug bounty programs. *Journal of Cybersecurity, 3*(2), 81–90.
18. Maillart, T., Sornette, D., Frei, S., Duebendorfer, T., & Saichev, A. (2011). Quantification of deviations from rationality with heavy-tails in human dynamics. *Physical Review E, 83*, 056101.
19. Malcai, O., Biham, O., Richmond, P., & Solomon, S. (2002). Theoretical analysis and simulations of the generalized Lotka-Volterra model. *Physical Review E, 66*, 031102.
20. Meier, R., Scherrer, C., Gugelmann, D., Lenders, V., & Vanbever, L. (2018). FeedRank: A tamper-resistant method for the ranking of cyber threat intelligence feeds. In *10th International Conference on Cyber Conflict(CyCon)*, pp. 321–344.
21. Meloni, S., Buscarino, A., Fortuna, L., Frasca, M., Gómez-Gardeñes, J., Latora, V., & Moreno, Y. (2009). Effects of mobility in a population of prisoner's dilemma players. *Physical Review E, 79*, 067101.
22. Mermoud, A., Keupp, M. M., Huguenin, K., Palmié, M., & Percia David, D. (2019). To share or not to share: A behavioral perspective on human participation in security information sharing. *Journal of Cybersecurity, 5*(1), tyz006.

23. Ostrom, E. (1990). *Governing the commons*. Cambridge University Press.
24. Safa, N., & Von Solms, R. (2016). An information security knowledge sharing model in organizations. *Computers in Human Behavior, 57*, 442–451.
25. Solomon, S. (1999). Generalized Lotka-Volterra (GLV) models and generic emergence of scaling laws in stock markets. arXiv:cond-mat/9901250.
26. Tosh, D., Sengupta, S., Kamhoua, C., Kwiat, K., & Martin, A. (2015). An evolutionary game-theoretic framework for cyber-threat information sharing. *IEEE International Conference on Communications (ICC), 2015*, 7341–7346.
27. Wagner C, Dulaunoy A, Wagener G, Iklody A (2016) MISP - The design and implementation of a collaborative threat intelligence sharing platform. In *Proceedings of the 2016 ACM Workshop on Information Sharing and Collaborative Security*, pp. 49–56.
28. Yang, X.-S., & He, X.-S. (2020). *Nature-inspired computation in data mining and machine learning*. Cham: Springer Nature.

Sébastien Gillard received an M.Sc. in Physics from the University of Fribourg (Switzerland) in 2016. He specializes in computational physics and statistics, in particular, data analysis and applied statistical modeling and analytical and numerical resolution methods for differential equations. His current research interest is the application of insights from recommender systems to critical infrastructure defense, including the development of code that can power deep learning algorithms.

Thomas Maillart holds a Master degree from the Swiss Federal Institute of Technology (EPFL) Lausanne (2005) and a Ph.D. from the Swiss Federal Institute of Technology (ETH) Zurich (2011). He received the 2012 Zurich Dissertation Prize for his pioneering work on cyber risks. Before joining the University of Geneva, he worked as a researcher at the Center for Law and Economics at ETH and as a post-doctoral researcher at the University of California at Berkeley. His research focuses on modeling and improving human collective intelligence, particularly in a context of a fast-expanding cyberspace.

Marcus M. Keupp is the editor of this volume. He chairs the Department of Defense Economics at the Military Academy of the Swiss Federal Institute of Technology (ETH) Zurich. He was educated at the University of Mannheim (Germany) and Warwick Business School (UK) and obtained his Ph.D. and habilitation from the University of St. Gallen (Switzerland). He has authored, co-authored, and edited twelve books and more than 30 peer-reviewed journal articles and received numerous awards for his academic achievements.

Chapter 3
Unsupervised Attack Isolation in Cyber-physical Systems: A Competitive Test of Clustering Algorithms

KuiZhen Su, Chuadhry Mujeeb Ahmed, and Jianying Zhou

3.1 The Attack Isolation Problem

In complex critical infrastructures such as water distribution or power-generating systems, input devices (sensors) convey information about physical parameters to output devices (actuators) which physically act upon this information [10].

When operators note a cyberattack, they must clarify whether a properly working actuator acts on spoofed sensor data, or whether sensor data are correct but the actuator itself is under attack. Additionally, a spoofed sensor may signal to the operator that the actuator is working normally when in fact it is under attack. A related problem is false alarms—the system can mislead operators into believing a sensor or actuator has been tampered with when in fact the system is operating normally. If operators are deceived by spoofed senor data and manually override an actuator they believe has been attacked when in fact it is operating normally, they may unintendedly contribute to the attack by this intervention.

Since both sensors and actuators are physically linked and generate live time series of status and flow data, the problem of fast attack isolation is key to noting and terminating cyberattacks in critical infrastructures. In the absence of a fast and precise classification that separates sensor and actuator data into two classes and judges which is under attack, operators cannot figure out where an attack actually takes place unless they perform manual inspections.

K. Su (✉) · J. Zhou
Singapore University of Technology and Design, Singapore, Singapore
e-mail: kuizhen_su@alumni.sutd.edu.sg

J. Zhou
e-mail: jianying_zhou@sutd.edu.sg

C. M. Ahmed
Computer and Information Sciences Department, University of Strathclyde, Glasgow, UK
e-mail: chuadhry@alumni.sutd.edu.sg

M. M. Keupp (ed.), *Cyberdefense*, International Series in Operations Research & Management Science 342,
https://doi.org/10.1007/978-3-031-30191-9_3

This attack isolation problem is key to the security of industrial control systems [21]. While prior research has explored options to automate anomaly detection methods (e.g., [12, 19]), and others have proposed methods to fuse or triangulate data sources to reduce false alarm rates (e.g., [3, 6]), supervised and semi-supervised machine learning methods still have two major disadvantages: Training results depend on subjective human labeling, and they are costly in terms of computation time. And while many machine learning methods can alarm operators that the system is attacked somewhere, they cannot identify the precise source of the anomaly [3].

Our approach therefore focuses on unsupervised methods since these can contribute to building anomaly detectors for industrial control systems [11]. While past research on unsupervised methods has focused on neural networks (e.g., [15, 16]), we explore the extent to which cluster analysis can yield accurate results which are cheap in terms of computation time. Clustering is one of the most popular unsupervised data mining methods. For a technical introduction into clustering algorithms for time series and their evaluation, see [5, 8, 13]. In particular, we want to explore methods that can treat attacks on sensors and actuators data simultaneously and correctly classify alarms according to whether there truly is an attack and which element of the system is targeted. Such perspectives are highly desirable since they have received relatively little attention. For example, [21] show how to isolate attacks but focus only on actuators.

Our approach draws on previous seminal work in time series analysis [1, 2], dataset construction [8] and clustering algorithms and computing [7, 18, 20]. We let four algorithms developed by this research, 1-nearest neighbors (1-NN), k-Means, k-Shape, and two-time clustering (TTC), compete in the Secure Water Treatment (SWaT) testbed which replicates a small water treatment plant.

3.2 Experimental Infrastructure, Data, and Analysis

SWaT is located at the iTrust Centre for Research in Cyber Security at the Singapore University of Technology and Design. For a detailed technical description of this testbed, see [10, 17]. Figure 3.1 details the six-stage water treatment process which is controlled and operated by 24 sensors and 27 actuators, all of which are detailed in [10]. Sensors inform operators both about water quantity (e.g., water level, flow, and pressure) and quality (e.g., pH, ORP, and conductivity). Actuators include mixers, motorized valves, and electric pumps.

SWaT controls a six-step physical water treatment process. These steps are labeled P1 through P6 in Fig. 3.1. First, raw water is taken in and stored in a tank (P1). Then, water quality is assessed and, if necessary, a static mixer adds HCl, NaOCl, or NaCl (P2). Impurities are ultrafiltrated by fine membranes (P3), and ultraviolet lamps dechlorinate the water (P4). Then, the water is pumped into a reverse osmosis system where contaminants are removed; a backwashing process uses the water produced by reverse osmosis to clean the ultrafiltration membranes (P5). In the final step P6,

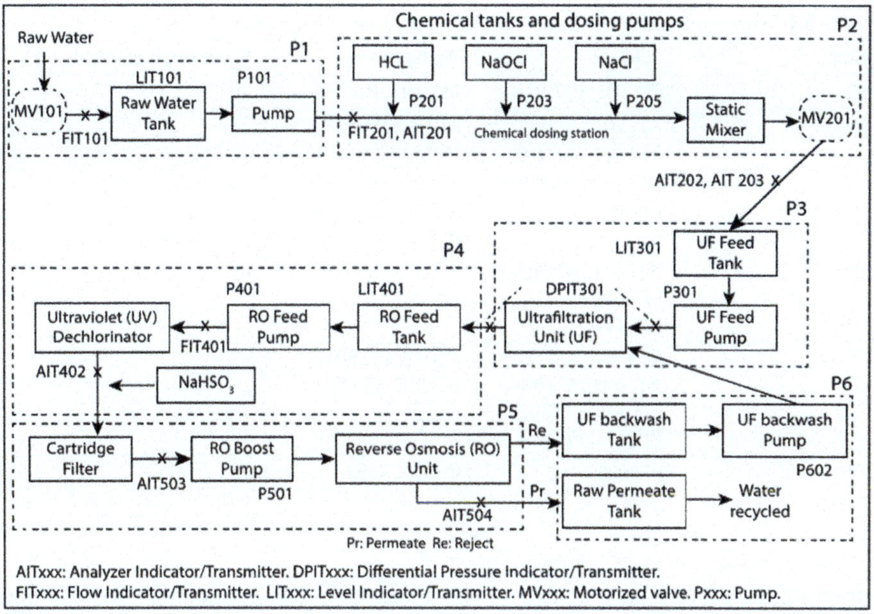

Fig. 3.1 Overview of SWaT testbed and water treatment process

the treated water is stored for subsequent distribution. The whole process is steered by a layered communications network, a set of dual PLCs controlled by a SCADA system, a human-machine interface, and a historian server which logs time series data.

Prior research has collected several large datasets with the SWaT testbed; we use the one described by [10]. In its original form, it comprises a total of 946,722 data points collected over an observation period of 11 days with all 51 sensors and actuators. After deleting backup attributes that had no data or duplicated values, a subset of 41 sensors and indicators remained which we used for all subsequent analyses (cf. Table 3.1). The last column informs about the share of all sensors and actuators in the respective step that our subset captures.

Since the first four hours of time series data are mostly duplicated in each process step to model the transition from one step to the next, we deleted these duplicated blocks. Hence, 482,400 observations per attribute remained for subsequent analysis. Before analysis, we applied z-normalization to the raw time series data to remove invariances.

In all subsequent analyses, we work with three pre-defined, fixed observation time spans m during which the clustering algorithms run. Since the dataset has a sampling rate of one second, m is a multiple of 60 s of observations. We choose values of 360, 720, and 1440 to analyze how the algorithms classify short, medium-length, and long time series typically observed in the original dataset. Using these values, we defined a set of 18 test sequences per step and m value which is used to

Table 3.1 Summary of SWaT sensors and actuators used in our analysis

Step	Sensors	Actuators	Share of all elements (%)
P1	FIT101, LIT101	MV101, P101	80
P2	AIT201, AIT202, AIT203, FIT201	MV201, P201*, P203, P205	72
P3	DPIT301, FIT301, LIT301	MV301, MV302, MV303, MV304, P302	89
P4	AIT401, AIT402, FIT401, LIT401	P403*, UV401*	67
P5	AIT501, AIT502, AIT503, AIT504, FIT501, FIT502, FIT503, FIT504	P501*, PIT501, PIT502, PIT503	92
P6	FIT601	P601*, P602	75

structure the performance analyses (viz. Table 3.2). These sequences provide both balanced and unbalanced sets of sensors and actuators (noted as "S/A ratio"). Further, we exclude the possibility that an object can belong to two clusters simultaneously ("hard clustering").

A comparison of multiple algorithms typically requires an objective public dataset as a reference frame. Since the SWaT data are unique, no ready-made baseline accuracy measure exists. Further, [6] note that even in the presence of an objective ground truth, unsupervised learning methods should still be trained since they cannot identify attacks they have not encountered before.

We therefore constructed a baseline dataset from the raw time series data and defined it as a base case against which the algorithms were trained. n denotes the number of time series considered in the respective analysis. We applied a fixed split ratio between training (60%) and test data series (40%). To evaluate the training set, we used 1-NN since a specification of $k = 1$ for a k-nearest neighbor algorithm implies the training sample has a zero error rate. We used Euclidian distance (ED) and conditional dynamic time warping (cDTW) to evaluate the initial training results. For a technical introduction into these measures, see [9]. Since unconstrained DTW is very costly in terms of computation time, we constrain DTW metrics to a window size of $w = 5$. The respective results for the training set are also shown in Table 3.2.

While we trained the algorithms, we also analyzed computation times by the `time.process_time()` function which returns the sum of both system and user CPU time the algorithm requires. The results of this analysis are summarized in Table 3.3. We set k-Means as the reference point against which we compared the performance of k-Shape and TTC. Euclidean distance measures require the least computation time. By comparison, k-Shape requires an average of 20 min to complete its run, whereas TTC with $w = 5$ requires about one hour.

Table 3.2 Summary of training results before clustering

Seq.	Step	m	Train($n_{.6}$)	Test($n_{.4}$)	S/A ratio	ED ($w = 0$)	cDTW ($w = 5$)
1	P1	360	804	536	2:2	0.2623	0.2377
2	P1	720	404	268	2:2	0.3765	0.3765
3	P1	1440	204	136	2:2	0.9808	0.9808
4	P2	360	804	536	4:4	0.7531	0.7253
5	P2	720	408	272	4:4	0.9036	0.8735
6	P2	1440	200	137	4:4	1.0000	1.0000
7	P3	360	800	536	3:5	0.4375	0.4175
8	P3	720	408	272	3:5	0.4759	0.4759
9	P3	1440	200	136	3:5	0.5800	0.5000
10	P4	360	804	534	4:2	0.8272	0.8272
11	P4	720	300	206	4:2	0.8621	0.8621
12	P4	1440	150	113	4:2	1.0000	1.0000
13	P5	360	804	540	11:1	0.2068	0.2068
14	P5	720	408	264	11:1	0.2048	0.8275
15	P5	1440	204	136	11:1	0.1635	0.1635
16	P6	360	804	537	1:2	0.8272	0.8242
17	P6	720	402	267	1:2	0.8375	0.8375
18	P6	1440	202	137	1:2	0.6569	0.6569

For the subsequent performance analysis, the k-Shape algorithm [18] was specified with a maximum number of iterations for k-Shape. The k-Means algorithm used both DTW and scalar-based distance (SBD) as distance measures and the arithmetic mean of time series coordinates for centroid computation. In every iteration of k-Shape and k-Means, the centroids of the previous run were used as reference points to refine the centroid computation of subsequent runs.

We measured the performance of all four algorithms by ED with a window size of $w = 0$ and cDTW with a window size of $w = 5$. For pairwise comparisons, we compute the Rand index and conditional entropy (see [4, 14] for a technical description of these measures). We report the average of both indices over 100 runs.

We programmed our analysis in Python with `Pycharm IDE` to obtain consistent evaluations. All classification reports and confusion matrices were generated with the `sklearn` library. We ran all analysis on a ready-made commercial laptop with a Dual Intel i5 CPU (4-core with 8 logical processors), 1.6GHz clock speed, and 8GB RAM.

Table 3.3 Computation time analysis

Seq.	Process	m	Train($n_{.6}$)	Test($n_{.4}$)	k-Means(Ref.)	k-Shape	TTC($w = 5$)
1	P1	360	804	536	0.1875	170x	10780x
2	P1	720	404	268	0.2188	30x	6393x
3	P1	1440	204	136	0.2188	28x	4941x
4	P2	360	804	536	0.1719	76x	5785x
5	P2	720	408	272	0.6094	24x	1443x
6	P2	1440	200	137	0.1250	55x	10138x
7	P3	360	800	536	0.1563	49x	17040x
8	P3	720	408	272	0.1719	286x	16551x
9	P3	1440	200	136	0.1250	82x	22489x
10	P4	360	804	534	0.0938	571x	28438x
11	P4	720	300	206	0.1719	95x	14394x
12	P4	1440	150	113	0.0781	1423x	27181x
13	P5	360	804	540	0.0781	7937x	60773x
14	P5	720	408	264	0.0625	9345x	81352x
15	P5	1440	204	136	0.0625	557x	51794x
16	P6	360	804	537	0.0469	16290x	63529x
17	P6	720	402	267	0.1094	5560x	24087x
18	P6	1440	202	137	0.0625	842x	60728x

3.3 Results

3.3.1 Comparative Accuracy

Table 3.4 details the overall accuracy of the four competing algorithms, i.e., the ratio of correctly predicted to total observations. In 10 out of 18 sequences, the respective accuracy exceeds the baseline. k-Shape realizes a top accuracy of 0.9111 when it clusters data from step P2 (sequence no. 5), while 1-NN has the worst accuracy of 0.00 in step P4 (sequence no. 6). Generally, algorithms that use DTW as their distance measure have better accuracy than those that do not. Among the three algorithms, k-Shape performs well although the data are intentionally not arranged in shape-based form.

3.3.2 Pairwise Comparison of k-Means and k-Shape

The accuracy distribution plot in Fig. 3.2 signals that k-Shape outperforms k-Means over most sequences, and particularly so for process step P2. Table 3.5 presents the related Rand index and entropy measures. k-Shape performs best in sequence no. 5, with a value of 0.9111, and worst in sequence no. 15, with a value of 0.0000.

Table 3.4 Summary of overall clustering accuracy

SN.	Process	Length(m)	1-NN(ED)	1-NN(cDTW)	k-Means	k-Shape	TTC($w = 5$)
1	P1	360	0.7377	**0.7623**	0.2313	0.4813	**0.2276**
2	P1	720	0.6235	**0.6235**	0.1418	0.1884	**0.1399**
3	P1	1440	0.0192	**0.0192**	0.2481	0.0224	**0.2836**
4	P2	360	**0.2469**	0.2747	0.3895	**0.5412**	0.3876
5	P2	720	**0.0964**	0.1265	0.4796	**0.9111**	0.4815
6	P2	1440	**0.0000**	0.0000	0.0074	**0.3333**	0.0298
7	P3	360	0.5625	**0.5825**	0.2276	0.4179	**0.1940**
8	P3	720	0.5241	**0.5241**	0.2610	**0.0257**	0.2279
9	P3	1440	0.4200	**0.5000**	0.0846	**0.0037**	0.0899
10	P4	360	0.1728	**0.1728**	**0.6214**	0.4660	0.5995
11	P4	720	0.1379	**0.1379**	0.5000	0.4735	**0.5029**
12	P4	1440	0.0000	**0.0000**	0.3333	0.3333	**0.3457**
13	P5	360	0.7932	**0.7932**	0.2482	0.3603	**0.1618**
14	P5	720	0.7952	**0.1725**	0.2647	0.4672	0.2336
15	P5	1440	0.8365	**0.8365**	0.2301	**0.0000**	0.2892
16	P6	360	0.1728	0.1758	0.1029	**0.0708**	**0.2264**
17	P6	720	0.1625	0.1625	0.1094	**0.5809**	**0.1068**
18	P6	1440	0.3431	0.3431	**0.3285**	0.3285	**0.3468**

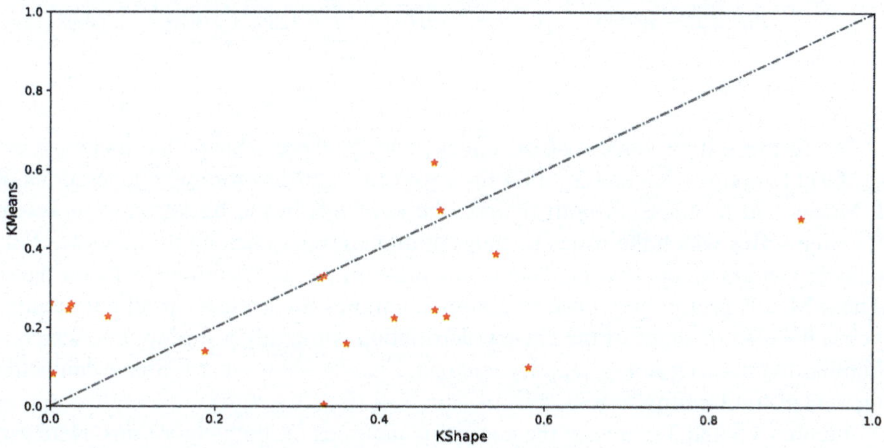

Fig. 3.2 Accuracy distribution plot of k-Shape versus k-Means

Table 3.5 Numerical performance comparison between k-Means and k-Shape

Seq.	Step(m)	k-Means	Rand index	cEntropy	k-Shape	Rand index	cEntropy
1	P1(360)	0.2313	0.52	0.00	**0.4813**	0.50	0.02
2	P1(720)	0.1418	0.54	0.01	**0.1884**	0.54	0.06
3	P1(1440)	**0.2481**	0.54	0.01	0.0224	0.51	0.03
4	P2(360)	0.3895	0.52	0.00	**0.5412**	0.50	0.02
5	P2(720)	0.4796	0.50	0.00	**0.9111**	0.84	0.58
6	P2(1440)	0.0074	0.55	0.02	**0.3333**	0.55	0.08
7	P3(360)	0.2276	0.51	0.00	**0.4179**	0.50	0.02
8	P3(720)	**0.2610**	0.53	0.01	0.0257	0.50	0.02
9	P3(1440)	**0.0846**	0.55	0.02	0.0037	0.50	0.02
10	P4(360)	**0.6214**	0.91	0.62	0.4660	0.50	0.02
11	P4(720)	**0.5000**	0.51	0.00	0.4735	0.50	0.02
12	P4(1440)	0.3333	0.55	0.02	0.3333	0.52	0.04
13	P5(360)	0.2482	0.50	0.00	**0.3603**	0.50	0.02
14	P5(720)	0.2647	0.52	0.00	**0.4672**	0.51	0.03
15	P5(1440)	**0.2301**	0.55	0.02	0.0000	0.51	0.02
16	P6(360)	**0.1029**	0.50	0.00	0.0708	0.51	0.03
17	P6(720)	0.1094	0.51	0.54	**0.5809**	0.51	0.03
18	P6(1440)	0.3285	0.52	0.02	0.3285	0.56	0.08

We further explored the case of sequence no. 5 where k-Shape has its best score of 0.9111. Figures 3.3 and 3.4 plot the respective cluster prototype generations of k-Means and k-Shape. In both figures, the red lines in the background represent the time series which the respective algorithm believes to belong to the same class. Cluster 1 refers to inputs (signal data), and cluster 2 refers to outputs (actuator data). The k-Means prototyping process simply computes the average of all data points, hence the overall shape of the cluster distribution is roughly a straight line which is highlighted in black in Fig. 3.3. By contrast, Fig. 3.4 shows that k-Shape can better recognize similar time series.

Figures 3.5 and 3.6 present the confusion matrices for both algorithms. Here and all subsequent matrices, the top-left value indicates the number of true positives, i.e., the number of positive observations (attacks) that were predicted accurately. The bottom right value represents the number of accurately predicted true negatives. The top-right corner collects false negatives (positive observations that the algorithm clustered as negative), and the bottom-left value collects false positives (negative observations that the algorithm clustered as positive).

The matrices suggest that both algorithms generate a high number of false alarms, but k-Shape has far greater accuracy. Therefore, the case of sequence no. 15 where k-Shape performs *worse* than any other algorithm seems surprising. Since sequence 15 has a highly skewed sensor/actuator ratio of 11:1 (viz. Table 3.2), we investigated this

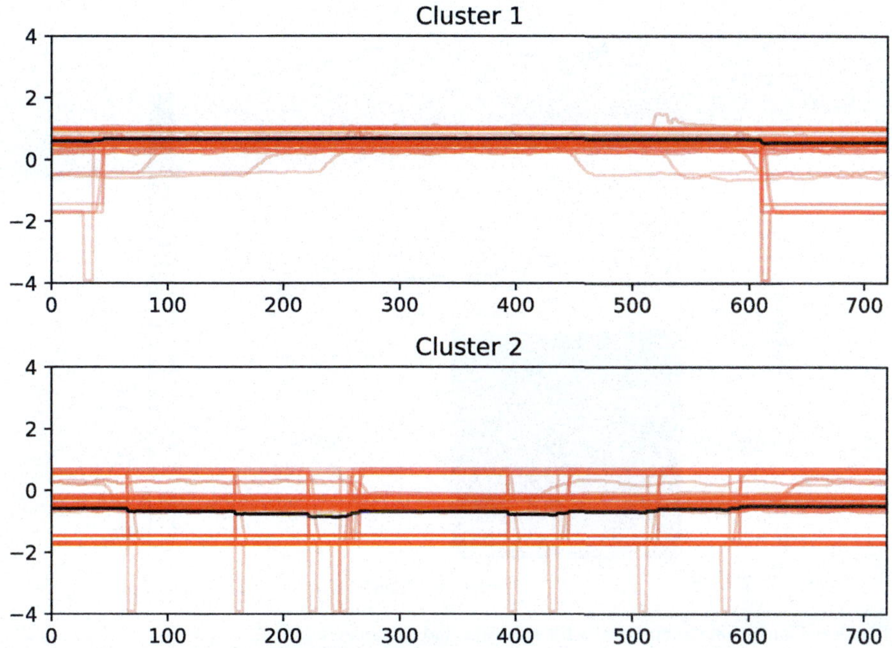

Fig. 3.3 Cluster prototypes rendered by k-Means

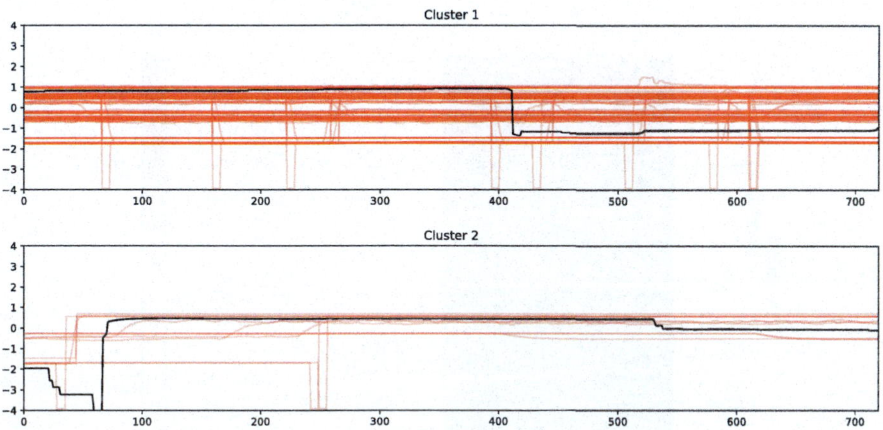

Fig. 3.4 Cluster prototypes rendered by k-Shape

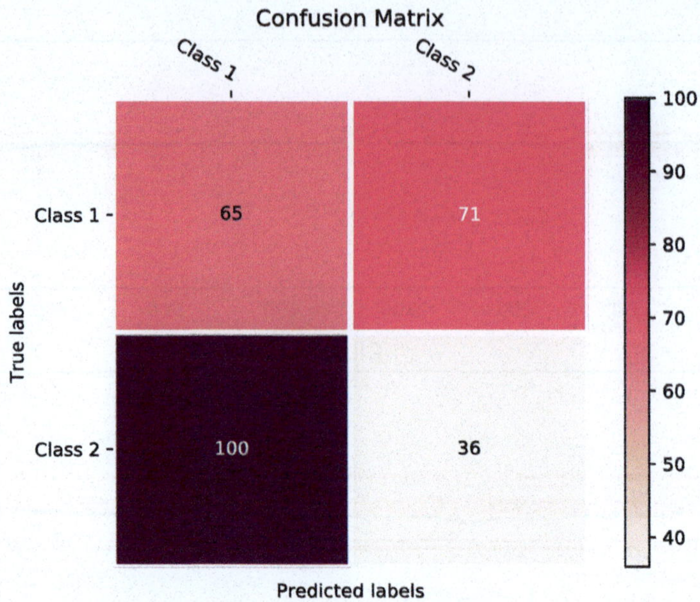

Fig. 3.5 Confusion matrix results for k-Means and sequence no. 5

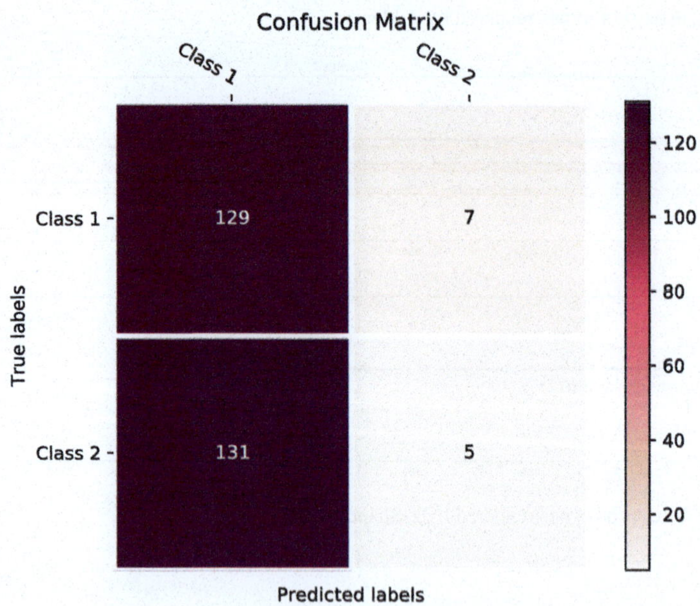

Fig. 3.6 Confusion matrix results for k-Shape and sequence no. 5

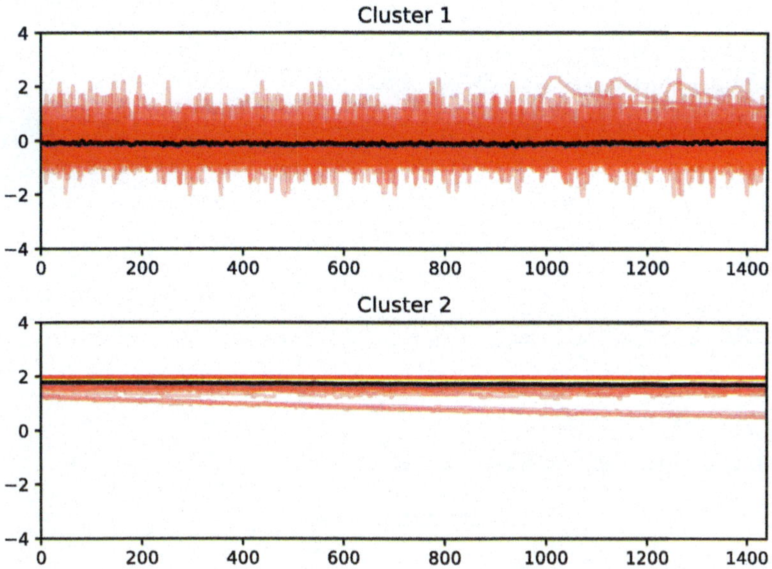

Fig. 3.7 Cluster prototypes rendered by k-Means

case further and compared it with the related performance of k-Means. Figures 3.7 and 3.8 detail the respective cluster prototype generations. Again, cluster 1 refers to inputs (signal data), and cluster 2 refers to outputs (actuator data).

Since the time series in this sequence produce much erratic noise (red lines), and since k-Means simply computes the average of all data points, the related cluster distribution (black line) reduces the noise. By comparison, when time series data feature this noise-like structure, k-Shape fails to perform appropriate abstraction and, by attempting to classify the noise, produces inaccurate clusters. In this particular case with highly skewed sensor-to-actuator data, an algorithm that oversimplifies would be a more efficient choice.

The related confusion matrices shown in Figs. 3.9 and 3.10 confirm this conclusion. The true positive rate of k-Shape is much lower than that of k-Means, and k-Shape fails to recognize many attacks.

3.3.3 Pairwise Comparison of k-Shape and TTC

In a second step, we compared the performance of k-Shape and TTC. The accuracy distribution plot in Fig. 3.11 signals that k-Shape outperforms TTC over most sequences. Table 3.6 presents the related Rand index and entropy measures.

We further explore the case of sequence no. 10 where TTC scores best and better than k-Shape. Figures 3.12 and 3.13 plot the respective cluster prototype generations

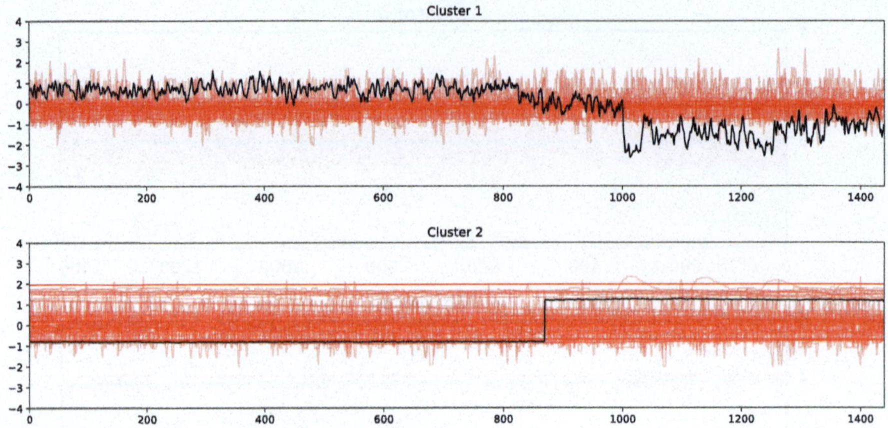

Fig. 3.8 Cluster prototypes rendered by k-Shape

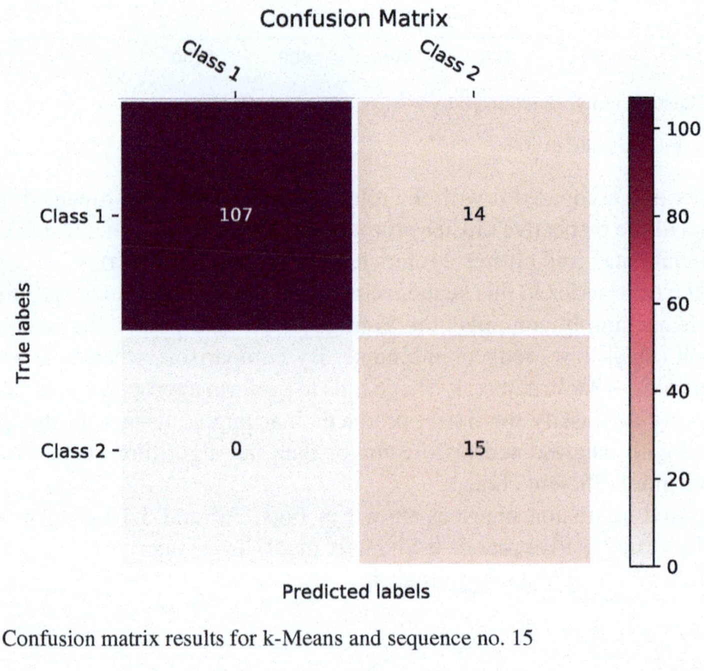

Fig. 3.9 Confusion matrix results for k-Means and sequence no. 15

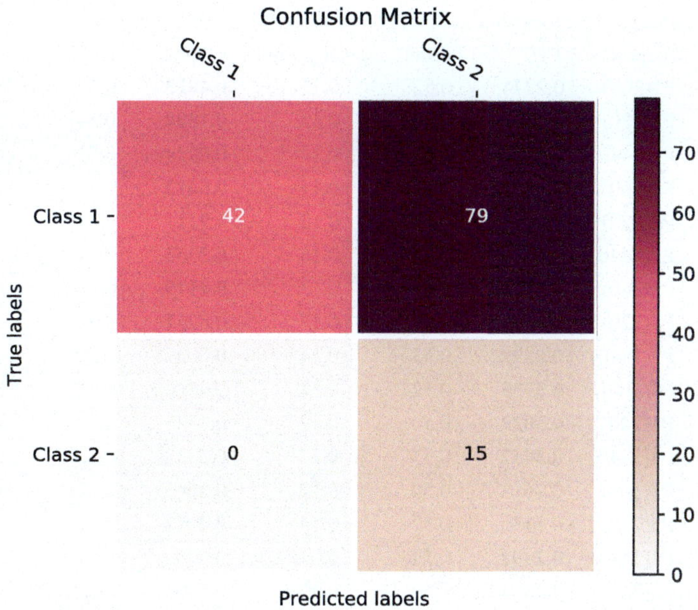

Fig. 3.10 Confusion matrix results for k-Shape and sequence no. 15

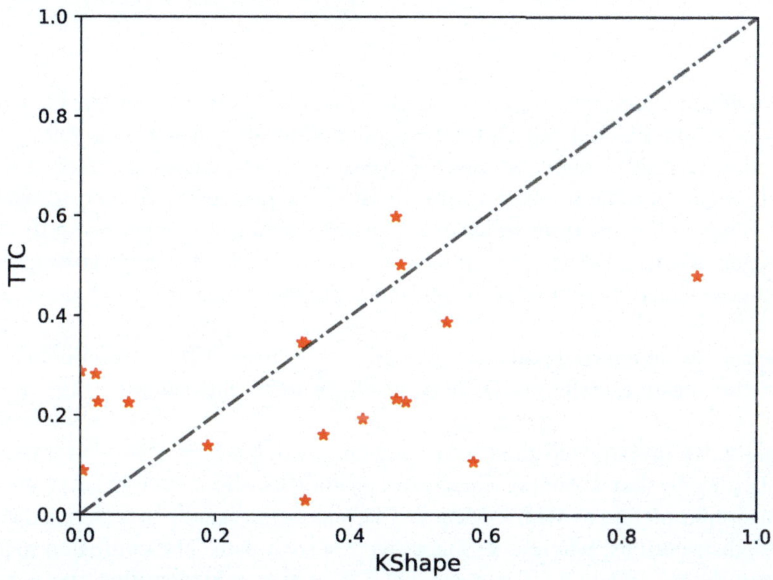

Fig. 3.11 Accuracy distribution plot for k-Shape versus TTC

Table 3.6 Numerical performance comparison between TTC and k-Shape

Seq.	Step(m)	TTC	Rand	cEntropy	k-Shape	Rand	cEntropy
1	P1(360)	0.2276	0.52	0.13	**0.4813**	0.50	0.02
2	P1(720)	0.1399	0.54	0.15	**0.1884**	0.54	0.06
3	P1(1440)	**0.2836**	0.53	0.14	0.0224	0.51	0.03
4	P2(360)	0.3876	0.52	0.14	**0.5412**	0.50	0.02
5	P2(720)	0.4815	0.50	0.12	**0.9111**	0.84	0.58
6	P2(1440)	0.0298	0.55	0.16	**0.3333**	0.55	0.08
7	P3(360)	0.1940	0.51	0.13	**0.4179**	0.50	0.02
8	P3(720)	**0.2279**	0.57	0.17	0.0257	0.50	0.02
9	P3(1440)	**0.0899**	0.53	0.14	0.0037	0.50	0.02
10	P4(360)	**0.5995**	0.52	0.14	0.4660	0.50	0.02
11	P4(720)	**0.5029**	0.50	0.12	0.4735	0.50	0.02
12	P4(1440)	**0.3457**	0.57	0.17	0.3333	0.52	0.04
13	P5(360)	0.1618	0.50	0.12	**0.3603**	0.50	0.02
14	P5(720)	0.2336	0.52	0.14	**0.4672**	0.51	0.03
15	P5(1440)	**0.2892**	0.52	0.14	0.0000	0.51	0.02
16	P6(360)	**0.2264**	0.50	0.12	0.0708	0.51	0.03
17	P6(720)	0.1068	0.55	0.16	**0.5809**	0.51	0.03
18	P6(1440)	**0.3468**	0.51	0.13	0.3285	0.56	0.08

of k-Means and k-Shape. Again, in both figures, the red lines in the background represent the time series which the respective algorithm believes to belong to the same class. Cluster 1 refers to inputs (signal data), and cluster 2 refers to outputs (actuator data). Similar to the case of k-Means in sequence 15, TTC performs better than k-Shape when the time series data is noisy because it tends to simplify cluster prototypes, whereas k-Shape attempts to over-fit the noise. Its shape abstraction has advantages when time series data are periodic, but they are less able to handle random noise.

The confusion matrix results confirm this assessment: TTC is excellent at recognizing true negatives, whereas k-Shape produces many false alarms (Figs. 3.14 and 3.15).

Finally, we investigated the case of sequence no. 6 where TTC performs worst, and much worse than k-Shape. The cluster prototypes, shown in Figs. 3.16 and 3.17, paint a similar picture as with k-Means: TTC can better handle time series data with "noisy" distributions, whereas k-Shape overfits such data. The confusion matrices, shown in Figs. 3.18 and 3.19, suggest that TTC adequately identifies true negatives, whereas k-Shape returns a high rate of false negatives.

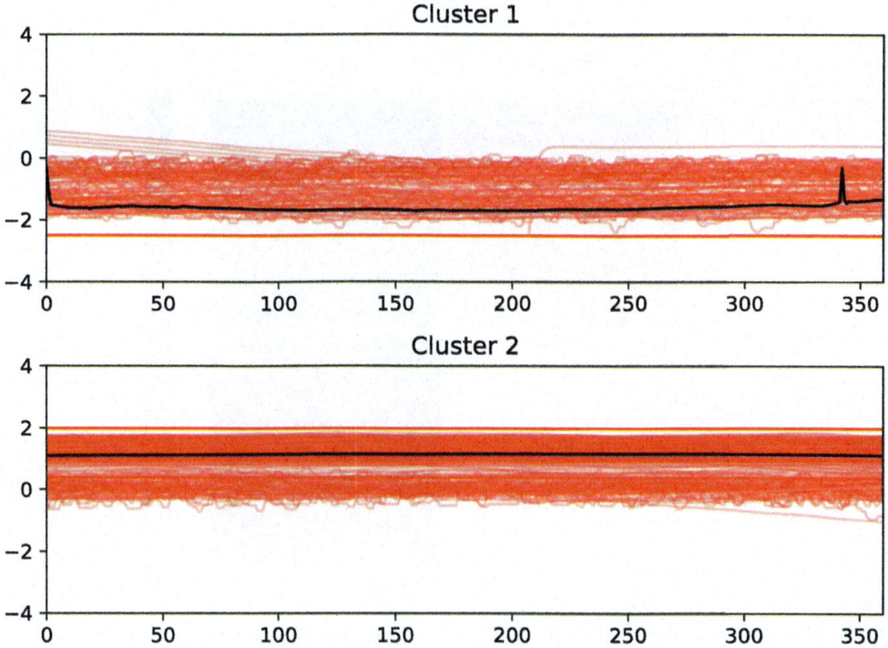

Fig. 3.12 Cluster prototypes rendered by TTC

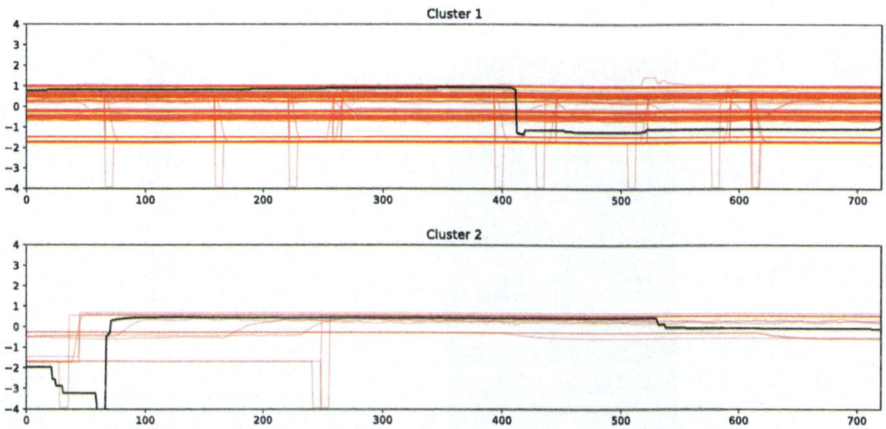

Fig. 3.13 Cluster prototypes rendered by k-Shape

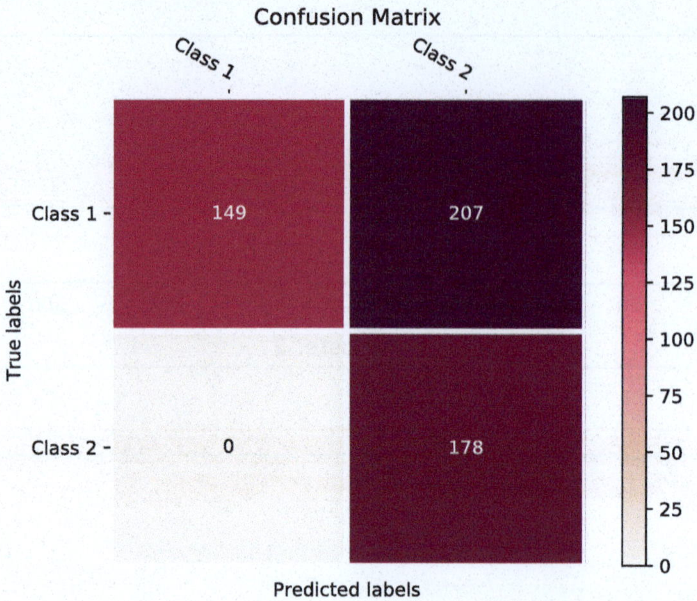

Fig. 3.14 Confusion matrix results for TTC and sequence no. 10

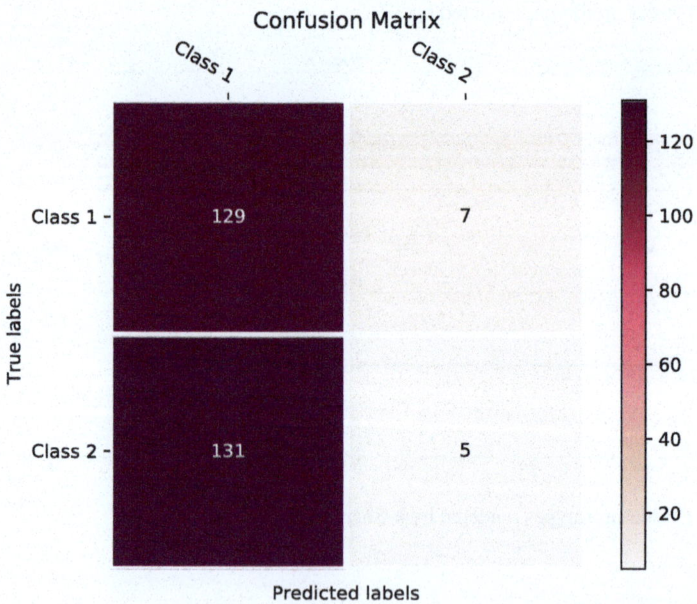

Fig. 3.15 Confusion matrix results for k-Shape and sequence no. 10

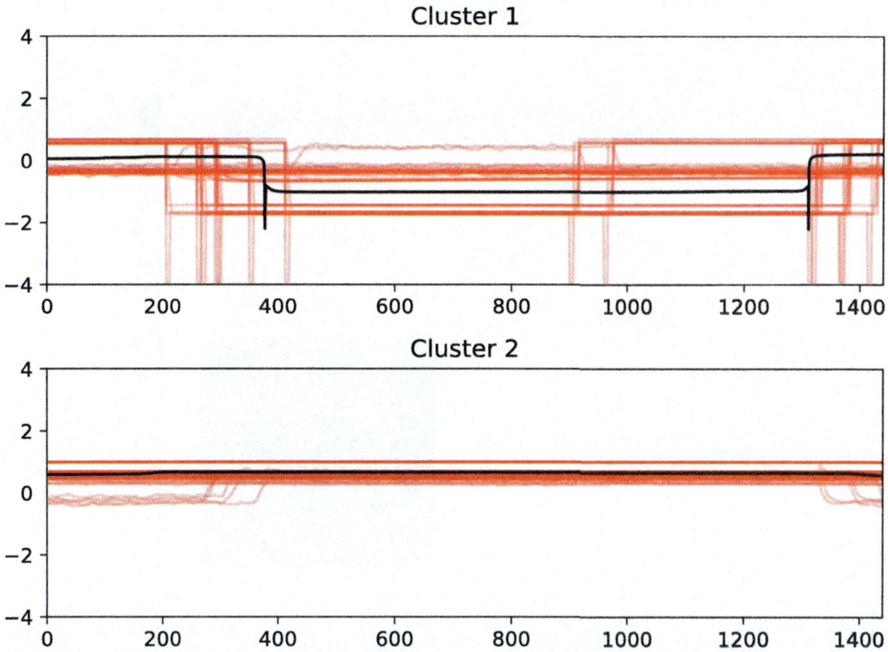

Fig. 3.16 Cluster prototypes rendered by TTC

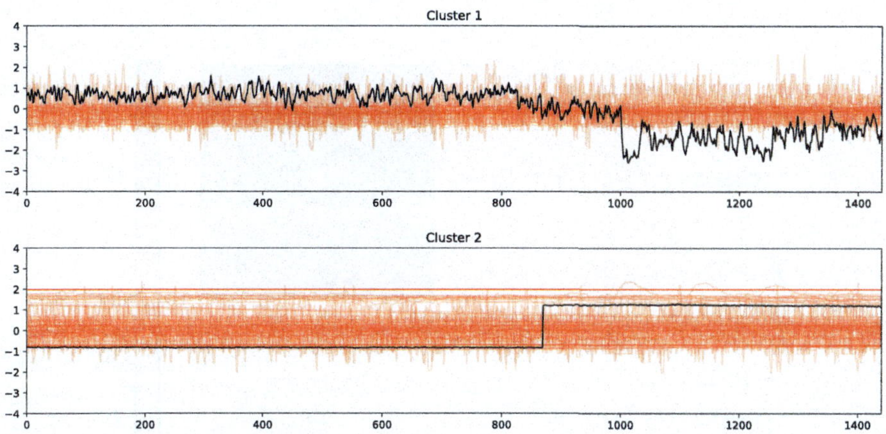

Fig. 3.17 Cluster prototypes rendered by k-Shape

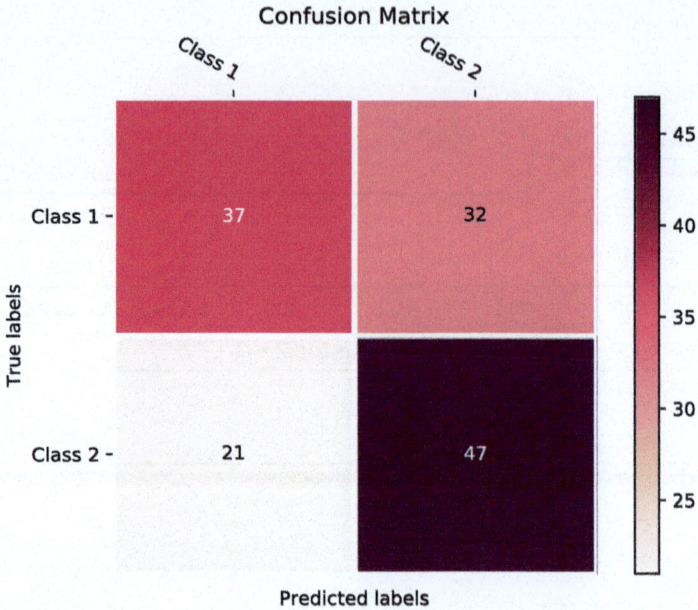

Fig. 3.18 Confusion matrix results for TTC and sequence no. 6

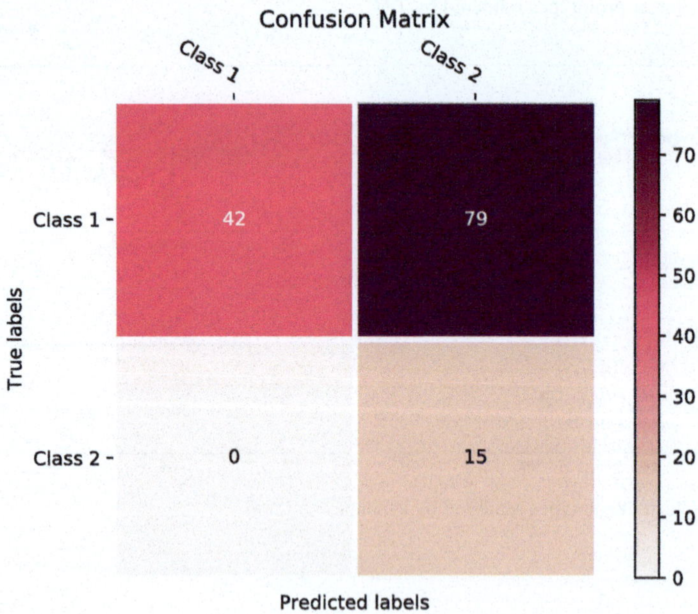

Fig. 3.19 Confusion Matrix results for k-Shape and sequence no. 6

3.4 Conclusion

Our findings generally support that the k-Shape algorithm has superior accuracy when it comes to attack isolation, except for the case of time series that are noisy. Overall, k-Shape merges the efficiency of ED with the accuracy of DTW; moreover, it is a domain-independent clustering algorithm for time series. Still, it has its shortcomings when the time series data do not exhibit clear patterns.

This problem points to an opportunity that [6] exploited by using a "superdetector" approach which fuses and triangulates different data sources. The above shortcomings of k-Shape may be mitigated by adding algorithms that can handle noisy data better, and by identifying ways of how the different detector data may be combined.

While this approach is beyond the scope of this contribution, such research would constitute a much-needed complement. Balaji et al. [6] note that their "superdetector" approach is a supervised one and hence requires extensive labeling and subjective human judgment. Future research could build on our findings to construct an unsupervised detector that combines different clustering algorithms which do not require such labeling.

Finally, the fundamental problem that attack data are sparse in comparison to normal operations data implies that attack data are rare events and hence might follow a Poisson or negative binomial distribution. Future research should therefore complement our computational approach with probabilistic methods to train detector algorithms with likelihoods of attack occurrence.

References

1. Aghabozorgi, S., Shirkhorshidi, A., & Wah, T. Y. (2015). Time-series clustering - A decade review. *Information Systems, 53*, 16–38.
2. Aghabozorgi S, Wah TY, Herawan T, Jalab H, Shayegan M, Jalali A (2014) A hybrid algorithm for clustering of time series data based on affinity search technique. The Scientific World Journal, 562194.
3. Ahmed, C. M., & Zhou, J. (2021). Bank of models: Sensor attack detection and isolation in industrial control systems. In D. Percia David, A. Mermoud, & T. Maillart (Eds.), *Critical Information Infrastructures Security* (pp. 3–23). Springer LNCS: Berlin, Heidelberg.
4. Amigó, E., Gonzalo, J., Artiles, J., & Verdejo, F. (2009). A comparison of extrinsic clustering evaluation metrics based on formal constraints. *Information Retrieval, 12*, 461–486.
5. Bagnall, A., Dau, H. A., Lines, J., Flynn, M., Large, J., Bostrom, A., Southam, P., & Keogh, E. (2018). The UEA multivariate time series classification archive. arXiv:1811.00075
6. Balaji, M., Shrivastava, S., Adepu, S., & Mathur, A. (2021). Super Detector: An ensemble approach for anomaly detection in industrial control systems. In D. Percia David, A. Mermoud, & T. Maillart (Eds.), *Critical Information Infrastructures Security* (pp. 24–43). Springer LNCS: Berlin, Heidelberg.
7. Batista, G., Keogh, E., Moses Tataw, O., & de Souza, V. (2014). CID: An efficient complexity-invariant distance for time series. *Data Mining and Knowledge Discovery, 28*, 634–669.
8. Dau, H. A., Bagnall, A., Kamgar, K., Yeh, C. C., Zhu, Y., Gharghabi, S., & Ratanamahatana CAm Keogh E. (2018). The UCR time series archive. arXiv:1810.07758

9. Ding, H., Trajcevski, G., Scheuermann, P., Wang, X., & Keogh, E. (2008). Querying and mining of time series data: Experimental comparison of representations and distance measures. *Proceedings of the VLDB Endowment, 1*(2), 1542–1552.
10. Goh, J., Adepu, S., Junejo, K. N., & Mathur, A. (2017). A dataset to support research in the design of secure water treatment systems. In G. Havarneanu, R. Setola, H. Nassopoulos, & S. Wolthusen (Eds.), *Critical Information Infrastructures Security* (pp. 88–99). Berlin, Heidelberg: Springer LNCS.
11. Inoue, J., Yamagata, Y., Chen, Y., Poskitt, C. M., & Sun, J. (2017). Anomaly detection for a water treatment system using unsupervised machine learning. In *Proceedings of the 2017 IEEE International Conference on Data Mining Workshops (ICDMW)*, pp. 1058–1065.
12. Junejo, K. N., Goh, J. (2016). Behaviour-based attack detection and classification in cyber physical systems using machine learning. In *Proceedings of the 2nd ACM International Workshop on Cyber-Physical System Security*, pp. 34–43.
13. Keogh, E., & Kasetty, S. (2003). On the need for time series data mining benchmarks: A survey and empirical demonstration. *Data Mining and Knowledge Discovery, 7*(4), 349–371.
14. Keogh, E., & Pazzani, M. (2000). A simple dimensionality reduction technique for fast similarity search in large time series databases. In T. Terano, H. Liu, & A. Chen (Eds.), *Knowledge Discovery and Data Mining* (pp. 122–133). Berlin, Heidelberg: Springer.
15. Kravchik, M., & Shabtai, A. (2018). Detecting cyber attacks in industrial control systems using convolutional neural networks. In *Proceedings of the 2018 Workshop on Cyber-Physical Systems Security and PrivaCy*, pp. 72–83.
16. Li, D., Chen, D., Jin, B., Shi, L., Goh, J., & Ng, S. K. (2019). MAD-GAN: Multivariate anomaly detection for time series data with generative adversarial networks. In I. V. Tetko, V. Kůrková, P. Karpov, & F. Theis (Eds.), *Artificial neural networks and machine learning - ICANN 2019: Text and time series* (pp. 703–716). Berlin, Heidelberg: Springer LNCS.
17. Mathur, A., & Tippenhauer, N. (2016). SWaT: A water treatment testbed for research and training on ICS security. In *Proceedings of the 2016 International Workshop on Cyber-physical Systems for Smart Water Networks (CySWater)*, pp. 31–36.
18. Paparrizos, J., & Gravano, L. (2016). k-Shape: Efficient and accurate clustering of time series. *ACM SIGMOD Record, 45*(1), 69–76.
19. Perales Gómez, A. L., Fernández Maimó, L., Huertas Celdrán, A., & García Clemente, F. J. (2020). MADICS: A methodology for anomaly detection in industrial control systems. *Symmetry, 12*(10), 1583.
20. Qureshi, M., Al-Madani, B., & Shawahna, A. (2019). Anomaly detection for industrial control networks using machine learning with the help from the inter-arrival curves. arXiv:1911.05692
21. Yang, T., Murguia, C., Kuijper, M., & Nešić, D. (2019). An unknown input multi-observer approach for estimation, attack isolation, and control of LTI systems under actuator attacks. In *Proceedings of the 18th European Control Conference (ECC)*, pp. 4350–4355.

KuiZhen Su graduated from the Master of Science Security by Design (MSSD) program at the Singapore University of Technology and Design (SUTD). He continues his passion in cyber security as a practitioner.

Chuadhry Mujeeb Ahmed is a Senior Lecturer (Assistant Professor) in cyber security at Newcastle University (UK) and a visiting fellow at the EECS department at the Georgia Institute of Technology. His research interests are in the security of cyber-physical systems, the internet of things, communication systems, and critical infrastructures. Before, he was a research fellow at the National Satellite of Excellence for Secure Critical Infrastructure at the Singapore University of Technology and Design.

Jianying Zhou is a professor and co-center director for iTrust at Singapore University of Technology and Design (SUTD). He received his Ph.D. in Information Security from Royal Holloway, University of London. His research interests are in applied cryptography and network security, cyber-physical system security, mobile and wireless security. He is a co-founder and steering committee co-chair of ACNS. He is also steering committee chair of ACM AsiaCCS, and steering committee member of Asiacrypt.

Chapter 4
Next Generation ISACs: Simulating Crowdsourced Intelligence for Faster Incident Response

Philipp Fischer and Sébastien Gillard

4.1 Limitations to Security Information Sharing

Few would argue that security information sharing, i.e., the voluntary exchange of information relevant to cybersecurity across different organizations, helps defenders to understand, mitigate, and prevent cyber attacks [1, 2, 7]. The European Union's agency for network and information security (ENISA) has proposed how such sharing could be stimulated [4, 5].

Among such proposals, information sharing and analysis centers (ISACs) stand out since they facilitate an interpersonal exchange of information between cybersecurity professionals. Since their emergence in the late 1990s, ISACs have become a dominant organizational model for security information sharing.

Still, security information sharing among human agents through ISACs is often slow and ineffective, both because of the transaction costs that physical meetings entail and because participants may purposefully withhold information when they do not trust each other [8, 13, 15, 22]. As a result, the contribution ISACs can make is limited [6, 17].

Since the value of cybersecurity information depreciates over time as attackers change tactics once compromised systems are reset [11], speed is of the essence

Supplementary Information The online version contains supplementary material available at https://doi.org/10.1007/978-3-031-30191-9_4.

P. Fischer (✉)
Department of Computer Science, Swiss Federal Institute of Technology Zurich, Zurich, Switzerland
e-mail: fischphi@student.ethz.ch

S. Gillard
Department of Defense Economics, Military Academy at the Swiss Federal Institute of Technology Zurich, Zurich, Switzerland
e-mail: sebastien.gillard@vtg.admin.ch

M. M. Keupp (ed.), *Cyberdefense*, International Series in Operations Research & Management Science 342,
https://doi.org/10.1007/978-3-031-30191-9_4

when it comes to sharing such information, and it is this aspect which motivates our research.

Recently, alternative platforms have attempted to overcome the problems that interpersonal interaction entails. These platforms provide human agents with the tools to share indicators of compromise (IoC) remotely and directly. We first describe and study two such "crowdsourced" platforms, *ThreatFox* and *MISP*, then we use the insights gained from this analysis to construct a hierarchical simulation model that studies how such platforms may facilitate the sharing of IoC. All subsequent analyses were implemented in `R`, and all plots were generated with the `ggplot2` package.

4.2 Crowdsourced Intelligence Sharing Platforms

4.2.1 ThreatFox

The online user community ThreatFox was founded in 2021. Its users, who are called "reporters," can anonymously and directly share information about cyber threats by entering IoC into an online database.[1] Any shared information is time-stamped, categorized, and immediately made available to all users. The community comprises both professionals and private individuals who have an interest in IT technology or cybersecurity. Besides an initial registration which can be associated with a Twitter handle, there is no restriction or screening process for new reporters who want to join the platform. Data entered by reporters are neither cross-checked nor verified. Detailed descriptive information on ThreatFox is available from [12].

We studied the IoC arrival and user onboarding on both platforms, both in order to understand their inner workings and to inform a simulation model that can predict the speed with which IoC are shared. We collected both the daily number of reporters and the daily number of IoC shared between March 2021 when the platform was inaugurated, and July 2022 when we began the analysis.

Figure 4.1 shows that the number of IoC shared exhibits a non-linear growth pattern. The black graph shows the actual growth of IoC, the fitted centered polynomial line in blue approximates the actual growth over time. Using non-linear least squares estimation, we estimated this growth has a non-constant rate of

$$\mathbb{E}[X_t] = \mu_t = \mu t^{\gamma} \tag{4.1}$$

where $t = 1, \ldots T$ denotes the day, X_t is the number of new IoC on a given day t, μ_t is the growth rate, and γ is an ancillary parameter we estimated at $\hat{\gamma} = 0.49$ for our particular dataset.

[1] See https://threatfox.abuse.ch/.

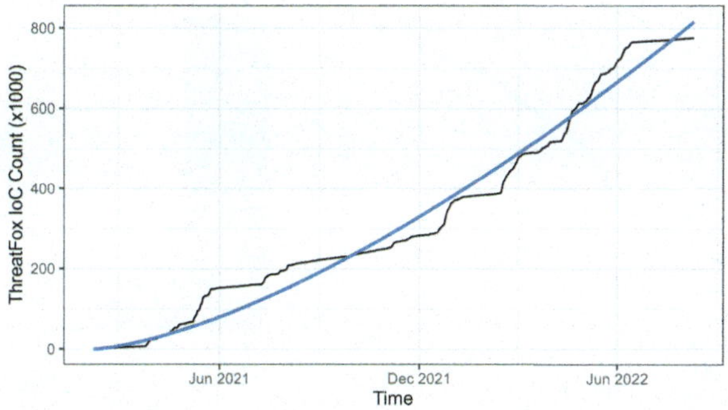

Fig. 4.1 Approximation of user growth on ThreatFox

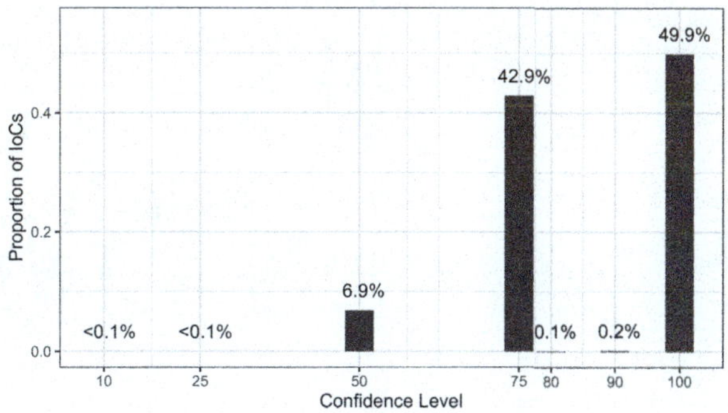

Fig. 4.2 Histogram of user confidence for all available IoC on ThreatFox

The platform allows users to assign a confidence level between 0 and 100 to their reported IoC which reflects how strongly the user believes the shared information is correct. Figure 4.2 shows our analysis of this attribute. About half of all IoC have a confidence level of 100%.

Finally, we found that the rate of reporter arrival is approximately constant (viz. Fig. 4.3, left-hand panel). The associated count data (right-hand panel) suggest that the arrival data are highly skewed; on most days, no new reporters arrive.

Let Y_t denote the number of reporters who join at time t. The total number of reporters then is $R_t = \sum_{j=1}^{t} Y_t$. The number of IoC that are shared daily per active reporter then is $\frac{X_t}{R_t}$. Under the assumptions that all reporters are independent and contribute equally, that IoC and reporters are independent, and that the constant growth rate is $\mathbb{E}[Y_t] = \lambda$, we can estimate the expected value of this ratio:

$$\mathbb{E}\left[\frac{X_t}{R_t}\right] = \frac{\mathbb{E}[X_t]}{\mathbb{E}[R_t]} = \frac{\mu_t}{\lambda t} = \frac{\mu}{\lambda} t^{\gamma - 1} \tag{4.2}$$

For our data, we estimated $(\hat{\gamma} - 1) = -0.51$, which implies that the number of IoC shared per reporter should slowly decrease over time. Figure 4.4 illustrates this

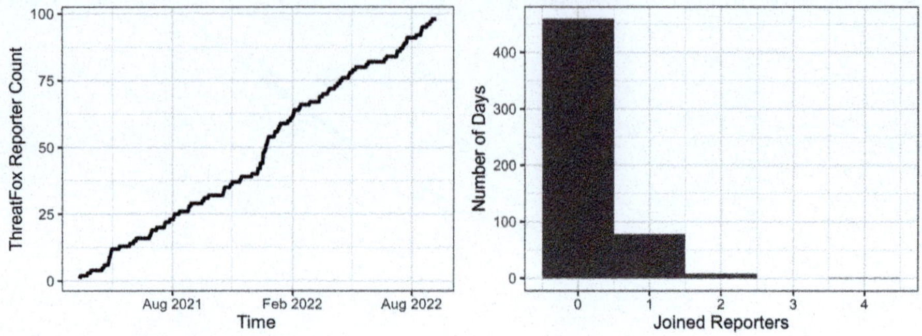

Fig. 4.3 Reporter arrival analysis

Fig. 4.4 Decreasing trend of IoC shared per reporter over time

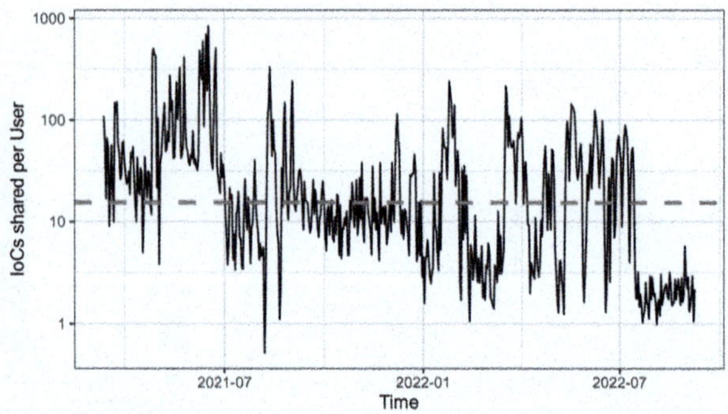

effect. The grey dashed line indicates the average rate; IoC counts slowly decrease relative to it.

Finally, we computed the empirical cumulative distribution function of the total number of IoC shared and took its complement to get the survival function. To estimate the power law exponent β, we used a weighted least squares scheme, so that reporters with a longer tenure on the platform have greater significance. We computed $\beta = 1.00$ with $R^2 = 0.98$. Figure 4.5 plots the survival function on a log-log scale.

The survival function suggests that reporters with a short tenure typically share more IoC per day, whereas for more senior contributors the number of IoC shared converges towards the estimate. This suggests that they share much information as they join, but converge towards the expected value over time.

4.2.2 MISP

Besides the relatively novel project ThreatFox, we also looked at a more established sharing platform to gain further insights for our subsequent simulation model. The Malware Information Sharing Platform (MISP) is an open-source platform where

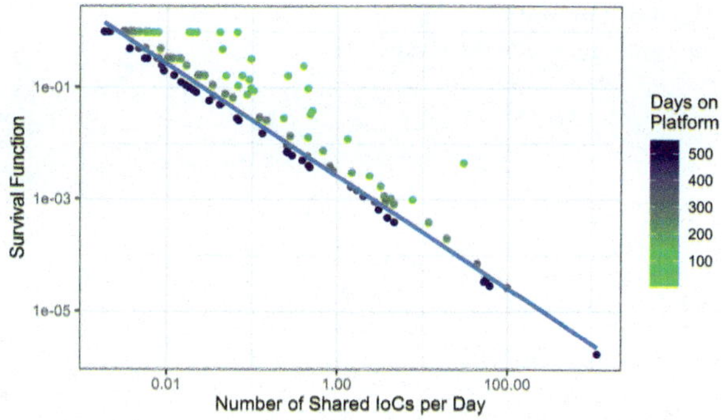

Fig. 4.5 Survival function of shared IoC per reporter

users can share any threat intelligence. It was developed in 2011, quickly popularized by European governments, and co-financed by the European Union.[2]

MISP collects decentrally entered IoC and collocates them over time into more complex threat warnings which are called "events." IoC are therefore published with delay. Its inner workings and user interaction have been richly explained before [3, 16, 21].

Compared to ThreatFox, MISP is more conservative. Contributors, who are called "organizations" (even if they are individuals), must undergo a verification and acceptance procedure before they are allowed to share information. MISP splits its user base into different communities, so that users must choose a particular community to which they want to contribute. Hence, users are not anonymous, and community membership exerts social pressure on them to verify and check any information before it is shared. Hence, one can assume that the IoC shared on MISP have a confidence level of 100%.

The operators of MISP provided us with a comprehensive dataset that contains over 86,000 events published by over 4,000 organizations between April 2014 and February 2022. We analyzed the distribution of users across all communities in this dataset and found it follows a power law distribution. Again, we computed the empirical probability distribution function and took its complement to get a corresponding survival function for MISP members. Figure 4.6 plots the result on a log-log scale.

We estimated the exponent $\beta = 1.66$ with $R^2 = 0.99$. The plot suggests that users are distributed quite asymmetrically across communities, which is plausible given the community size follows a power law, i.e., many communities have but a few users while very few communities attract a large number of users. Our simulation model takes this non-linear user-community distribution into account.

[2] See https://www.misp-project.org/.

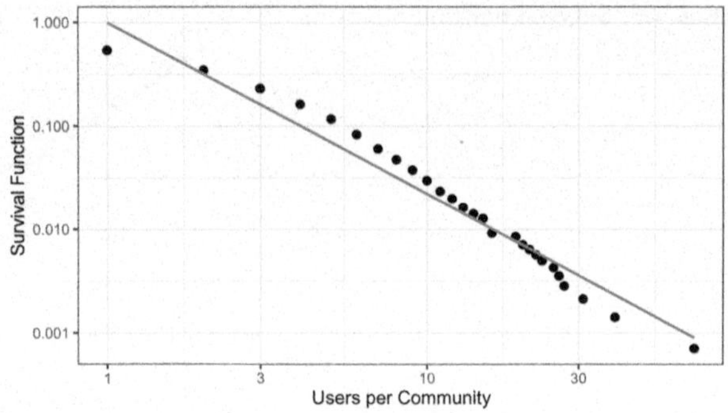

Fig. 4.6 Survival function of the community size on MISP

4.3 Hierarchical Simulation Model

We now use the observations we made on ThreatFox and MISP to inform a hierarchical simulation model that should replicate the actual observations as closely as possible. It mimics a fictitious platform on which users organize themselves in communities and share IoC according to three subprocesses: "user arrival" describes the onboarding of users on the platform, "IoC arrival" features a hidden Markov process by which the emergence of IoC is simulated, and "user behavior" describes the propensity of users to share IoC with others. The set of parameters introduced by these subprocesses is shown in Table 4.1.

In our model, a Dirichlet process with ancillary parameters α and θ controls both the arrival and the distribution of users across communities. Typically, such a process would only use a single parameter θ (implying that $\alpha = 0$) to assign users to communities according to an exponential law, so that the probability of joining a community is proportional to the number of users in that community. However, since Fig. 4.6 suggests that the actual distribution of users on MISP follows a power law, we introduce a second parameter α, so that we can increase the concentration of the largest communities and further decrease the chance that a user will join a small community. Thus, while higher values of α encourage users to either join the largest community or start a new one, higher values of θ imply that more communities are created. Note that for $\theta = \alpha = 0$, there is just a single community, hence ThreatFox emerges as a special case of MISP. For the case of more than one community, we used the data on 2,408 MISP communities to estimate $\hat{\theta} = 14.9$ and $\hat{\alpha} = 0.89$.

4.3.1 User Arrival Subprocess

We let $\mathcal{Y}_t$ capture the set of all active users at time $t = 1, \ldots, T$. Hence, the number of elements in this set is $R_t = |\mathcal{Y}_t| = \sum_{j=1}^{t} Y_t$ and the number of daily new arrivals is $|\mathcal{Y}_t| - |\mathcal{Y}_{t-1}| = Y_t$.

Table 4.1 Parameters used in our hierarchical model

Parameter	Defined in	Value or estimate	Description
λ	$\mathbb{R}^+$	$\hat{\lambda} = 0.18$	User arrival rate estimated with ThreatFox data, remains fixed in simulation model
θ	$\mathbb{R}^+$	$\hat{\theta} = 14.9$	Concentration parameter; describes how strongly users would rather create a new community than join an existing one
α	$[0, 1]$	$\hat{\alpha} = 0.89$	Discount parameter which controls the distribution of users into communities
μ_A, μ_B	$\mathbb{R}$	$\hat{\mu}_A = 283$, $\hat{\mu}_B = 3639$	IoC arrival rates for hidden Markov process states, both remain fixed in simulation model
p_A, p_B	$[0, 1]$	$\hat{p}_A = 0.29$, $\hat{p}_B = 0.11$	Transition probabilities for hidden Markov process states, both remain fixed in simulation model
δ	$\mathbb{R}^+$	$\delta \in \{1, 100\}$	Risk to user reputation if IoC is shared, assumed to be $\delta = 1$ for ThreatFox and $\delta = 100$ for MISP
κ	$[0, 1]$	$\kappa = 0.5$	Average fraction of users who already know about a particular IoC, assumed to be $\kappa = 0.5$

If, like in the case of MISP, the total number of users increases linearly over time with a constant rate of $\mathbb{E}[Y_t] = \lambda$, we can assume that the number of new arrivals per day has a Poisson distribution. The maximum likelihood estimator of the rate parameter is then given by the average daily arrival number $\hat{\lambda} = \frac{1}{T}\sum_{t=1}^{T} Y_t$ and the estimated cumulative user count is given by the observed linear function $\hat{R}_t = \hat{\lambda}t$ with $\hat{\lambda} = 0.18$ users per day. This Poisson process also facilitates the sampling procedure since we only need to sample a new Poisson random variable Y_t for each day and add the number of new users obtained thereby to the set of all users $\mathcal{Y}_t$.

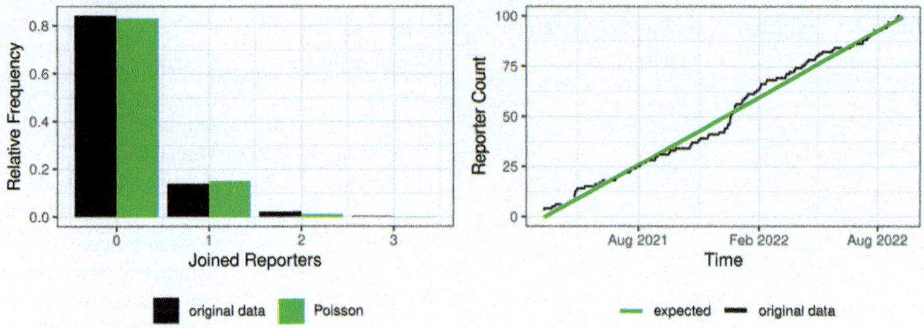

Fig. 4.7 Comparison of MISP user arrival and Poisson process prediction

We checked the plausibility of our assumptions by comparing this Poisson process to the original MISP data (viz. Fig. 4.7). It compares the relative frequency of daily user arrival in the MISP data with the frequencies given by the Poisson model (left-hand panel) as well as the expected values of cumulative reporter counts over time (right-hand panel).

We further aligned the user arrival process with the actual MISP structure by grouping users to communities. The variable $\ell = 1, \ldots, L_t$ captures the number of communities at time t, and $\mathcal{Y}_t^\ell$ with size $Y_t^\ell = |\mathcal{Y}_t^\ell|$ records the set of all users in a particular community at time t. The original set $\mathcal{Y}_t = \bigcup_{\ell=1}^{L} \mathcal{Y}_t^\ell$ then defines the number of all users across all communities. We assume any user can join but one discrete community, so $\mathcal{Y}_t^\ell \cap \mathcal{Y}_t^{\ell'} = \emptyset$ for all $\ell \neq \ell'$. Therefore $\{\mathcal{Y}_t^\ell\}_\ell$ is a partition of the set of all active users.

We let a Dirichlet process assign users to communities. It assumes that the probability ω_1 of a newly arriving user to be assigned to a community is proportional to the number of users already present in that community, so $\omega_1 = \frac{Y_t^\ell}{Y_t}$ for community ℓ. Hence, we capture a typical concentration process by which a few communities grow the faster the larger they are already, whereas most communities will have relatively few users.

While this process can model a fixed number of communities, we also want to discuss the case where users organize themselves in new communities, the probability of which we denote as $\omega_2 = \frac{\theta}{Y_t+\theta}$, where $\theta > 0$ is an ancillary parameter. Since users can now choose to start new communities instead of joining an extant community ℓ, the probability of joining the latter is $\omega_3 = \frac{Y_t^\ell}{Y_t+\theta}$.

Finally, we consider the measured distribution of community size which we found follows a power law. The probability that a new community emerges then is $\omega_4 = \frac{\theta+\alpha L}{Y_t+\theta}$, where L is the number of extant communities at that time, and the probability that a user joins community ℓ is $\frac{Y_t^\ell-\alpha}{Y_t+\theta}$.

Figure 4.8 plots the community building process which has a Pareto distribution. With the data on all 2,408 MISP communities, we estimated a Pareto index of $\beta = 1.66$ and $\hat{\alpha} = 0.89$.

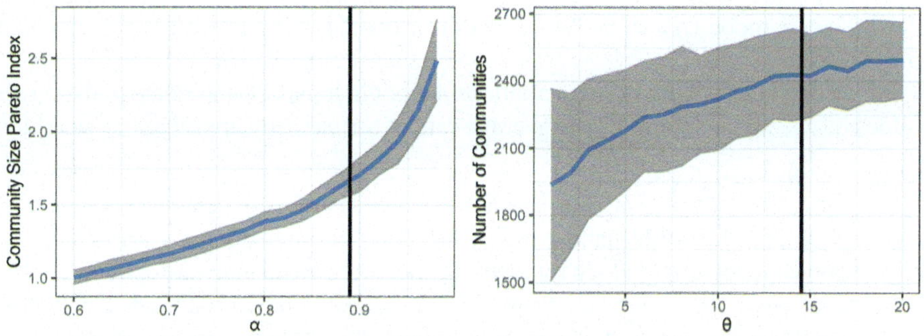

Fig. 4.8 Optimal parameters for the community building process

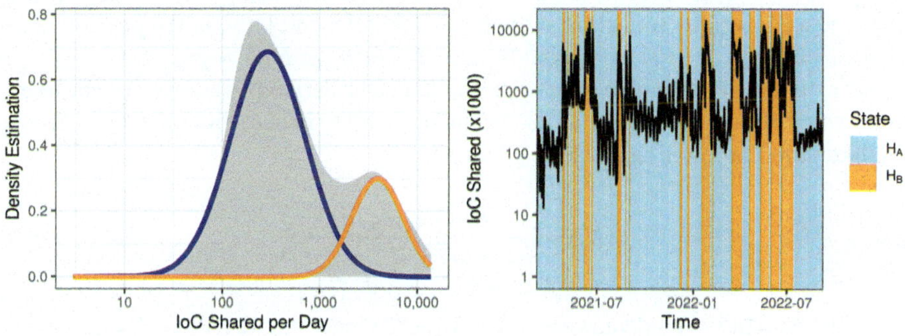

Fig. 4.9 Counts and density estimation of IoC shared on ThreatFox per day

4.3.2 IoC Arrival Subprocess

Next, we simulate the arrival of all IoC that the users have chosen to share with their community. We denote by X_t the number of IoC added to the sharing platform at time t which is measured in days, so the total number of IoC available by that time is $S_t = \sum_{j=1}^{t} X_t$, and the set of all IoC shared on the platform at time t is $\mathcal{X}_t$ with size $|\mathcal{X}_t| = S_t$. Since the daily number of IoC arriving on ThreatFox is numerically large (viz. Fig. 4.9, right-hand panel), we will use a continuous approximation for the discrete count data in X_t.

In both datasets, the density of the logarithms $\log X_t$ exhibit an approximately normal distribution (viz. Fig. 4.9, left-hand panel). We therefore posit that X_t is distributed according to a weighted sum of log-normal distributions with mixture weight p in logspace:

$$\log X_t \sim (1-p)\mathcal{N}\left(\log \mu_A, \sigma_A^2\right) + p\mathcal{N}\left(\log \mu_B, \sigma_B^2\right) \tag{4.3}$$

We assumed that μ_B corresponds to the larger mode $\mu_B > \mu_A$ and used the ThreatFox data to estimate parameters for the first mode ($\hat{\mu}_A = 284; \hat{\sigma}_A^2 = 0.71$) and for the larger mode ($\hat{\mu}_B = 3639$; $\hat{\sigma}_B^2 = 0.38$). For the mixture weight we obtained $\hat{p} = 0.25$.

Since the means of the two distributions are not in logspace and relate to the direct values of X_t, we can compute the average rate of arrival μ by applying the weighted geometric mean $\mu = \sqrt{\mu_A^{1-p} \mu_B^p}$.

On Threatfox, IoC arrival is irregular over time: Periods of relatively low arrival counts (viz. Fig. 4.9, right-hand panel, state H_A) are interspersed with periods of highly intensive reporting which typically begins when novel malware appears (right-hand panel, state H_B). In order to model the autocorrelation associated with this effect, we introduce a hidden Markov chain with these two modes H_A and H_B. The sequence h_t, $t = 1, \ldots, T$ assigns to each day t one of the states $h_t \in \{H_A, H_B\}$. Then, the probability that the state of the subsequent day changes from H_A to H_B or vice versa is given by transition probabilities that depend only on the previous day: $\mathbb{P}\left[h_{t-1} = H_B | h_t = H_A\right] = p_B$ and $\mathbb{P}\left[h_{t-1} = H_A | h_t = H_B\right] = p_A$.

An estimate of the hidden state sequence h_t can be derived by comparing the likelihood ratios of each day. Under a log-normal probability density function $f(x; \mu, \sigma^2)$, the likelihood ratio for each day is given by

$$r(X_t) = \frac{p f(X_t; \mu_B, \sigma_B^2)}{(1-p) f(X_t; \mu_A, \sigma_A^2)} \tag{4.4}$$

Using the ThreatFox data, we estimated that the hidden state is $\hat{h}_t = H_B$ if $r(X_t) > 1$. With this estimate, we counted the number of transitions and obtained transition probabilities of $\hat{p}_A = 0.29$ and $\hat{p}_B = 0.11$.

However, the above calculation does not yet consider that the number of IoC shared on ThreatFox exhibits a non-linear growth pattern (viz. Eq. 4.1). Since the right-hand panel of Fig. 4.9 suggests that the frequency of IoC arrivals is higher during state H_B while the sequence of the modes is rather stable, we fit the model with fixed rates μ_A and μ_B.

4.3.3 Behavioral Subprocess

Finally, we consider that an IoC can only arrive at the platform if and only if the user chooses to share it. Hence, IoC visible on the platform represent but a subsample of all IoC that users are aware of. They may choose to withhold a particular IoC due to a lack of trust in other members of their community, or they may fear to publish a weakness that is critical to their business interests.

We follow [9] and frame the user's decision to share an IoC as an economic problem. IoC that are already broadly known by a subset of users $\mathcal{I} \subset \mathcal{Y}_t$ in the community have little value for that community if they are shared again. Vice versa, the fewer users $I(x) = |\mathcal{I}(x)|$ already know about an IoC, the more valuable it is to the community. Hence, the raw value of a particular IoC $x \in X_t$ can be expressed in terms of the number of all users who do not yet know about it. Following the example of ThreatFox, we multiply this raw value by a confidence score $c(x) \in [0, 1]$, so that the value of an IoC is reduced proportionately to the sharer's lack of confidence in its novelty or relevance. The value of a particular IoC $x \in \mathcal{X}_t$ then is

$$v_t(x) = c(x)\left(1 - \frac{|\mathcal{I}(x)|}{|\mathcal{Y}_t|}\right) = c(x)\left(1 - \frac{I(x)}{Y_t}\right) \tag{4.5}$$

Since only shared IoC can be observed, the true distribution of $v_t(x)$ cannot be known. A simple approach to this limitation is to assume that $I(x)$ has a uniform distribution $I(x) \sim \text{Uni}\{1, \ldots, Y_t\}$. By defining a parameter $\kappa \in [0, 1]$ which captures the average fraction of users who already know about the IoC, we can further refine the distributional assumption and assign a Beta distribution to this fraction: $\frac{I(x)}{Y_t} \sim \text{Beta}(\kappa, 1 - \kappa)$. A small κ thus implies that very few users already know about an IoC and vice versa.

We now model the behavioral aspects that co-determine a user's willingness to share a particular IoC: benefit expectation (U_v), reputation (U_p), and specificity (U_r). To exclude the possibility that worthless IoC are shared excessively, we introduce an exponential scaling with a factor of 4 for all three aspects, so that IoC of very little value are unlikely to be shared (note that $e^{-4} < 0.02$).

First, a user is likely to share an IoC if it is worth less than the average value of all IoC on the platform. In this case, the user gives up relatively little value but can benefit from more valuable IoC shared by others. Since there are X_t IoC on the platform at time t and the average value of all IoC on the platform at time t is $\frac{1}{X_t}\sum_{z \in \mathcal{X}_t} v_t(z)$, the probability that a user shares a particular IoC x of value $v_t(x)$ is

$$\mathbb{P}[U_v(x) = 1] = \exp\left(-4\left(v_t(x) - \frac{1}{X_t}\sum_{z \in \mathcal{X}_t} v_t(z)\right)\right) \tag{4.6}$$

Second, we posit that highly reputable users are unlikely to share IoCs of little value since they would risk their reputation in the user community, not the least because mutual trust is a significant antecedent to the willingness to share [15]. We therefore introduce an ancillary parameter $\delta > 0$ which assigns a reputational risk to users. Reputational risk grows with δ, hence a numerically large δ implies a high risk that user damage their reputation if they share irrelevant or low-value IoC. We compare the value of a given IoC with the average value of all IoC shared by a particular user $y \in \mathcal{Y}_t$. This average can be computed by introducing the set of IoC shared by user y, $\mathcal{X}_t(y) \subseteq \mathcal{X}_t$, and then only use the IoC in this set to compute their average value of $\bar{v}(y) = \frac{1}{|\mathcal{X}_t(y)|}\sum_{z \in \mathcal{X}_t(y)} v_t(z)$. We scale this value with reputational risk δ, so that the probability that a user shares an IoC subject to his or her reputation is:

$$\mathbb{P}\left[U_p(x, y) = 1\right] = \exp\left(4\delta\left(v_t(x) - \bar{v}(y)\right)\right) \tag{4.7}$$

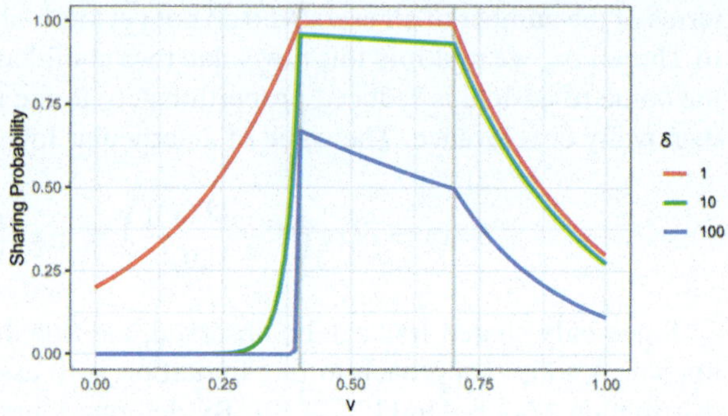

Fig. 4.10 Sharing probability for different values of an IoC

Third, a user's propensity to share an IoC is likely co-determined by the specificity of this IoC. We argued before that a particular IoC $x \in \mathcal{X}_t$ is more valuable to a community the fewer users in that community already know about it. Hence, the few users that do know may be reluctant to share it since the specificity of the IoC may point to vulnerabilities [10, 18, 19]. They would probably only share such information in smaller communities where only a handful of users interact who trust each other and who can be relied upon to handle such IoC discreetly. Therefore, the value of an IoC $v_t(x)$ must be scaled at time t by the size of the community Y_t^ℓ in relation to the number of all users on the platform Y_t with a factor of $\frac{Y_t^\ell - 1}{Y_t - 1}$. Note the subtraction of 1 filters out user communities with just one member which do exist on the MISP platform. Hence, the probability that an IoC is shared within a specific community, subject to reputational risk δ, is

$$\mathbb{P}\left[U_r(x) = 1\right] = \exp\left(-4\delta \frac{Y_t^\ell - 1}{Y_t - 1} v_t(x)\right) \tag{4.8}$$

Finally, we posit that all three aspects must be present cumulatively for an IoC to be shared: Users should expect to realize a benefit from sharing it, they will only do so if they really believe it is valuable, and if their fears regarding sensitivity are alleviated. Hence, we can express the decision to share an IoC as a single Bernoulli variable with probability $U(x, y) = U_v(x) \cdot U_p(x, y) \cdot U_r(x)$. Figure 4.10 plots its range subject to different levels of IoC value v and reputational risk δ.

The plot suggests that high values of δ decrease the probability of sharing because of reputational risk: the higher a user's reputation in the community, the less likely it is that a user shares IoC below a certain value threshold—much unlike users with a low reputation. But those users are also more likely to share IoCs of higher value than users who are concerned about their reputation.

4.3.4 Sampling Procedure

In order to combine the above subprocesses into a full model, we sequentially sample from them in three steps, using one day as unit of discretization. We first sample a number of users from the user arrival subprocess and assign them to a community. The parameters associated with this first step are the arrival rate λ, and the community concentration and dispersion parameters θ and α. Since we estimated these on the basis of ThreatFox and MISP data, they will be fixed at their estimated values.

In the second step, we sample a number of IoC from the IoC arrival subprocess. Using the IoC distribution with mean μ, we assign the sampled IoC to some users at random. The hidden Markov chain is sampled with different means μ_A and μ_B for the two states H_A and H_B, and we use the respective transition probabilities p_A and p_B we estimated with ThreatFox and MISP data before. The number of sharing users is scaled with $\sqrt{Y_t}$ to simulate the effect that users leave over time. The specific users are selected with a probability proportional to the number of IoC they have already shared. The third and final step evaluates the sharing probabilities for all selected users and sampled IoC. In this step we scale the sharing probability using value and reputation, and we scale the number of selected users to match the real IoC we observed being shared on ThreatFox as closely as possible.

Figure 4.11 provides an illustration of how the sampling process matches simulated to actual data. It shows a single time series of simulated IoC counts and compares them to the real data we observed on ThreatFox. The simulation is calibrated such that after $T = 550$ days, the number of simulated IoC shared is close to the actual observed number, and the measured exponent of daily IoC counts with reputational risk parameter $\delta = 1$ matches exactly the observed $\gamma = 0.49$.

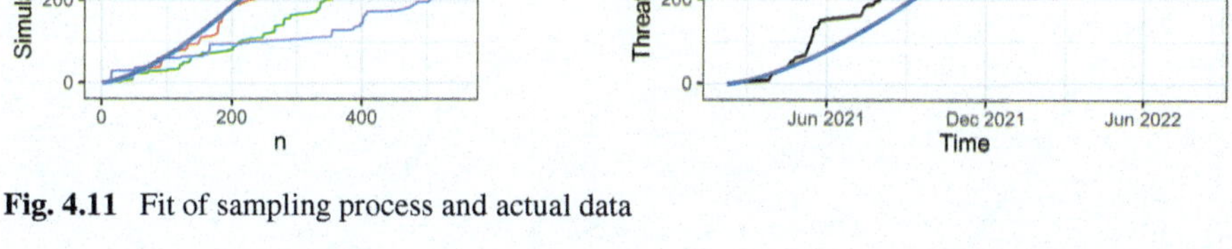

Fig. 4.11 Fit of sampling process and actual data

4.4 Simulation Results

We generated all the following results by replicating the simulation six times for a total number of $T = 4000$ steps. The plots show the mean values of these six replications as dots. To facilitate the depiction of trends and patterns, we fitted cubic splines to all results in order to obtain smooth lines.

In a first simulation, we let the reputational risk parameter δ vary across two platforms, one with a single and one with multiple communities, and analyzed how different levels of reputational risk influenced the total number of IoC shared (left-hand panel) and the average value of the IoC shared (right-hand panel). Figure 4.12 presents the results.

We find that on a single-community platform, users are reluctant to share IoC when reputational risk is high, so that relatively few sensitive IoC are shared and the average IoC value falls with increasing reputational risk. In contrast, this reputational risk effect is much smaller on a multiple-community platform, and the average value even increases with reputational risk, implying that users are confident and trust each other when they share high-value IoC. This implies that a platform with a single user community like ThreatFox will likely attract users who put less emphasis on reputation and share more, but less valuable IoC. In contrast, multiple-community platforms like MISP can expect to perform better in regard to the sharing of high-value IoC.

In a second step, we let the parameters θ and α vary in order to detail this result. Figure 4.13 shows the corresponding results. Note the vertical bar is set at the estimate of $\hat{\theta} = 14.9$ we obtained from the MISP data.

Both the number and the average value of the IoC shared increase with the number and the dispersion of the communities on the platform. We let the parameter θ vary to study the effect of the number of communities. An isolated effect can only be measured when $\alpha = 0$, but we added the base case of MISP ($\alpha = 0.89$) in Fig. 4.13 with dashed lines for the sake of completeness. Clearly, as the number of communities grows, so does the number of shared IoC, regardless of reputational risk.

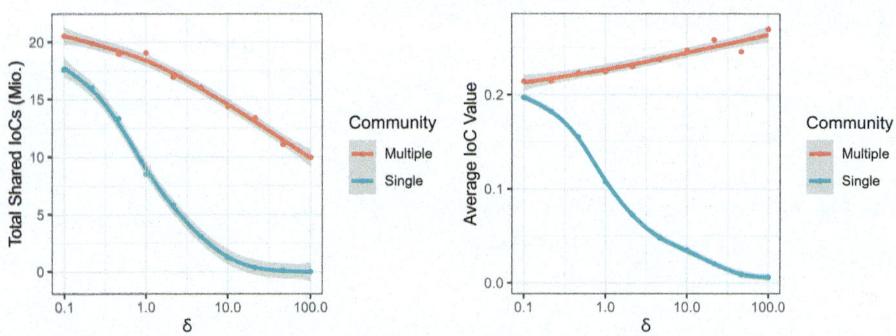

Fig. 4.12 IoC shared and average IoC for different levels of δ and platform designs

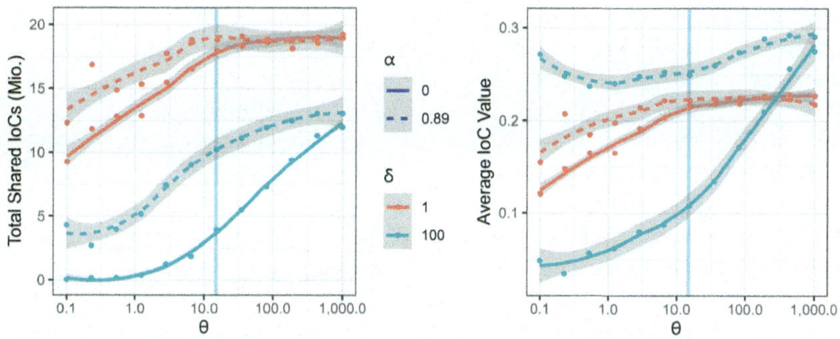

Fig. 4.13 IoC shared and average IoC value for different levels of θ and α

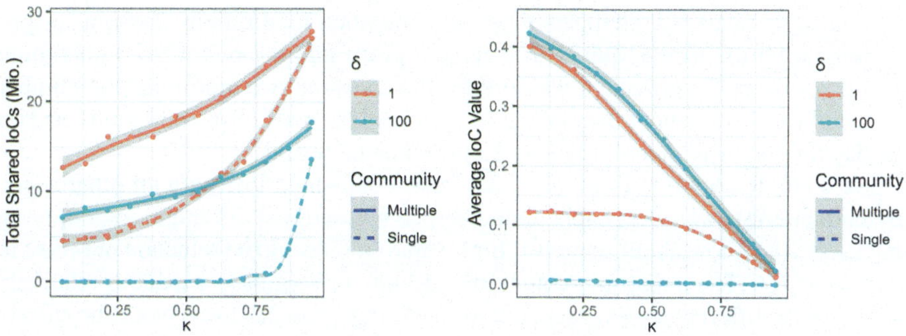

Fig. 4.14 IoC shared and average IoC value for different levels of κ

We presume that, when this risk is low, this number likely saturates when θ exceeds some threshold, and then other factors likely deter users from sharing.

The right-hand panel of Fig. 4.13 shows that IoC value increases with the number of communities, and more strongly so the higher the reputational risk is. Thus, many small communities would be required to reap the full benefit a high value IoC offers, since the line for $\delta = 1$ is only exceeded for high values of θ. Note, however, that this analysis does not strictly hold for MISP which has $\alpha = 0.89$, implying that the case for high reputational risk is always above the one for low reputational risk.

In a third simulation, we let the parameter κ vary by platform design and reputational risk. Since κ is the average fraction of users who already know about a particular IoC, the term $(1 - \kappa)$ is the average value of an IoC. Figure 4.14 shows that when κ is small, implying an IoC has a high value, many more IoC are shared on a multiple-community compared to a single-community design, and this effect is stable for different levels of reputational risk.

Vice versa, when κ is large, the average value of IoC shared decreases quickly, on both platform designs but quicker for a single-community setting with low reputational risk, implying that many IoC of low value are shared by users who are not too much concerned about damaging their reputation by doing so.

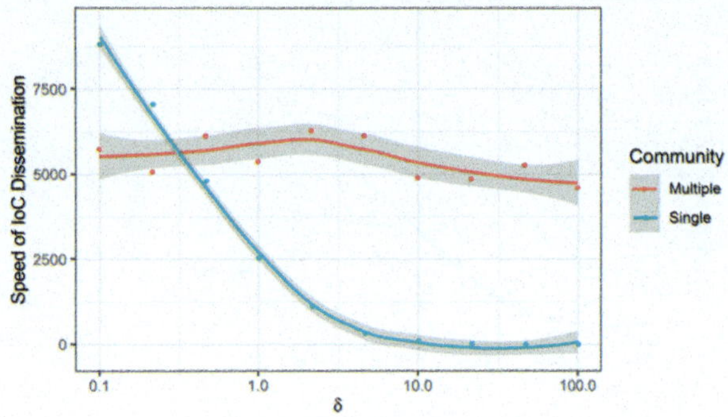

Fig. 4.15 Dissemination speed by platform community design

Finally, we analyzed the speed of IoC dissemination for different platform designs by simulating the time required to convey a given number of IoC to a maximum number of users. To provide a measure for this question, we multiplied the number of shared IoC by day with the number of members the respective community had on the day the IoC was shared. Figure 4.15 presents the results.

For a single-community design where users can share IoC with all other users, dissemination speed quickly approaches zero as reputational risk increases, implying that users who know about sensitive (high-value) IoC would be reluctant or refuse to share such IoC. For a multiple-community design, dissemination speed is relatively stable across different levels of reputational risk, implying that users would be willing to share high-value IoC within specialized communities without much hesitation.

4.5 Conclusion

Our results point to a trade-off between the speed with which IoC are shared, and the average value of those IoC. Single-community designs like ThreatFox are less associated with reputational risk, and hence IoC sharing is fast, but the average value of what is shared remains limited. On multiple-community designs like MISP, high-value IoC are shared provided users can organize themselves in specialized communities in which they probably trust each other and minimize the sharing of low-value IoC since their reputation is at stake. At the same time, such communities seem to facilitate the exchange of high-value IoC that might be too sensitive to be shared.

For future platform managers, this trade-off implies that a design which facilitates anonymous and speedy exchange will probably set limits on the value of the IoC shared, whereas IoC sharing in multiple-community designs is probably slower, associated with more transaction cost, but of higher value to cyberdefense. Hence, unilateral praises of the superiority of collective online interaction and open-community collaboration models (e.g., [14, 20, 23]) should be taken with a pinch of salt.

Our simulation suggests that a multiple-community approach for users who are sensitive to reputational risk leads to a slower but more valuable exchange. Hence, this design could be used in settings where IoC are associated with structural vulnerabilities that enable targeted attacks. In contrast, a single, anonymous community could quickly share information on relatively low-key events, such as the emergence of malware that targets average web users.

Nevertheless, future platform architects may also evaluate how these two different approaches to sharing information may be combined in a single platform. For example, a hybrid platform could offer users a choice to share a particular IoC either personally within a closed community or anonymously with all users.

References

1. Böhme, R. (2016). Back to the roots: Information sharing economics and what we can learn for security. In *Proceedings of the 2016 ACM Workshop on Information Sharing and Collaborative Security,* (pp. 1–2).
2. Böhme, R. (Ed.). (2013). *The economics of information security and privacy*. Springer.
3. Dulaunoy, A., Wagener, G., Iklody, A., Mokaddem, S., & Wagner, C. (2018). An indicator scoring method for MISP platforms. In *Proceedings of the 2018 TNC conference, Trondheim (Norway).*
4. ENISA. (2017). *Information sharing and analysis centres (ISACs): Cooperative models*. European Union Agency For Network and Information Security.
5. ENISA. (2010). *Incentives and barriers to information sharing*. European Union Agency for Network and Information Security.
6. Falco, G., et al. (2019). Cyber risk research impeded by disciplinary barriers. *Science, 366*(6469), 1066–1069.
7. Gal-Or, E., & Ghose, A. (2005). The economic incentives for sharing security information. *Information Systems Research, 16*, 186–208.
8. Garrido-Pelaz, R., González-Manzano, L., Pastrana, S. (2016). Shall we collaborate? A model to analyse the benefits of information sharing. In *Proceedings of the 2016 ACM Workshop on Information Sharing and Collaborative Security,* (pp. 15–24).
9. He, M., Devine, L., & Zhuang, J. (2018). Perspectives on cybersecurity information sharing among multiple stakeholders using a decision-theoretic approach. *Risk Analysis, 38*(2), 215–225.
10. Horák, M., Stupka, V., & Husák, M. (2019). GDPR compliance cybersecurity software: A case study of DPIA in information sharing platform. In *Proceedings of the 14th ACM International Conference on Availability, Reliability and Security* (pp. 1–8).
11. Iklody, A., Wagener, G., Dulaunoy, A., Mokaddem, S., & Wagner, S. (2018). Decaying indicators of compromise. arXiv:1803.11052.
12. Jollès, E., & Mermoud, A. (2022). Building collaborative cybersecurity for critical infrastructure protection: Empirical evidence of collective intelligence information-sharing dynamics on ThreatFox. In *Proceedings of the 17th International Conference on Critical Information Infrastructures Security (CRITIS), forthcoming*.
13. Laube, S., & Böhme, R. (2017). Strategic aspects of cyber risk information sharing. *ACM Computing Surveys, 50*(5), 77: 1–36.
14. Malone, T. W. (2019). *Superminds: How hyperconnectivity is changing the way we solve problems*. Oneworld Publications.
15. Mermoud, A., Keupp, M. M., Huguenin, K., Palmié, M., & Percia David, D. (2019). To share or not to share: A behavioral perspective on human participation in security information sharing. *Journal of Cybersecurity, 5*(1), tyz006.

16. Mokaddem, S., Wagener, G., Dulaunoy, A., & Iklody, A. (2019). Taxonomy driven indicator scoring in MISP threat intelligence platforms. arXiv:1902.03914.
17. Moore, T. (2010). The economics of cybersecurity: Principles and policy options. *International Journal of Critical Infrastructure Protection, 3*, 103–117.
18. Murdoch, S., & Leaver, N. (2015). Anonymity vs. trust in cyber-security collaboration. In *Proceedings of the 2nd ACM Workshop on Information Sharing and Collaborative Security* (pp. 27–29).
19. Pang, R., Allman, M., Paxson, V., & Lee, J. (2006). The devil and packet trace anonymization. *ACM SIGCOMM Computer Communication Review, 36*(1), 29–38.
20. Postmes, T., & Brunsting, S. (2002). Collective action in the age of the internet: Mass communication and online mobilization. *Social Science Computer Review, 3*, 290–301.
21. Wagner, C., Dulaunoy, A., Wagener, G., & Iklody, A. (2016). MISP—The design and implementation of a collaborative threat intelligence sharing platform. In *Proceedings of the 2016 ACM Workshop on Information Sharing and Collaborative Security* (pp. 49–56).
22. Webster, G. D., Harris, R. L., Hanif, Z. D., Hembree, B. A., Grossklags, J., & Eckert, C. (2018). Sharing is caring: Collaborative analysis and real-time enquiry for security analytics. In *Proceedings of the 2018 IEEE International Conference on Internet of Things* (pp. 1402–1409).
23. Woolley, A. W., Chabris, C., Pentland, A., Hashmi, N., & Malone, T. W. (2010). Evidence for a collective intelligence factor in the performance of human groups. *Science, 330*(6004), 686–688.

Philipp Fischer received his Bachelor's degree in Computational Science and Engineering in 2019 and is currently completing his Master's degree in Data Science, both at the Swiss Federal Institute of Technology (ETH) Zurich. His professional expertise in data science spans algorithm development, statistical modeling and visualization, specifically for IoT data. His research interests focus on statistical computing and the development of data analytics tools and software.

Sébastien Gillard received an MSc in Physics from the University of Fribourg (Switzerland) in 2016. He specializes in computational physics and statistics, in particular, data analysis and applied statistical modeling and analytical and numerical resolution methods for differential equations. His current research interest is the application of insights from recommender systems to critical infrastructure defense, including the development of code that can power deep learning algorithms.

Part II
Foresight

Chapter 5
Identification of Future Cyberdefense Technology by Text Mining

Dimitri Percia David, William Blonay, Sébastien Gillard, Thomas Maillart, Alain Mermoud, Loïc Maréchal, and Michael Tsesmelis

5.1 Introduction

Few would doubt that firms should identify technologies today that will prove to be important for cyberdefense tomorrow, and that they should evaluate such technologies thoroughly and objectively so they can make informed investment decisions

Supplementary Information The online version contains supplementary material available at https://doi.org/10.1007/978-3-031-30191-9_5.

D. Percia David (✉)
Institute of Entrepreneurship & Management, University of Applied Sciences Valais, Sierre, Switzerland
e-mail: dimitri.perciadavid@hevs.ch

T. Maillart
Information Science Institute, GSEM, Université de Genève, Genève, Switzerland
e-mail: thomas.maillart@unige.ch

W. Blonay · A. Mermoud · M. Tsesmelis
Cyber-Defence Campus, armasuisse Science and Technology, Thun, Switzerland
e-mail: william.blonay@ar.admin.ch

A. Mermoud
e-mail: alain.mermoud@ar.admin.ch

M. Tsesmelis
e-mail: michael.tsesmelis22@imperial.ac.uk

S. Gillard
Department of Defense Economics, Military Academy at ETH Zurich, Birmensdorf ZH, Switzerland
e-mail: sebastien.gillard@vtg.admin.ch

L. Maréchal
Department of Information Systems, HEC lausanne, University of Lausanne, 1005 Lausanne, Switzerland
e-mail: loic.marechal@unil.ch

M. M. Keupp (ed.), *Cyberdefense*, International Series in Operations Research & Management Science 342,
https://doi.org/10.1007/978-3-031-30191-9_5

[18, 23]. However, this proposition is easier written than realized, since firms are subject to bias and misjudgment as they invest in technology for cyberdefense.

When firms defer investment for too long, or if procurement procedures are highly bureaucratic, the acquired technology is already outdated when it is finally deployed [41]. When they buy too early, they acquire technology that may fail to provide effective protection. Vendors often forego security issues as they put underdeveloped technology to market early and then use clients as beta-testers who must identify and patch vulnerabilities [1], not the least both because creating secure technology requires high investments, and profitability decreases with time-to-market [1, 7].

Many firms follow the advice of consultancy firms or vendors when making investment decisions, so they are prone to any bias that such advice entails [16, 42], all the more since human information processing is often more influenced by psychological tendencies than by objective analysis [33]. It is therefore not surprising that many qualitative models and indicators that rely on subjective assessments have failed to correctly predict the emergence and relevance of future technologies [3, 8, 26].

Such misjudgments are not only costly since firms must forego the sunk cost of ineffective investment, but they also threaten the efficacy of future cyberdefense. While the literature abounds with attempts to improve technology forecasting (for recent reviews, see [9, 22, 28], these problems are surprisingly persistent. In an attempt to overcome them, we propose that big data bibliometric analysis ("text mining") can provide firms with open source-based information about the maturity, security, and relevance of any technology. Firms can then use this information to make informed investment decisions.

5.2 Bibliometric Method

Our approach builds on prior work in bibliometrics and automated text mining [13, 14, 25, 37]. These methods have been successfully used to forecast and extrapolate technological trends, if with relatively small samples (e.g., [6, 20]).

We follow recent suggestions to complement such approaches with big data analytics (e.g., [19, 30]) and bibliometric methods (e.g., [14, 37]; Jaewoo et al. 2014). We propose an automated analysis of the `arXiv` repository which collects scholarly working papers, pre-prints, technical reports, post-proceedings, and journal publications.[1] These contributions ("e-prints") can be seen as a proxy for present and emerging technological knowledge.

With such a measure, we capture the amount of attention that the scientific community gives to specific cyberdefense technologies. In the scientific field of computer science, uploading e-prints on the *arXiv* repository–once they are ready for submission in a scientific conference or a scientific journal—is a common practice.

[1] See https://arxiv.org/.

Consequently, we argue that most scientific advances are captured through the uploaded e-prints of the *arXiv* platform.

We downloaded the full text of all 1,858,293 e-prints uploaded between August 14, 1991 and December 31, 2020, by a mirror of the repository which is accessible through Cornell University.[2] We isolated those e-prints that the `arXiv` moderators had grouped into the domain `.cs` (computer science). Authors who wish to upload e-prints must choose a category that best describes the subject matter of their work. Since authors have no apparent incentive to misclassify their own work, and since moderators also check the classification consistency, we believe the resulting taxonomy is accurate.[3]. However, not all contributions in this domain are necessarily relevant for cyberdefense. Since the `arXiv` moderators have further subdivided the `.cs` domain into more specific clusters, we selected those clusters whose technology was discussed in the section *Defenses* in Wikipedia's information security portal.[4] This selection procedure yielded a population of twenty clusters. Table 5.1 presents them together with their respective number of e-prints. We also de-seasonalized publication frequencies in all clusters by applying the LOESS (STL) method [12].

We first defined a set Ω_x for all clusters which was used in all subsequent analyses. While we use monthly frequencies for the purpose of this analysis, the set can be scaled to any time frequency.

$$\Omega_x = \{m \in \mathbb{N}^* \mid m \leq N\} \text{ with } N \in \mathbb{N}^* \tag{5.1}$$

where x is a cluster and

- m represents a month between the date of the first e-print in a given cluster x and the date of the last e-print in that cluster;
- N is the number of months between the date of the first e-print in a given cluster x and the date of the last e-print in that cluster.

While `arXiv` is popular today, it was relatively unknown in 1991, and hence many e-prints may have been uploaded well after their original date of creation. We therefore cannot readily assume the repository shows a constant rate of attention. We therefore based all subsequent analyses on the publication (and not the upload) date. Further, we normalized the number of e-prints in each cluster by dividing the total number of e-prints per cluster and month by the corresponding count of all e-prints in the repository per month.[5] Table 5.2 gives descriptive statistics for normalized numbers of e-prints in each cluster obtained thereby.

[2] See www.kaggle.com/Cornell-University/arxiv.

[3] For more information about the classification process, see https://arxiv.org/category_taxonomy This taxonomy substantially relies on the 2012 ACM Computing Classification System, see https://arxiv.org/corr/subjectclasses.

[4] See https://en.wikipedia.org/wiki/Information_security.

[5] Raw data for monthly download statistics are available from https://arxiv.org/stats/monthly_downloads.

Table 5.1 Overview of clusters and e-prints

`arXiv` category	Description	# e-prints...	... which discuss security issues	Percentage
|cs.AI|	Artificial intelligence	38620	11447	29.64
|cs.AR|	Hardware architecture	2573	971	37.73
|cs.CC|	Computational complexity	8492	1216	14.31
|cs.CL|	Computation and language	29528	8536	28.90
|cs.CR|	Cryptography and security	19784	14952	75.57
|cs.CV|	Computer vision and pattern recognition	64696	21852	33.77
|cs.DB|	Databases	6269	2341	37.34
|cs.DC|	Distributed, parallel, and cluster computing	14955	5686	38.02
|cs.DS|	Data structures and algorithms	18269	3458	18.92
|cs.GT|	Computer science and game theory	7992	2279	28.51
|cs.HC|	Human-Computer interaction	8774	2753	31.37
|cs.IR|	Information retrieval	10407	3216	30.90
|cs.LG|	Machine learning	94024	30142	32.05
|cs.NE|	Neural and evolutionary computing	10155	2649	26.08
|cs.NI|	Networking and internet architecture	16606	6826	41.10
|cs.OS|	Operating systems	652	303	46.47
|cs.PL|	Programming languages	5731	1937	33.79
|cs.RO|	Robotics	16187	6055	37.40
|cs.SE|	Software engineering	10032	4109	40.95
|cs.SY|	Systems and control	18347	6845	37.30

Table 5.2 Descriptive statistics by cluster

Cluster	Mean	Median	std. dev.	Skewness	Kurtosis
cs.AI	1.013	0.473	1.421	3.532	20.656
cs.AR	0.085	0.048	0.147	7.417	79.602
cs.CC	0.412	0.414	0.191	0.212	−0.281
cs.CL	1.071	0.333	1.459	1.98	4.308
cs.CR	0.683	0.548	0.674	1.873	6.728
cs.CV	1.731	0.274	2.959	2.871	13.908
cs.DB	0.257	0.238	0.194	1.282	4.701
cs.DC	0.55	0.429	0.448	0.823	0.296
cs.DS	0.676	0.653	0.539	0.261	−1.347
cs.GT	0.332	0.366	0.249	0.294	−0.525
cs.HC	0.272	0.135	0.346	2.354	7.817
cs.IR	0.35	0.233	0.345	1.365	1.476
cs.LG	2.333	0.361	4.321	2.644	7.741
cs.NE	0.349	0.207	0.355	1.05	0.119
cs.NI	0.673	0.78	0.487	0.019	−1.454
cs.OS	0.028	0.025	0.027	0.683	−0.35
cs.PL	0.242	0.229	0.158	0.526	−0.14
cs.RO	0.447	0.12	0.827	4.617	35.723
cs.SE	0.36	0.263	0.416	5.389	54.764
cs.SY	0.964	0.84	0.875	3.295	21.205

5.3 Maturity

The literature consistently suggests that technological lifecycles follow a logistic or sigmoid shape [6, 32, 39]. We therefore analyzed the development state of the technologies in each of the 20 clusters by fitting sigmoid curves to the observed counts of e-prints over time. The sigmoid curve is attractive to fit "S-shaped" distributions because it is generated by a bounded, differentiable, and real function that is defined for all real input values, has a non-negative derivative at each point and exactly one inflection point [24]. The idea behind this approach is simple: If the curve fits the observed counts, the technology is maturing, and an inflection point can be found. If no fit is possible, the technology is still in its exponential growth phase, but the likely inflexion point can still be predicted from the model goodness-of-fit statistic. We specified the sigmoid curve as

$$\sigma(t) = \frac{L}{1 + e^{-k(t-t_0)}} \tag{5.2}$$

where $t \in \Omega_x$ and

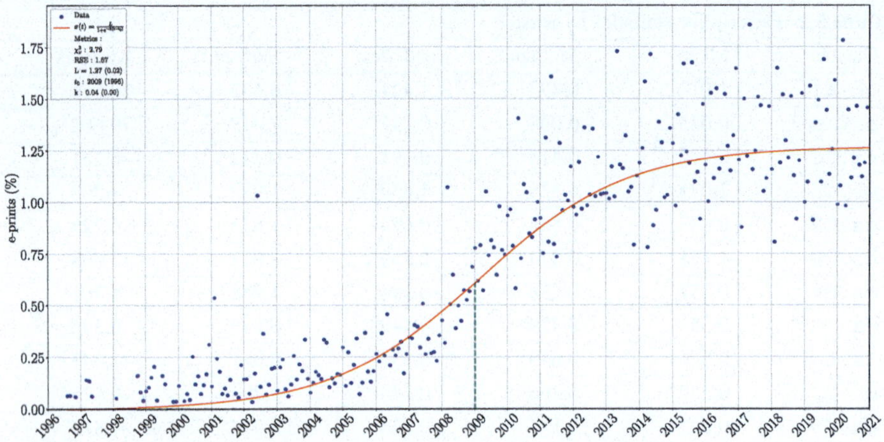

Fig. 5.1 Sigmoid fitting for cluster `cs.DS`

- t_0 is the maximum of the first derivative of the function, i.e., the time when the inflection has occurred (or will occur in the future);
- L is the curve's maximum limit value $L = \lim_{t \to +\infty} \sigma(t)$;
- k is the sigmoid growth rate of the curve.

We used the Python `.optimize.curve_fit` procedure that comes with the `scipy` package to compute the curvature, its ancillary parameters, and goodness-of-fit statistics. The procedure finds the optimal values of the parameters L, k, and t_0 as well as their respective standard errors by minimizing non-linear least squares errors through the Levenberg-Marquardt algorithm. We assessed the goodness-of-fit of the sigmoid model (i.e., the extent to which the fitted sigmoid curve adequately captures the distribution of e-prints in each cluster) by computing the squared root of the reduced chi-squared statistic χ^2_ν. If $\chi^2_\nu \approxeq 1$, a sigmoid fitting is appropriate. A $\chi^2_\nu < 1$ indicates that the model is over-fitting the data by improperly fitting noise or overestimating the error variance, whereas a $\chi^2_\nu > 1$ indicates that the fit has not fully captured the data or that the error variance has been underestimated, and a $\chi^2_\nu \gg 1$ indicates a poor model fit [5].

Accordingly, the amplitude of the standard errors of the curve parameters diverges: while the standard errors of L, k, and t_0 are relatively low in those clusters where a sigmoid curve can be fitted, they are much greater in those clusters where such fitting is not supported (viz. Table 5.3).

Table 5.3 shows good sigmoid fit for fourteen clusters; in each of these we have $\chi^2_\nu > 1$. Figures 5.1 and 5.2 plot the respective curves for the clusters `cs.DS` and `cs.CV`.[6]

[6] Due to limited space, only selected figures are shown for different χ^2_ν fit values. The complete set of figures for all fitted curves is available from the corresponding author.

Table 5.3 Ancillary parameters and goodness-of-fit statistics

Cluster	χ^2_ν	*s.e.*	L	k	t_0
`cs.AI`	10.062	3.172	49908.902	0.015	2071
`cs.AR`	1.889	1.375	1297.227	0.016	2065
`cs.CC`	2.588	1.609	0.489	0.032	2004
`cs.CL`	12.145	3.485	5.568	0.039	2019
`cs.CR`	3.013	1.736	10.783	0.015	2028
`cs.CV`	4.966	2.228	13.626	0.037	2019
`cs.DB`	2.454	1.567	0.461	0.025	2010
`cs.DC`	2.178	1.476	1.665	0.020	2015
`cs.DS`	2.788	1.670	1.273	0.037	2009
`cs.GT`	1.969	1.403	0.524	0.054	2009
`cs.HC`	2.275	1.508	1766.652	0.020	2051
`cs.IR`	2.137	1.462	8.690	0.015	2031
`cs.LG`	12.952	3.599	12463.478	0.030	2039
`cs.NE`	3.042	1.744	1.298	0.025	2016
`cs.NI`	2.383	1.544	1.125	0.046	2008
`cs.OS`	0.893	0.945	78.830	0.007	2115
`cs.PL`	2.712	1.647	0.423	0.022	2011
`cs.RO`	3.762	1.940	6.918	0.032	2022
`cs.SE`	3.297	1.816	0.855	0.025	2013
`cs.SY`	10.444	3.232	2.963	0.031	2018

Note that our method predicts the inflection point even if the right leg of the sigmoid curve will only emerge in the future (viz. t_0 in Table 5.3). For example, from Fig. 5.2 and Table 5.4, evaluators can conclude that the technological evolution in the cluster `cs.CV` is past the point of maximum growth since inflection has occurred in 2019. This implies that the technology in this cluster is now in its maturation phase, even if the full sigmoid curve is yet to emerge in the future.

For the remaning six clusters, no sigmoid function fits the data. In the cluster `cs.OS` where $\chi^2_\nu < 1$, the distribution shows a high dispersion in the e-print data, and although the number of contributions has grown, there is no clear trend towards maturity, implying that technological evolution is still uncertain (viz. Fig. 5.3).

In the five clusters where $\chi^2_\nu \gg 1$, e-prints grow exponentially. In these clusters, technology is still evolving, implying that any significant investment would be premature, even if the inflection point seems close in some clusters. Figures 5.4 and 5.5 provide illustrations for the clusters `cs.AR` and `cs.LG`.

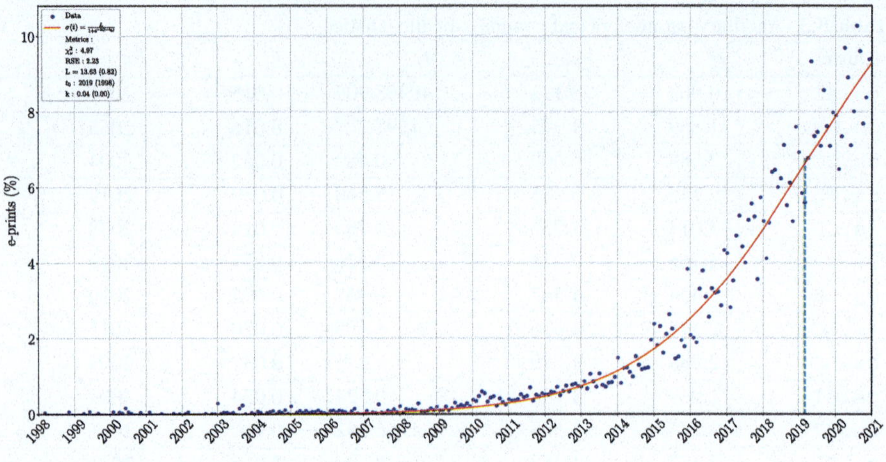

Fig. 5.2 Sigmoid fitting for cluster `cs.CV`

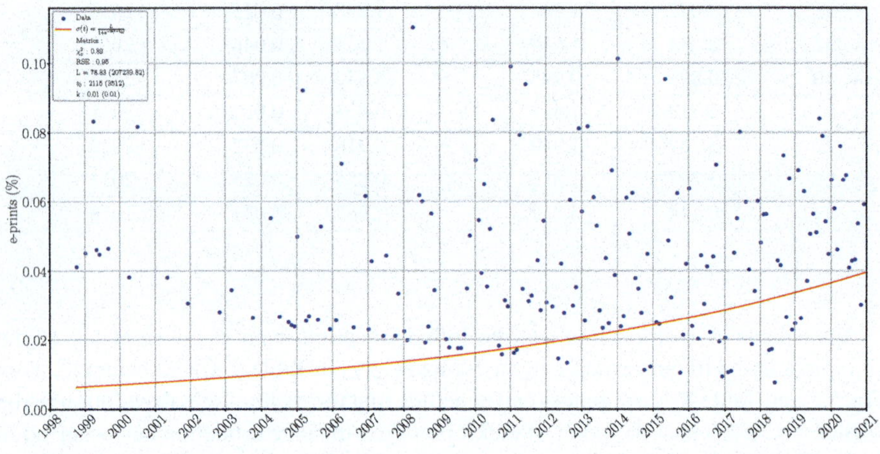

Fig. 5.3 Non-sigmoid dispersion in cluster `cs.OS`

5.4 Security Issues

As any technology moves from an initial growth phase to a consolidation phase, security issues come to the fore as the technology is adopted on an industry-wide basis. For firms, the emergence of this trend signals that an initial "hype" phase is gradually replaced by a more risk-and investment-related perspective. We would therefore expect that the growth of e-prints which specifically discuss security issues lags the growth of all e-prints.

We use natural language processing to assess which fraction of all e-prints in the respective clusters is discusses security issues. This method is often used to

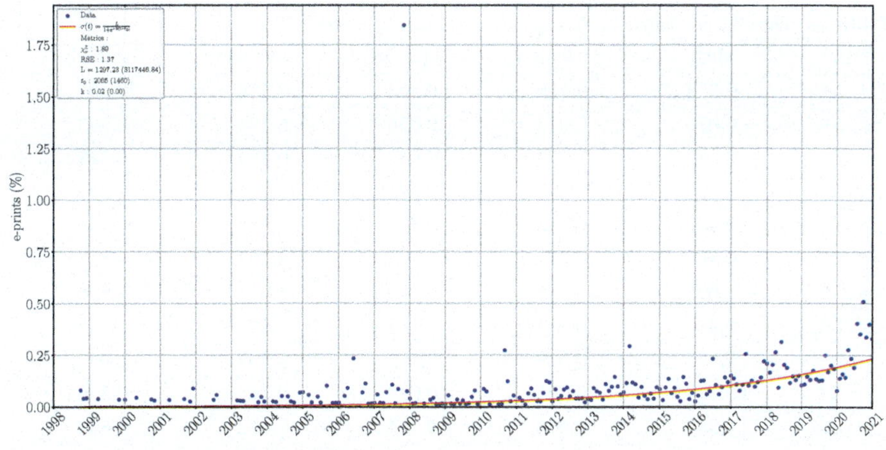

Fig. 5.4 Onset of exponential growth in cluster `cs.AR`

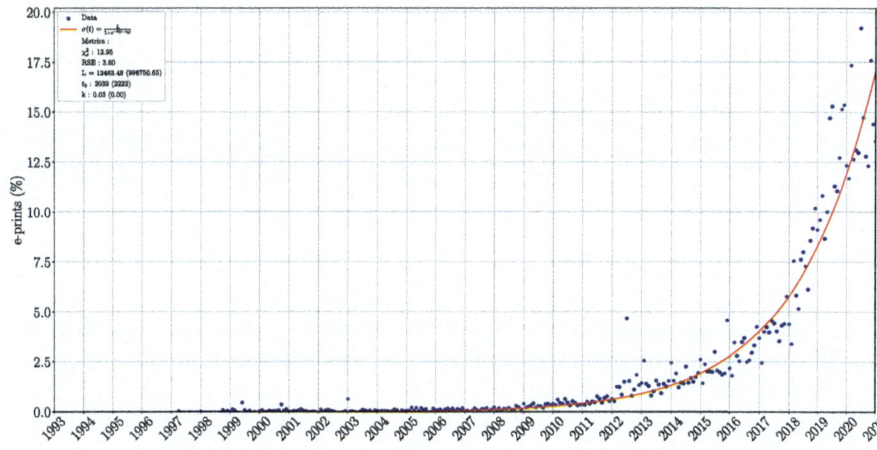

Fig. 5.5 Ongoing exponential growth in cluster `cs.LG`

predict market trends [4] and to capture risk assessments among users and technology evaluators [21, 43], because natural language conveys the judgment, thinking, and attitudes of individuals toward a given topic [6, 10, 17]. In particular, security-related discussions can be captured by this method [36].

Following [11, 38], we used those keywords from Wikipedia's information security portal that related to confidentiality, integrity, availability, and non-repudiation—*secure*, *security*, *safe*, *reliability*, *dependability*, *confidential*, *confidentiality*, *integrity*, *availability*, *defense*, *defence*, *defensive*, and *privacy*. We then authored a Python script that queried the API of the `arXiv` repository with these keywords and collected all e-prints that contained at least one of them. Table 5.4 shows detailed statistics for these e-prints with security issues.

Table 5.4 Descriptive statistics for e-prints with security issues

Cluster	Mean	Median	std. dev.	Skewness	Kurtosis
cs.AI	0.278	0.116	0.463	4.488	32.157
cs.AR	0.029	0.013	0.056	6.234	60.993
cs.CC	0.057	0.055	0.04	0.454	0.348
cs.CL	0.301	0.08	0.442	2.111	5.057
cs.CR	0.502	0.388	0.53	1.888	6.558
cs.CV	0.58	0.07	1.108	3.797	24.809
cs.DB	0.095	0.086	0.079	1.011	1.806
cs.DC	0.2	0.134	0.187	1.176	1.755
cs.DS	0.125	0.099	0.113	0.509	–0.939
cs.GT	0.1	0.091	0.079	0.76	0.836
cs.HC	0.083	0.038	0.115	2.472	8.883
cs.IR	0.106	0.066	0.114	1.365	1.335
cs.LG	0.713	0.082	1.46	2.976	10.415
cs.NE	0.089	0.045	0.103	1.178	0.358
cs.NI	0.26	0.275	0.211	0.285	–1.143
cs.OS	0.012	0.0	0.016	1.126	0.438
cs.PL	0.078	0.065	0.063	0.883	1.215
cs.RO	0.168	0.034	0.338	4.826	37.944
cs.SE	0.142	0.097	0.182	5.545	56.079
cs.SY	0.343	0.252	0.368	3.188	17.82

For each cluster, we plotted the distribution of such e-prints with security issues over all e-prints and over time. Figures 5.6 and 5.7 illustrate the results for the clusters cs.CV and cs.LG.[7]

Both figures suggest that the discussion of security issues lags the growth trend of the respective technology. Firms therefore should be wary of this effect and weigh the risk of investing early against the risk of waiting until the growth trend of the security discussion also exhibits an inflection point.

5.5 Expert Opinion

Firms can mitigate investment risk by considering the opinion of qualified experts in the field before making a decision. Eventually, singular expert opinions converge to a (positive or negative) consensus [15, 29], and that consensus is related to the maturity and market-readiness of a technology [44]. Hence, a positive (negative) expert consensus about a particular technology makes investment more attractive

[7] Due to limited space, only selected figures for the growth of e-prints with security issues. The complete set of figures for the growth of security issues is available from the corresponding author.

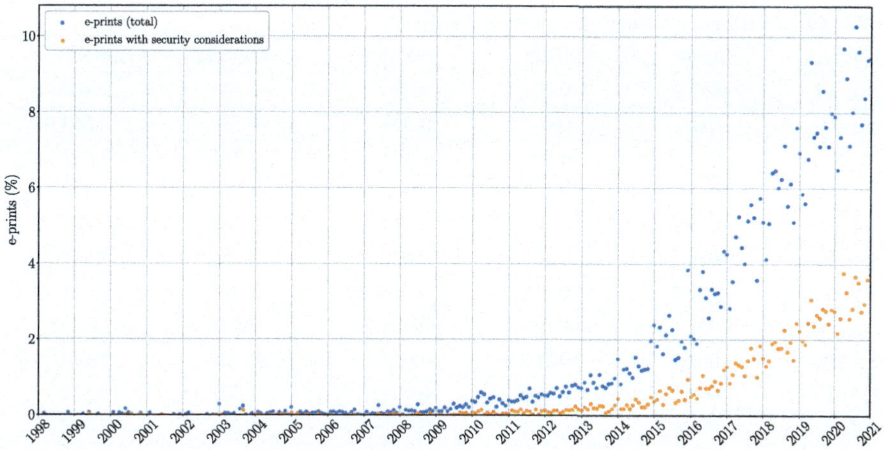

Fig. 5.6 Deferred onset of security issues in cluster `cs.CV`

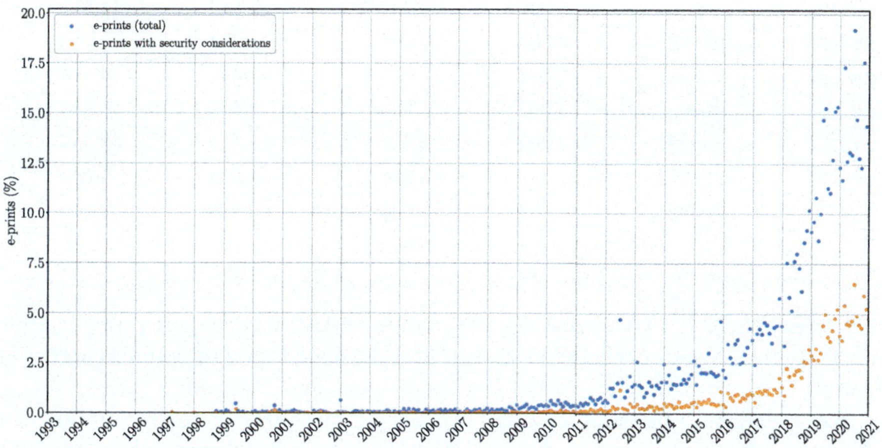

Fig. 5.7 Deferred onset of security issues in cluster `cs.LG`

(risky). Given that e-print authors can be considered experts in the technology field they help develop, the semantics they use to describe and comment on a particular technology can be analyzed to extract a quantitative measure for expert sentiment [31].

By using Python's English language labeled thesaurus (NLTK), we transformed the raw text of each e-print into machine-readable tokens by removing special characters, stop words, and punctuation. We also lowered upper-cases. These normalized tokens were then "lemmatized," i.e., morphologically transformed to their canonical form. Following [40], we then applied a standard cumulative-sentiment function that classified each token into either a positive or negative sentiment and summed up the result across all tokens in each e-print. We then normalized these counts on a score

Table 5.5 Distribution statistics for opinion dispersion

Cluster	Mean	Median	std. dev.	Skewness	Kurtosis
cs.AI	–0.002	–0.001	0.006	–1.341	2.809
cs.AR	–0.0	0.0	0.007	–1.592	7.664
cs.CC	–0.009	–0.009	0.005	–0.967	3.658
cs.CL	0.004	0.005	0.003	–1.038	3.462
cs.CR	–0.006	–0.005	0.014	–10.379	140.804
cs.CV	–0.003	–0.002	0.007	–2.053	7.548
cs.DB	0.001	0.001	0.006	–0.077	9.936
cs.DC	–0.0	0.0	0.005	–1.57	11.395
cs.DS	–0.004	–0.003	0.005	–0.008	9.114
cs.GT	0.002	0.003	0.008	–1.379	14.532
cs.HC	0.004	0.005	0.007	–1.261	5.772
cs.IR	0.006	0.007	0.007	–3.64	22.239
cs.LG	–0.002	–0.001	0.006	–1.737	10.354
cs.NE	–0.003	–0.001	0.007	–2.538	13.56
cs.NI	–0.002	–0.001	0.005	–1.774	13.112
cs.OS	–0.003	–0.001	0.01	–1.441	4.284
cs.PL	0.002	0.002	0.006	–3.476	40.685
cs.RO	–0.003	–0.002	0.007	–3.337	18.244
cs.SE	–0.001	0.0	0.006	–1.022	5.65
cs.SY	–0.005	–0.005	0.004	–0.529	7.064

that ranges from -1 (strongest negative sentiment) to 1 (strongest positive sentiment). Table 5.5 presents detailed statistics for the distribution of opinions across all e-prints.

We plotted these statistics to visualize how opinion shifts and trends over time.[8] In all figures, black dots represent the median, and the shaded areas cover the second and third quartiles of the opinion dispersion across all e-prints in the respective cluster.

In Fig. 5.8, expert opinion has shifted from a neutral stance to a more negative view about the cluster `cs.CV`. In Fig. 5.9, positive and negative opinions regarding the cluster `cs.SE` are balanced, and no trend has emerged yet. In Fig. 5.10, expert opinion has converged to a positive trend, but only after much initial criticism and predominantly negative views as regards cluster `cs.AI`.

Firms should therefore carefully observe such shifts over a longer period of time before making an investment decision since initial optimism or pessimism can reverse to the opposite. Moreover, the opinion dispersion suggests that initial discussions are likely more heated as opinions diverge more, and that considerable time may be required before a consensus emerges. Given that opinion convergence is indicated by

[8] Due to limited space, only selected figures are shown for basic patterns of opinion dispersion. The complete set of figures is available from the corresponding author.

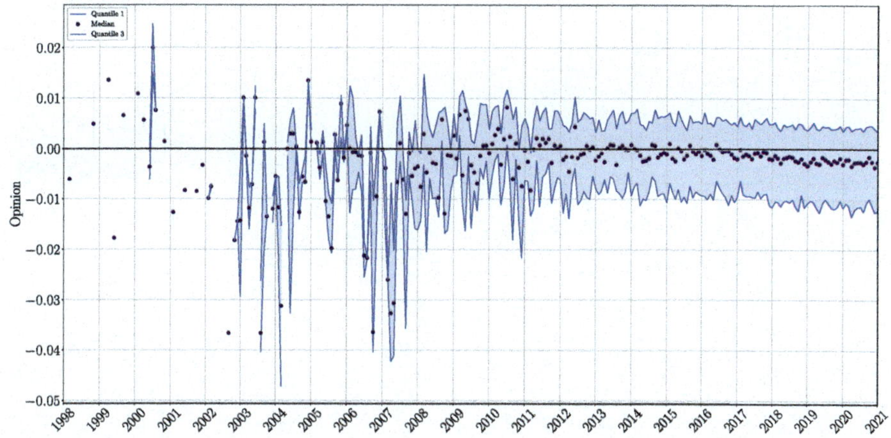

Fig. 5.8 Negative opinion trend in cluster `cs.CV`

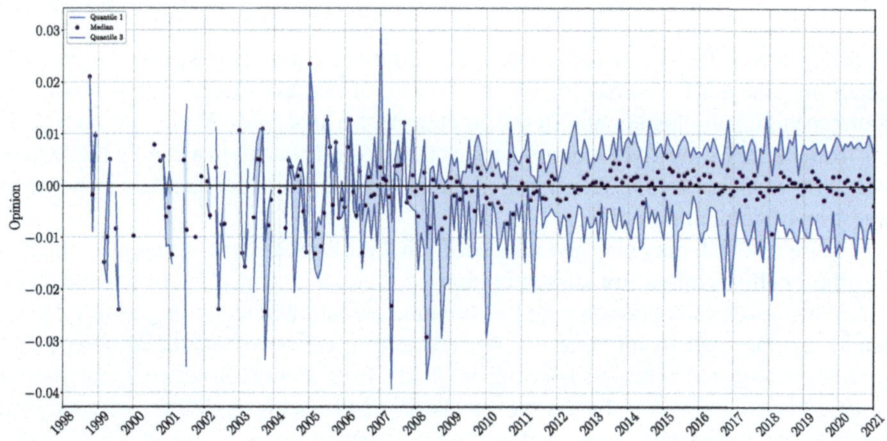

Fig. 5.9 Non-trending expert discussion in cluster `cs.SE`

a decreasing standard deviation of opinion dispersion [27], firms should recalculate opinion patterns regularly and follow the evolution of the respective trends before they make investment decisions.

5.6 Conclusion

In this article, we have shown how big data bibliometric analysis can help firms to make more informed and unbiased investment decisions. The methods we have proposed are scalable to different sample sizes and temporal frequencies. They can

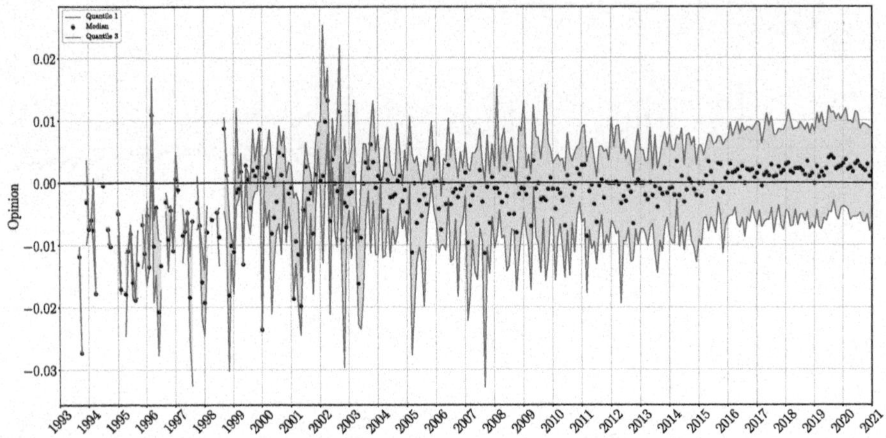

Fig. 5.10 Positive opinion shift in cluster `cs.AI` after initial negative views

be realized with freely available open data. Future research may want to expand and detail our analysis by increasing the granularity of our analysis, e.g., by identifying more specific sub-clusters within the 20 clusters we analyzed. While our analysis is far from being exhaustive, it demonstrates that powerful analytics can be realized at very low transaction cost. Extending our analysis to even larger samples is merely a question of computing power.

Future research may also generate additional bibliometric measures, e.g., regarding the quality, content, or dissemination of `arXiv` e-prints. More sophisticated functions which can better capture the dynamic evolution of technologies (e.g., [35]) could also be used to improve the sigmoid fitting we have calculated here. Also, more sophisticated machine-learning methods such as neural networks or probabilistic classifiers may enhance the precision of the analysis. While we analyzed open source information, our methods are not specific to any particular repository. Firms and scholars alike may apply our proposed method to even larger databases such as *Web of Science* or *Semantic Scholar*.

We caution the reader that `arXiv` e-prints are not necessarily peer-reviewed since authors can upload any type of technological information. Hence, in a strict scholarly sense, e-prints do not constitute validated scientific knowledge, but rather information and opinions about technologies. Some ideas featured in these e-prints may never materialize; on the other hand, creative and unusual thought that would probably not survive a mainstream review process can be harnessed. As the global scientific landscape shifts away from publisher-bound to open access formats, future research may also target open access journals as a source of bibliometrics-empowered technology evaluation.

Acknowledgements This research was awarded a *Cyber Defence Campus Fellowship* from the Research Office of the Swiss Federal Institute of Technology Lausanne (EPFL). We thank Vincent

Lenders and three anonymous reviewers of the WEIS 2021 conference for their comments on an earlier draft of this manuscript.

References

1. Anderson, R. (2020). *Security engineering: A guide to building dependable distributed systems* (3rd ed.). Wiley
2. Anderson, R., & Moore, T. (2006). The economics of information security. *Science, 314*(5799), 610–613.
3. Bagozzi, R. P. (2007). The legacy of the technology acceptance model and a proposal for a paradigm shift. *Journal of the Association for Information Systems, 8*(4), 244–254.
4. Bai, X. (2011). Predicting consumer sentiments from online text. *Decision Support Systems, 50*(4), 732–742.
5. Bevington, P. R., & Robinson, D. K. (2003). *Data reduction and error analysis*. McGraw Hill.
6. Bengisu, M., & Nekhili, R. (2006). Forecasting emerging technologies with the aid of science and technology databases. *Technological Forecasting and Social Change, 73*(7), 835–844.
7. Böhme, R. (2013). *The economics of information security and privacy*. Springer.
8. Bruno, I., Lobo, G., Covino, B., Donarelli, A., Marchetti, V., Panni, A. S., & Molinari, F. (2020). Technology readiness revisited: A proposal for extending the scope of impact assessment of European public services. In *ACM Proceedings of the 13th International Conference on Theory and Practice of Electronic Governance,* (pp. 369–380).
9. Calleja-Sanz, G., Olivella-Nadal, J., & Solé-Parellada, F. (2020). Technology forecasting: Recent trends and new methods. In C. Machado, & J. P. Davim (Eds.), *Research methodology in management and industrial engineering,* (pp. 45–69).
10. Chang, W. L., & Wang, J. Y. (2018). Mine is yours? Using sentiment analysis to explore the degree of risk in the sharing economy. *Electronic Commerce Research and Applications, 28*, 141–158.
11. Cherdantseva, Y., & Hilton, J. (2013). A reference model of information assurance security. In *Proceedings of the 2013 International Conference on Availability, Reliability and Security,* (pp. 546–555).
12. Cleveland, R. B., Cleveland, W. S., McRae, J. E., & Terpenning, I. (1990). STL: A seasonal trend decomposition. *Journal of Official Statistics, 6*(1), 3–73.
13. Choi, J., & Hwang, Y. S. (2014). Patent keyword network analysis for improving technology development efficiency. *Technological Forecasting and Social Change, 83*, 170–182.
14. Dotsika, F., & Watkins, A. (2017). Identifying potentially disruptive trends by means of keyword network analysis. *Technological Forecasting and Social Change, 119*, 114–127.
15. Dou, R., Zhang, Y., & Nan, G. (2017). Iterative product design through group opinion evolution. *International Journal of Production Research, 55*(13), 3886–3905.
16. Ena, O., Mikova, N., Saritas, O., & Sokolova, A. (2016). A methodology for technology trend monitoring: The case of semantic technologies. *Scientometrics, 108*(3), 1013–1041.
17. Fang, X., & Zhan, J. (2015). Sentiment analysis using product review data. *Journal of Big Data* 2, article 5.
18. Fleming, T. C., Qualkenbush, E. L., & Chapa, A. M. (2017). The secret war against the United States: The top threat to national security and the American dream. *The Cyber Defense Review, 2*(3), 25–32.
19. Goyal, D., Goyal, R., Rekha, G., Malik, S., & Tyagi, A. K. (2020). Emerging trends and challenges in data science and big data analytics. In *Proceedings of the 2020 International Conference on Emerging Trends in Information Technology and Engineering,* (pp. 1–8).
20. Guo, W., Wang, H., Tian, Y., & Xian, M. (2019). Research on cyberspace security testing and evaluation of technology development trends. In *Proceedings of the 2019 IEEE International Conference on Communications, Information Systems and Computer Engineering,* (pp. 363–367).

21. Gurung, A., & Raja, M. K. (2016). Online privacy and security concerns of consumers. *Information & Computer Security, 24*(4), 348–371.
22. Haleem, A., Mannan, B., Luthra, S., Kumar, S., & Khurana, S. (2019). Technology forecasting (TF) and technology assessment (TA) methodologies: A conceptual review. *Benchmarking, 26*(1), 48–72.
23. Hallman, R. A., Major, M., Romero-Mariona, J., Phipps, R., Romero, E., John, M., & Miguel, S. (2020). Return on cybersecurity investment in operational technology systems: Quantifying the value that cybersecurity technologies provide after integration. In *Complex is 2020,* (pp. 43–52).
24. Han, J., & Moraga, C. (1995). The influence of the sigmoid function parameters on the speed of backpropagation learning. *Lecture Notes in Computer Science* (pp. 195–201). Springer.
25. Hao, J., Yan, Y., Gong, L., Wang, G., & Lin, J. (2014). Knowledge map-based method for domain knowledge browsing. *Decision Support Systems, 61*, 106–114.
26. Héder, M. (2017). From NASA to EU: The evolution of the TRL scale in public sector innovation. *The Innovation Journal, 22*(2), 1–23.
27. Huang, J., Boh, W. F., & Goh, K. H. (2019). Opinion convergence versus polarization: Examining opinion distributions in online word-of-mouth. *Journal of the Association for Information Science and Technology, 70*(11), 1183–1193.
28. Lee, C. (2021). A review of data analytics in technological forecasting. *Technological Forecasting and Social Change, 166*, 120646.
29. Lehrer, K., & Wagner, C. (2012). *Rational consensus in science and society*. Springer Science & Business Media
30. Li, X., Xie, Q., Daim, T., & Huang, L. (2019). Forecasting technology trends using text mining of the gaps between science and technology: The case of perovskite solar cell technology. *Technological Forecasting and Social Change, 146*, 432–449.
31. Liu, B. (2012). *Sentiment analysis and opinion mining (synthesis lectures on human language technologies*. Morgan & Claypool.
32. Lotfi, A., Lotfi, A., & Halal, W. E. (2014). Forecasting technology diffusion: A new generalisation of the logistic model. *Technology Analysis & Strategic Management, 26*(8), 943–957.
33. Maidullah, S., & Sharma, A. (2019). Decision making in the era of infobesity: A study on interaction of gender and psychological tendencies. *Humanities & Social Sciences Reviews, 7*(5), 571–586.
34. Maks, I., & Vossen, P. (2013). Sentiment analysis of reviews: Should we analyze writer intentions or reader perceptions?. In *Proceedings of the 2013 International Conference on Recent Advances in Natural Language Processing RANLP 2013,* (pp. 415–419).
35. Meyer, P. S., & Ausubel, J. H. (1999). Carrying capacity: A model with logistically varying limits. *Technological Forecasting and Social Change, 61*(3), 209–214.
36. Pletea, D., Vasilescu, B., & Serebrenik, A. (2014). Security and emotion: Sentiment analysis of security discussions on github. In *Proceedings of the 11th Working Conference on mining software repositories,* (pp. 348–351).
37. Rezaeian, M., Montazeri, H., & Loonen, R. (2017). Science foresight using life-cycle analysis, text mining and clustering: A case study on natural ventilation. *Technological Forecasting and Social Change, 118*, 270–280.
38. Ritzdorf, H., Wust, K., Gervais, A., Felley, G., & Capkun, S. (2018) TLS-N: Non-repudiation over TLS enabling ubiquitous content signing. In *Proceedings of the 2018 Network and Distributed System Security Symposium, San Diego CA*.
39. Rogers, E. M. (2010). *Diffusion of innovations*. Simon and Schuster.
40. Serrano-Guerrero, J., Olivas, J. A., Romero, F. P., & Herrera-Viedma, E. (2015). Sentiment analysis: A review and comparative analysis of web services. *Information Sciences, 311*, 18–38.
41. Schoeni, D. E. (2017). Still too slow for cyber warfare: Why extension of the rapid acquisition authority and the special emergency procurement authority to cyber are half measures. *Public Contract Law Journal, 46*(4), 833–852.

42. Wang, X., Qiu, P., Zhu, D., Mitkova, L., Lei, M., & Porter, A. L. (2015). Identification of technology development trends based on subject-action-object analysis: The case of dye-sensitized solar cells. *Technological Forecasting and Social Change, 98*, 24–46.
43. Yang, J., Sarathy, R., & Lee, J. K. (2016). The effect of product review balance and volume on online shoppers' risk perception and purchase intention. *Decision Support Systems, 89*, 66–76.
44. Yüzügüllü, E., & Deason, J. P. (2007). Structuring objectives to facilitate convergence of divergent opinion in hydrogen production decisions. *Energy Policy, 35*(1), 452–460.

Dimitri Percia David is an Assistant Professor of Data Science and Econometrics at the University of Applied Sciences Valais (Switzerland) where he applies data science and machine learning to the field of technology mining. Prior to this position, he was a postdoctoral researcher at the Information Science Institute of the University of Geneva, and the first recipient of the Distinguished CYD Postdoctoral Fellowship. He earned his Ph.D. in Information Systems from the Faculty of Business and Economics (HEC) at the University of Lausanne, and he has more than eight years of professional experience in the commodities trading industry and as a scientific collaborator at the Military Academy at Swiss Federal Institute of Technology (ETH) Zurich.

William Blonay is a cybersecurity researcher at the Cyber Defence Campus of armasuisse Science and Technology in Lausanne (Switzerland). He is also a cybersecurity researcher at the NATO Cooperative Cyber Defence Centre of Excellence. His main research interests are in the area of internet networks, cellular networks and internet of things.

Sébastien Gillard received an MSc in Physics from the University of Fribourg (Switzerland) in 2016. He specializes in computational physics and statistics, in particular, data analysis and applied statistical modeling and analytical and numerical resolution methods for differential equations. His current research interest is the application of insights from recommender systems to critical infrastructure defense, including the development of code that can power deep learning algorithms.

Thomas Maillart holds a Master degree from the Swiss Federal Institute of Technology (EPFL) Lausanne (2005) and a Ph.D. from the Swiss Federal Institute of Technology (ETH) Zurich (2011). He received the 2012 Zurich Dissertation Prize for his pioneering work on cyber risks. Before joining the University of Geneva, he worked as a researcher at the Center for Law and Economics at ETH and as a post-doctoral researcher at the University of California at Berkeley. His research focuses on modeling and improving human collective intelligence, particularly in a context of a fast-expanding cyberspace.

Alain Mermoud is the Head of Technology Monitoring and Forecasting at the Cyber Defence Campus of armasuisse Science and Technology. He obtained his Ph.D. in Information Systems from the University of Lausanne (Switzerland). He has more than five years of professional experience in the banking industry. His research interests span emerging technologies, disruptive innovations, threat intelligence and the economics of security.

Loïc Maréchal is a researcher at the University of Lausanne (Switzerland) and the Cyber Defence Campus of armasuisse Science and Technology. He is also a visiting lecturer in finance at the University of Geneva, ESSEC, and Les Roches Business Schools. He holds a Ph.D. in finance from the University of Neuchâtel and has over ten years of commodity markets experience, including working on trading desks as a quantitative analyst. His research interest is in the application of financial models to cybersecurity and alternative investment spaces, particularly commodity derivatives and private equity markets.

Michael Tsesmelis is an MSc student in Computational Science and Engineering at Imperial College London. Before, he was a researcher at the Cyber Defence Campus of armasuisse Science and Technology, and he also served as a cybersecurity expert in the Cyber Battalion of the Swiss Armed Forces. His research focuses on economic data science, cybersecurity and computational physics.

Chapter 6
A Novel Algorithm for Informed Investment in Cybersecurity Companies and Technologies

Anita Mezzetti, Loïc Maréchal, Dimitri Percia David, William Blonay, Sébastien Gillard, Michael Tsesmelis, Thomas Maillart, and Alain Mermoud

6.1 Problem

We consider a setting where investors acquire technology for cyberdefense directly by investing in one or more companies that develop such technology, rather than by purchasing commercially available products from vendors. The problem these

---

Supplementary Information The online version contains supplementary material available at https://doi.org/10.1007/978-3-031-30191-9_6.

A. Mezzetti
Credit Suisse, Uetlibergstrasse 231, Zurich, Switzerland

L. Maréchal (✉)
Department of Information Systems, Université de Lausanne, HEC, Lausanne, Switzerland
e-mail: loic.marechal@unil.ch

W. Blonay · M. Tsesmelis · A. Mermoud
Cyber-Defence Campus, armasuisse Science and Technology, Thun, Switzerland
e-mail: william.blonay@ar.admin.ch

M. Tsesmelis
e-mail: michael.tsesmelis22@imperial.ac.uk

A. Mermoud
e-mail: alain.mermoud@ar.admin.ch

S. Gillard · T. Maillart
Information Science Institute, Geneva School of Economics and Management, University of Geneva, Geneva, Switzerland
e-mail: sebastien.gillard@vtg.admin.ch

T. Maillart
e-mail: thomas.maillart@unige.ch

D. Percia David
Institute of Entrepreneurship & Management, University of Applied Sciences Valais, Sierre, Switzerland
e-mail: dimitri.perciadavid@hevs.ch

M. M. Keupp (ed.), *Cyberdefense*, International Series in Operations Research & Management Science 342,
https://doi.org/10.1007/978-3-031-30191-9_6

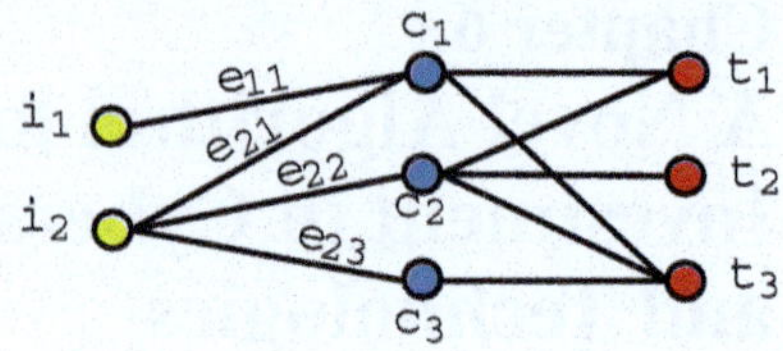

Fig. 6.1 Schematic tripartite graph of investors, companies, and technologies

investors face is twofold: They must decide on which technologies to focus, and they must inform themselves about the companies which specialize in these technologies. Since investors have both limited financial and intellectual resources, they cannot invest simultaneously in all companies or understand all existing and emerging technologies. Moreover, they have individual preferences about companies and technologies which co-determine their decision. As investors may make biased choices in the absence of objective quantitative information, they may misread the market and hence invest in companies that prove to be unprofitable, or in technologies that are ineffective when deployed against cyberattackers, and particularly so as they evaluate start-up companies [22]. It is therefore paramount that investors are well-informed before they make decisions about equity stakes or technology procurement [2].

Figure 6.1 structures this problem schematically by a tripartite graph in which investors (i) want to evaluate a set of companies (c), each of which is involved with one or more cybersecurity technologies (t). There are hence bipartite relationships between investors and companies, and also between companies and technologies, but only indirect links exist between investors and technologies since technologies are nested in companies. Hence, investors can prefer a particular technology, but they can only access it by investing in the particular firm that is involved with it.

Subject to their investment policy and technological preferences, investors wish to identify those companies which can generate economic value from the technologies they are involved with, because investment in such companies will likely prove to be profitable. At the same time, they want to identify relevant technologies which can enable effective cyberdefense. Both points are by no means certain, since many companies—in particular, startups—create technology but fail economically, and because the effectiveness of any technology against future cyberattacks is unknown. Investors therefore require rankings in which companies and technologies score the higher the more they respond to investors' requirements.

This setting shares some commonality with the basic problem all web users face: among billions of websites, they want to quickly identify those which are most relevant to the queries they submit. Users require a ranking of all websites in which those with the highest relevance to their query appear topmost. Past contributions have developed algorithms that solve this problem, most notably, *PageRank* that powers Google's search engine [16].

However, the ranking problem is more complicated in our tripartite setting. First, the market for cyberdefense technology is a complex landscape in which companies and technologies co-evolve [7]. Hence, the rankings of companies and technologies are co-determined, so they must be calculated simultaneously. Whereas simple ranking algorithms only consider unipartite entities (e.g., websites), our setting involves two different types of entities—companies and technologies—which require different scores. Second, much prior research has studied directed graphs (e.g., [1, 5, 19]), but our setting requires a solution for an undirected graph. Third, recent work suggests that rankings of companies or technologies as targets for investment are inadequate unless the algorithm also considers investor preferences [4, 14]. The algorithm we propose in the following addresses all three points.

6.2 Algorithm

Building on the work of [10, 13], we propose *TechRank*, a recursive random walk algorithm that evaluates the relative importance of companies and technologies in a tripartite network ('landscape'). The reader is referred to these contributions for a more detailed introduction to these design ideas behind the proposed algorithm. Table 6.1 provides an overview of the notation and key variables the algorithm uses.

Its purpose is to simultaneously compute separate but correlated scores w_c and w_t by which companies and technologies in the landscape are ranked subject to investor preferences. Whereas w_c captures the expertise a particular company has in the landscape, w_t gives the relevance a particular technology has in that system. The algorithm calculates these scores as follows.

We denote the total number of companies in the landscape by n^c and the total number of technologies by n^t. In the adjacency matrix $M^{CT}_{c,t}$, which has a dimension of $n^c \times n^t$, entries take a value of 1 if a particular company c is involved with a particular technology t, and 0 otherwise. We initialize the scores based on the thought that a company with a high relevance in the landscape should have more relationships with its neighbors. Similarly, a highly relevant technology should attract many companies [3, 6, 17]. Hence, the algorithm is initialized with the respective degrees of each entity c and t:[1]

$$\begin{cases} w_c^0 &= \sum_{t=1}^{n^t} M^{CT}_{c,t} = k_c \\ \\ w_t^0 &= \sum_{c=1}^{n^c} M^{CT}_{c,t} = k_t \end{cases} \tag{6.1}$$

After initialization, the algorithm performs a random walk which, at each iteration, incorporates information about a company expertise and technology relevance. The transition probabilities $G_{c,t}$ and $G_{t,c}$ describe the extent to which the significance of a company or technology changes as the iteration progresses, formally:

[1] The symbols k_c and k_t are introduced here to facilitate the display of the subsequent formulae.

Table 6.1 Model parameters and variables

Variable	Definition range	Description
$n^{(C)}$	$\mathbb{N}$	Number of external features available for companies
n^c	$\mathbb{N}$	Number of companies
$n^{(T)}$	$\mathbb{N}$	Number of external features available for technologies
n^t	$\mathbb{N}$	Number of technologies
$p_i^{(C)}$	[0, 1]	Percentage of interest in company preference factor i
$p_j^{(T)}$	[0, 1]	Percentage of interest in technology preference factor j
$f_i^{(C)}$	$\mathbb{R}^{n^c}$	Vector associated with company preference factor i
$f_j^{(T)}$	$\mathbb{R}^{n^t}$	Vector associated with the technology preference factor j
n^i	$\mathbb{N}$	Number of investors
$M_{c,t}^{CT}$	$\mathbb{R}^{n^c \cdot n^t}$	Adjacency matrix of the C-T bipartite network
$M_{c,t}^{IC}$	$\mathbb{R}^{n^i \cdot n^c}$	Adjacency matrix of the I-C bipartite network
$\gamma_t^{i,c}$	$\mathbb{R}$	Funding investor i provides to company c at time t
e^{IC}	$\mathbb{R}^{n^i \cdot n^c}$	Total investments all investors made in all companies
e^C	$\mathbb{R}^{n^c}$	Total investments each company collected
e^T	$\mathbb{R}^{n^t}$	Total investments each technology collected
$e_{\max}^C$	$\mathbb{R}$	Maximum of total investments in all companies
$e_{\max}^T$	$\mathbb{R}$	Maximum of total investments in all technologies
f_c^C	[0, 1]	Factor of previous investments in company c
f_t^T	[0, 1]	Factor of previous investments in technology t

$$\begin{cases} G_{c,t}(\beta) &= \dfrac{M_{c,t}^{CT} k_c^{-\beta}}{\sum_{c'=1}^{n^c} M_{c',t}^{CT} k_c'^{-\beta}} \\ \\ G_{t,c}(\alpha) &= \dfrac{M_{c,t}^{CT} k_t^{-\alpha}}{\sum_{t'=1}^{n^t} M_{c,t'}^{CT} k_t'^{-\alpha}}, \end{cases} \tag{6.2}$$

where the parameters α and β capture the extent to which a firm c also creates economic value when it works with technology t. We introduce these parameters since interactions between companies and technologies need not necessarily be productive. Klein et al. [13] emphasize that Wikipedia editors can engage in prolonged edit wars that destroy rather than create value. By way of analogy, firms can invest a lot of funds into creating technology but subsequently fail to generate any economic value from these investments. Both probabilities are recomputed in every recursive step. Using (8.1) with (8.2), we can describe the n-th recursive step as

$$\begin{cases} w_c^{n+1} & = \sum_{t=1}^{n^t} G_{c,t}(\beta) w_t^n \\ w_t^{n+1} & = \sum_{c=1}^{n^c} G_{t,c}(\alpha) w_c^n \end{cases} \tag{6.3}$$

Hence, the algorithm is a Markov process. Any step w^n only depends on the information available in the previous step w^{n-1}. As it is the case with the *PageRank* algorithm, the recursion terminates when the score values converge. However, this preliminary ranking is incomplete unless the algorithm also considers the preferences investors have about companies and technologies since these likely influence the choices they make. Therefore, we introduce two ground truth scores

$$\hat{w}_c$$

and

$$\hat{w}_c$$

which capture specific features that investors consider as they make actual choices about companies and technologies. We define these ground truth scores as

$$\begin{cases} \hat{w}_c = \sum_{i=1}^{n^{(C)}} p_i^{(C)} f_i^{(C)} = p^{(C)} \cdot f^{(C)} \\ \hat{w}_t = \sum_{i=1}^{n^{(T)}} p_i^{(T)} f_i^{(T)} = p^{(T)} \cdot f^{(T)} \end{cases} \tag{6.4}$$

where $f^{(C)} = f_1^{(C)}, \ldots, f_{n^{(C)}}^{(C)}$ is a vector of a number of company-specific features $n^{(C)}$ which investors consider and weight with a percentage of interest $p_i^{(C)}$ with $\sum_{i=0}^{n^{(C)}} p_i^{(C)} = 1$. If investors dislike a particular feature, the evaluation enters the score with a negative sign. Similarly, $f^{(T)} = f_1^{(T)}, \ldots, f_{n^{(T)}}^{(T)}$ is a vector of technology-specific features $n^{(T)}$ which investors consider and weight with a percentage of interest $p_i^{(T)}$, with $\sum_{i=0}^{n^{(T)}} p_i^{(T)} = 1$. For companies and technologies alike, these evaluations are converted to scalars $f_i^{(C)} \in [0, 1]$ and $f_i^{(T)} \in [0, 1]$, so that the ground truth scores $\hat{w}_c$ and $\hat{w}_c$ are conditioned on values $\in [0, 1]$.

We then compute Spearman correlations between the random walk scores and the ground truth scores in order to evaluate how well the algorithm fits investor preferences. Since these correlations ρ_c for companies and ρ_t for technologies depend on the parameters α and β, we want to identify those parameters for which the respective correlation is maximized, formally:

$$\begin{cases} (\alpha^*, \beta^*) = \arg\max_{\alpha,\beta} \rho_c(\alpha, \beta) \\ (\alpha^*, \beta^*) = \arg\max_{\alpha,\beta} \rho_t(\alpha, \beta), \end{cases} \tag{6.5}$$

This optimization problem is solved by a grid search. The vector notation in Eq. (6.4) allows the analyst to capture a very large array of attributes, but to keep the computational complexity low. We restrict our demonstration to a small selection of such preferences: The accumulated investment a company or technology has received from all investors in the landscape to date, and the geographical distance between investor and company. These are modeled as follows.

We believe that investors would be willing to invest in firms which have already received significant funding in the past, since such funding would signal that other investors have confidence in this particular company. We capture this information by weighting the edges e as shown in Fig. 6.1 by the sum of all previous investments that an investor i has made in company c until the current time period $\mathcal{T}$. These relationships between investors and companies are captured in the adjacency matrix $M^{IC}_{c,t}$.

We define the amount of a single investment from i to c at time t by $\gamma_t^{i,c}$. The weight of the edge $i - c$ is given by $e_{i,c} = \sum_{t=0}^{\mathcal{T}} \gamma_t^{i,c}$. We then sum the contribution of all investors to find the attribute $f_c^C \in [0, 1]$ for a company c. We then normalize and divide all investments by the maximum investment. By generalizing this procedure, we obtain

$$\begin{cases} e^{IC}_{i,c} = \sum_{t=0}^{\mathcal{T}} \gamma_t^{i,c} & \forall i, c \\ e^C_c = \sum_{i=1}^{n^i} e_{i,c} M^{IC}_{i,c} & \forall c \\ e_{\max} = \max\limits_c e^C_c \\ f^{(C)}_c = e^C_c / e_{\max}, \end{cases} \tag{6.6}$$

for each $c \in 1, \ldots, n^c$. Hence, Eq. (6.6) gives a scalar for each company that summarizes the amount of previous investments that company has obtained. The sub-algorithm no.1 which computes this scalar is shown in the technical appendix. By the same token, the sum of previous investments $f_c^{(C)}$ that a particular technology has obtained is calculated as

$$\begin{cases} e^{(I,C)}_{i,c} = \sum_{t=0}^{(\mathcal{T}} \gamma^t_{i,c} & \forall i, c \\ e^C_c = \sum_{i=1}^{n^i} e_{i,c} & \forall c \\ e^T_t = \sum_{c=1}^{n^c} e_c M^{CT}_{c,t} \\ e_{\max} = \max\limits_t e^T_t \\ f^{(T)}_t = e^T_t / e_{\max} \end{cases} . \tag{6.7}$$

The sub-algorithm no. 2 which computes this scalar is shown in the technical appendix. Finally, we consider the geographical distance between investor and company locations since investors may prefer companies they can see and visit at low transaction cost. Following [12], we calculate the Haversine distance between investor and company locations $h_{i,c}$ by sub-algorithm 3 which is set out in the technical appendix. By implication, the scalar $f_c^{(C)} \in [0, 1]$ should approach a value of 1 as the distance decreases to zero.

We programmed all three sub-algorithms as well as the TechRank algorithm in Python, using the libraries `numPy` [9], `pandas` [15, 18], `networkX` [8], `matplotlib` [11], and `seaborn` [20]. We ran the code on a machine with a 16-core Intel Xeon CPU E5-2620 v4 @ 2.10GHz and 128GB of memory.

6.3 Evaluation

We used data from the platform *Crunchbase*, a crowdsourced, international repository of information about start-up companies and their investors, to compare how well our proposed algorithm ranks them. Crunchbase records both the identity and location of companies and investors and uses a proprietary algorithm that ranks their significance. In particular, the database tracks all funding provided by each investor to each company in the database. It also delivers the required data for the two features that investors consider in our demonstration—previous investment and company and investor location data.[2]

We selected all companies in the database whose description contained at least two of the keywords *cybersecurity*, *confidentiality*, *integrity*, *availability*, *secure*, *security*, *safe*, *reliability*, *dependability*, *confidential*, *confidentiality*, *integrity*, *availability*, *defence*, *defensive*, and *privacy*.[3]

This query yielded a landscape of 2429 companies which were involved with 477 technologies. For purposes of illustration, Fig. 6.2 plots selected bipartite relationships between companies (red) and technologies (blue) in this landscape. The size of the respective node is proportional to its degree.

The ranking for companies (technologies) converged after 723 (1120) iterations which took 16,890.26 (12,779.62) s. While the scores fluctuated significantly during the first 100 iterations, they quickly converged afterwards. The number of iterations needed for convergence appears to be independent from the number of entities, but since there more companies than technologies in our sample, technology ranking takes longer to converge. Figures 6.3 and 6.4 display the convergence for companies and technologies, respectively. Entities starting with a high score do not significantly change rank. Thus, the algorithm assigns high scores to entities with a high degree (i.e., high network centrality). However, entities starting with a low degree may significantly change their score, especially in the case of technologies. Therefore, *TechRank* does not only recognize the importance of the most established entities, it also allows the analyst to identify emerging technologies.

---

[2] See www.crunchbase.com/. Data were downloaded by the daily *.csv export file on April 28, 2021. about.crunchbase.com/blog/influential-companies/ gives more specific information about the ranking procedure.

[3] The choice of these keywords was motivated by Wikipedia's information security portal. See https://en.wikipedia.org/wiki/Information_security.

Fig. 6.2 Sub-area of a selected landscape of companies and technologies

Fig. 6.3 Convergence of ranking for companies

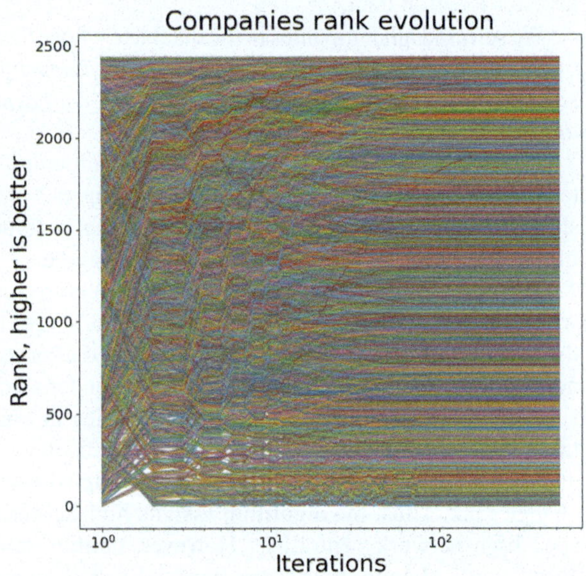

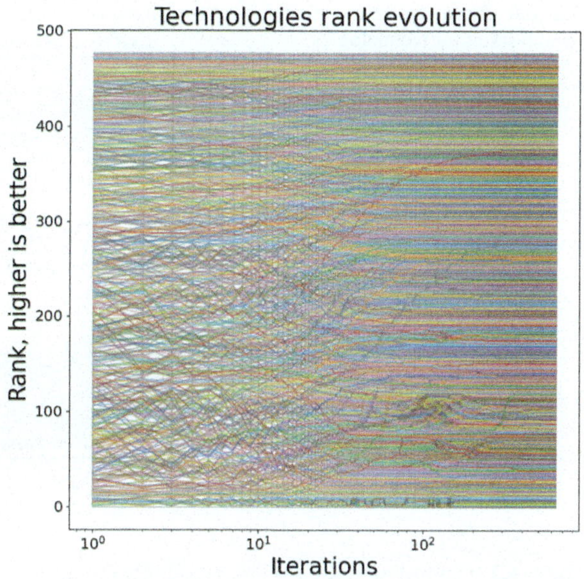

Fig. 6.4 Convergence of ranking for technologies

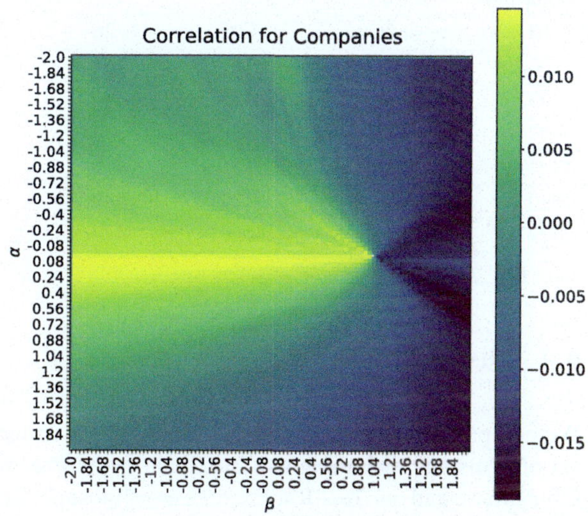

Fig. 6.5 Parameter grid search result for companies

Figures 6.5 and 6.6 depict the results of the grid search that optimizes the parameters α and β for a maximum correlation between the ranks obtained by the algorithm and the ground truth scores.

Table 6.2 identifies the optimal sets of α^* and β^* for companies (0.04; -1.88) and technologies (0.48; -2.00) and shows how these sets evolved during convergence.

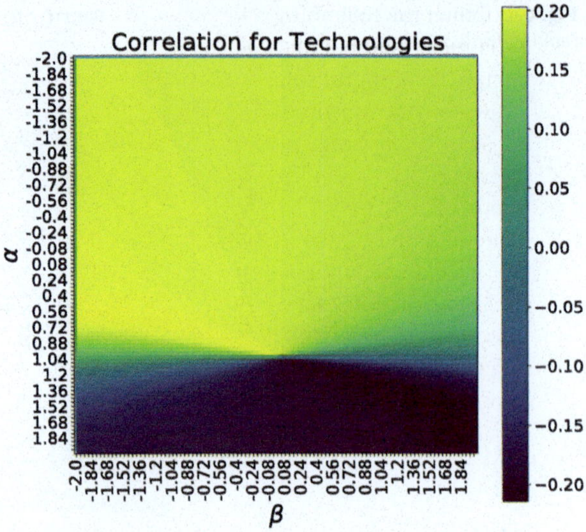

Fig. 6.6 Parameter grid search result for technologies

Table 6.2 Optimal parameters for alpha and beta for the landscape in our sample

Companies	$\alpha^*(C)$	$\beta^*(C)$	Technologies	$\alpha^*(T)$	$\beta^*(T)$
10	–0.36	1.92	26	–2.00	0.00
100	–0.04	0.92	134	0.52	–1.04
499	–0.08	0.88	306	0.68	–1.36
997	–0.12	0.80	371	–2.00	0.00
1494	–0.12	0.80	416	0.92	–0.12
1990	–0.04	0.92	449	0.56	–2.00
2429	0.04	–1.88	477	0.48	–2.00

6.4 Discussion

We compared the results with the ranking that Crunchbase provided for the same set of firms and technologies. The Spearman correlation of 0.014 suggests that the Crunchbase and our TechRank scores are almost perfectly uncorrelated. The Crunchbase ranking procedure is unipartite since it ranks firms by investment but does not consider the co-evolution of firms and technologies. It is therefore unsurprising that our and Crunchbase ranking results are correlated little. Our approach does not interpret the Crunchbase algorithm as a ground truth against which the performance of our algorithm could be measured; rather, we propose that we are using a different and more complex ranking procedure for which independent ground truths must be identified for future performance evaluations. We do emphasize that the ranking result crucially depends on the way technologies in the landscape are linked with companies. To ignore this multipartite setting implies to generate flawed rankings.

In particular, the technology ranking allows investors who are interested in a certain technological field but unaware of the industry landscape to express their preference and obtain meaningful solutions. Our algorithm can analyze complex landscapes at a very low cost; the run-time requirements are negligible. Our approach is parsimonious in the sense that it requires no weights for the bipartite edges between companies and technologies, and that the algorithm optimizes the ranking by a simple random walk procedure.

Moreover, the Crunchbase rank focuses on the company's level of activity and not on its market influence. It considers all companies in the database, while our illustration only covers a subset of a particular landscape. Still, even when we varied investor preferences, we never obtained correlation coefficients above 2%. Finally, the Crunchbase algorithm is not open source, so there is no objective way to identify the reasons for this divergence.

Our approach does not only consider firms and investors, but a tripartite nested setting in which investors fund companies in which technologies are nested. This approach responds to prior calls for research (e.g., [1, 5, 13, 19]). It also confirms call that have proposed to replace time-series analyses of static indicators with graph-based methods (e.g., [21]). Our results demonstrate that the topological structure of the landscape co-determines the ranking results.

As opposed to the Crunchbase ranking, our algorithm considers investor preferences about companies and technologies. In so doing we also follow prior calls for research (e.g., [14]). We believe that future work could expand our algorithm by considering additional investor preferences, or by refining the method by which these are operationalized. For example, ethical investors may want to know about companies' gender and diversity policies, investors with personal exposure may emphasize social media policy, and business angels may want to focus on incubators and accelerators [4].

Future research should expand our approach by refining the text-based search we used to identify relevant companies. More sophisticated techniques, such as natural language processing, may provide more accurate selections. Further, more detailed data about the technologies these firms produce would be helpful to refine the analysis of why investors would want to invest in them. Future research may extend our proposed algorithm beyond investor preferences, so that the topology of any cybersecurity landscape can be captured with greater granularity. For example, in our Crunchbase sample there is no information about how each company allocates its resources among all the technologies it is working on. Since firms may concurrently work on several technologies, but assign different priorities (and hence different budgets) to them, it would be very helpful to understand the extent to which specific funds are reserved for specific technologies. Finally, since both our algorithm and the Crunchbase ranking are static, future research should consider how the tripartite network of companies, technologies, and investors evolves over time.

Acknowledgements This chapter features results from a research project funded by the Cyber Defence (CYD) Campus which is run and funded by the science and technology division of the Swiss Federal Office for Defense Procurement *armasuisse*.

Technical Appendix

Algorithm 6.1: Previous investments factor for companies

$e^C \leftarrow [0] \cdot len(c\_names)$
for $c \in range(c\_names)$ **do**
  for $i \in range(i\_names)$ **do**
    for $c \in range(i\_names)$ **do**
      $e^{IC}_{i,c} \leftarrow \sum_{t=0}^{T} \gamma_t^{i,c}$ // $\gamma^t_{i,c}$ is the amount of the investment from i to c at time t
      $e^C[c] \leftarrow e^C[c] + e^{IC}_{i,c}$
$e^C_{max} \leftarrow \max(e^C)$
$f^C \leftarrow e^C / e_{max}$ // f^C: list of previous investments for each technology
return f^C

Algorithm 6.2: Previous investments factor for technologies

$e^C \leftarrow [0] \cdot len(c\_names)$
for $c \in range(c\_names)$ **do**
  for $i \in range(i\_names)$ **do**
    $e^{IC}_{i,c} \leftarrow \sum_{t=0}^{(T)} \gamma_t^{IC}$ // $\gamma^t_{i,c}$ is the amount of the investment from i to c at time t
    $e^C[c] \leftarrow e^C[c] + e^{IC}_{i,c}$
$e^T \leftarrow e^C \cdot M^{CT}$ // Matrix multiplication
$e_{max} \leftarrow \max(e^T)$
$f^T \leftarrow e^T / e_{max}$ // f^T: list of previous investments for each technology
return f^T

References

1. Benzi, M., Estrada, E., & Klymko C (2012) Ranking hubs and authorities using matrix functions. arXiv:1201.3120.
2. Byrne, T., & Gingras, J. (2017). *The right way to select technology*. Rosenfeld
3. Canito, J., Ramos, P., Moro, S., & Rita, P. (2018). Unfolding the relations between companies and technologies under the big data umbrella. *Computers in Industry, 99*, 1–8.
4. Dalle, J. M., den Besten, M., & Menon, C. (2017). Using Crunchbase for economic and managerial research. OECD Science, Technology and Industry Working Papers 2017/08

Algorithm 6.3: Geographic coordinates factor

```
h_dict ← {}
for c_name, c_address ∈ c_locations do
    lat ← c_address.latitude
    lon ← c_address.longitude
    h ← haver_dist(lat, lon, lat_inv, lon_in)    // haver_dist is a function
        we have created
    h_dict[c_name] ← 1/h
h_max ← max (h_dict)
for c_name, h ∈ h_dict do
    h_dict[c_name] ← 1 − h/h_max
return h_dict
```


5. Donato, D., Laura, L., Leonardi, S., & Millozzi, S. (2004). Large scale properties of the Webgraph. *European Physical Journal B, 38*(2), 239–243.
6. Gold, A. H., Malhotra, A., & Segars, A. H. (2001). Knowledge management: An organizational capabilities perspective. *Journal of Management Information Systems, 18*, 185–214.
7. Gordon, L. A., Loeb, M. P., Lucyshyn, W., & Zhou, L. (2018). Empirical evidence on the determinants of cybersecurity investments in private sector firms. *Journal of Information Security, 9*(2), 133–153.
8. Hagberg, A. A., Schult, D. A., & Swart, P. J. (2008). Exploring network structure, dynamics, and function using NetworkX. In *Proceedings of the 7th Python in Science Conference*, (pp. 11–15)
9. Harris, C. R., et al. (2020). Array programming with NumPy. *Nature, 585*(7825), 357–362.
10. Hidalgo, C. A., Hausmann, R., & Dasgupta, P. S. (2009). The building blocks of economic complexity. *Proceedings of the National Academy of Sciences, 26*, 10570–10575.
11. Hunter, J. D. (2007). Matplotlib: A 2D graphics environment. *Computing in Science & Engineering, 9*(3), 90–95.
12. Ingole, P. V., & Nichat, M. K. (2013). Landmark based shortest path detection by using Dijkestra algorithm and Haversine formula. *International Journal of Engineering Research and Applications, 3*, 162–165.
13. Klein, M., Maillart, T., & Chuang, J. (2015). The virtuous circle of Wikipedia: Recursive measures of collaboration structures. In *Proceedings of the 18th ACM Conference on Computer Supported Cooperative Work & Social Computing*, (pp. 1106–1115)
14. Liang, Y., & Yuan, D. (2016). Predicting investor funding behavior using Crunchbase social network feature. *Internet Research, 26*, 74–100.
15. McKinney, W. (2010). Data structures for statistical computing in Python. In *Proceedings of the 9th Python in Science Conference*, (pp. 56–61)
16. Page, L., Brin, S., Motwani, R., & Winograd, T. (1999). *The PageRank citation ranking: Bringing order to the web*. Stanford InfoLab, Technical Report 1999-66.
17. Saxena, A., & Iyengar, S. (2020). Centrality measures in complex networks: A survey. arXiv:2011.07190.
18. The pandas development team (2020). pandas-dev/pandas: Pandas, zenodo. 3509134.
19. Tu, X., Jiang, G. P., Song, Y., & Zhang, X. (2018). Novel multiplex PageRank in multilayer networks. *IEEE Access, 6*, 2807778.
20. Waskom, M. L. (2021). Seaborn: Statistical data visualization. *Journal of Open Source Software, 60*(6), 3021.
21. You, H., Li, M., Hipel, K. W., Jiang, J., Ge, B., & Duan, H. (2017). Development trend forecasting for coherent light generator technology based on patent citation network analysis. *Scientometrics, 111*(1), 297–315.

22. Zhong, H., Chuanren, L., Zhong, J., & Xiong, H. (2018). Which startup to invest in: A personalized portfolio strategy. *Annals of Operations Research 263*, 339–360

Anita Mezzetti currently works as a quant engineer, modelling the price of structured products at Credit Suisse. She holds a Bachelor in Mathematics for Engineering from Polytechnic of Turin, where she was supported by a full scholarship for the top students, and she earned a Master in Financial Engineering at the Swiss Federal Institute of Technology (EPFL) in 2020. She completed her Master Thesis, supported by a CYD fellowship, at the Cyber Defence Campus of armasuisse Science and Technology.

Loïc Maréchal is a researcher at the University of Lausanne (Switzerland) and the Cyber Defence Campus of armasuisse Science and Technology. He is also a visiting lecturer in finance at the University of Geneva, ESSEC, and Les Roches Business Schools. He holds a Ph.D. in finance from the University of Neuchâtel and has over ten years of commodity markets experience, including working on trading desks as a quantitative analyst. His research interest is in the application of financial models to cybersecurity and alternative investment spaces, particularly commodity derivatives and private equity markets.

Dimitri Percia David is an Assistant Professor of Data Science and Econometrics at the University of Applied Sciences Valais (Switzerland) where he applies data science and machine learning to the field of technology mining. Prior to this position, he was a postdoctoral researcher at the Information Science Institute of the University of Geneva, and the first recipient of the Distinguished CYD Postdoctoral Fellowship. He earned his Ph.D. in Information Systems from the Faculty of Business and Economics (HEC) at the University of Lausanne, and he has more than eight years of professional experience in the commodities trading industry and as a scientific collaborator at the Military Academy at Swiss Federal Institute of Technology (ETH) Zurich.

William Blonay is a cybersecurity researcher at the Cyber Defence Campus of armasuisse Science and Technology in Lausanne (Switzerland). He is also a cybersecurity researcher at the NATO Cooperative Cyber Defence Centre of Excellence. His main research interests are in the area of internet networks, cellular networks and internet of things.

Sébastien Gillard received an MSc in Physics from the University of Fribourg (Switzerland) in 2016. He specializes in computational physics and statistics, in particular, data analysis and applied statistical modeling and analytical and numerical resolution methods for differential equations. His current research interest is the application of insights from recommender systems to critical infrastructure defense, including the development of code that can power deep learning algorithms.

Michael Tsesmelis is an MSc student in Computational Science and Engineering at Imperial College London. Before, he was a researcher at the Cyber Defence Campus of armasuisse Science and Technology, and he also served as a cybersecurity expert in the Cyber Battalion of the Swiss Armed Forces. His research focuses on economic data science, cybersecurity and computational physics.

Thomas Maillart holds a Master degree from the Swiss Federal Institute of Technology (EPFL) Lausanne (2005) and a Ph.D. from the Swiss Federal Institute of Technology (ETH) Zurich (2011). He received the 2012 Zurich Dissertation Prize for his pioneering work on cyber risks. Before joining the University of Geneva, he worked as a researcher at the Center for Law and Economics at ETH and as a post-doctoral researcher at the University of California at Berkeley. His research focuses on modeling and improving human collective intelligence, particularly in a context of a fast-expanding cyberspace.

Alain Mermoud is the Head of Technology Monitoring and Forecasting at the Cyber Defence Campus of armasuisse Science and Technology. He obtained his Ph.D. in Information Systems from the University of Lausanne (Switzerland). He has more than five years of professional experience in the banking industry. His research interests span emerging technologies, disruptive innovations, threat intelligence and the economics of security.

Chapter 7
Identifying Emerging Technologies and Influential Companies Using Network Dynamics of Patent Clusters

Michael Tsesmelis, Ljiljana Dolamic, Marcus M. Keupp, Dimitri Percia David, and Alain Mermoud

7.1 The Challenge of Predicting Emerging Technology

With accelerating innovation cycles, stakeholders in both industry and government have an increasing need for dependable and real-time insights on technological paradigm shifts, so that they can adapt both business models and public policy to accommodate technological change. In particular, since cybersecurity technology must monitor and defend computer systems, operators need to know how both these systems and the opportunities to attack them evolve. Hence, the cybersecurity industry is extremely reliant on timely information about emerging technologies. However, although data-backed solutions to modern technology monitoring and identification are improving, they rely heavily on subjective and qualitative assessments without any scientific foundation. For instance, some consultancy firms continue to use the

Supplementary Information The online version contains supplementary material available at https://doi.org/10.1007/978-3-031-30191-9_7.

M. Tsesmelis (✉) · L. Dolamic · A. Mermoud
Cyber-Defence Campus, armasuisse Science and Technology, Thun, Switzerland
e-mail: michael.tsesmelis22@imperial.ac.uk

L. Dolamic
e-mail: ljiljana.dolamic@ar.admin.ch

A. Mermoud
e-mail: alain.mermoud@ar.admin.ch

M. M. Keupp
Military Academy at the Swiss Federal Institute of Technology Zurich, Birmensdorf, Switzerland
e-mail: marcus.keupp@milak.ethz.ch

D. Percia David (✉)
Institute of Entrepreneurship and Management, University of Applied Sciences Valais, Sierre, Switzerland
e-mail: dimitri.perciadavid@hevs.ch

M. M. Keupp (ed.), *Cyberdefense*, International Series in Operations Research & Management Science 342,
https://doi.org/10.1007/978-3-031-30191-9_7

Delphi method to predict future business and technology trends. Others regularly publish lists of emerging technologies with very little indication of the exact methods and assumptions by which these lists are created.

Many publications attempt to define the concept of 'emerging technology', and the semantic confusion obfuscates rather than clarifies the debate. Some authors (e.g., [5, 7, 9, 15, 18]) believe a technology is deemed emerging when its potential impact on the economy or society is high, a terminology which includes both evolutionary change as well as disruptive innovations. Others focus on the extent to which the future potential is ambiguous (e.g., [3]). Another group underlines novelty and growth as key determinant factors (e.g., [21]). Still others believe that emerging technologies arise through evolutionary processes upon novel combinations of extant technological fields (e.g., [22]). Yet, quantitative studies of emerging technologies generally agree that semantic differences may be less important than defining a valid proxy measure which can adequately capture technological change. While it might be hard to define whether one particular technology is emerging, it is much easier to compute the relative importance of technologies.

We use patent data as such a proxy, since they provide extensive information on hardware, software, and services innovation. Hence, they are often used to predict emerging technologies. Therefore, we regard emerging technologies as those with the highest growth rates in citations and patent count. Hence, in our framework, emerging technologies are not necessarily new, but witness the fastest changes in interest from researchers and patent applicants.

However, our approach also differs from the prior literature in methodological terms. Many contributions have analyzed or text-mined patent data by bibliometric methods and S-curve growth models to predict emerging technology (e.g., [1, 2, 6, 10, 11, 17, 19]).

In contrast, our approach proposes a fully automated recommender system in which machine learning techniques are used to conduct large-scale patent data analysis. The system ranks technologies and companies according to novel indicators, analyzes near-past dynamics, and predicts current and near-future technological trends. By this approach, we follow recent research which highlights how artificial intelligence methods can help to predict emerging technologies. For example, [12] used supervised learning on citation graphs from the United States Patent and Trademark Office (USPTO) data to automatically label and forecast emerging technologies with high precision. Similarly, [23] applied supervised deep learning on world-wide patent data. Lee et al. [13] extracted 21 indicators from the USPTO data and used neural networks to predict emergence.

Moreover, few contributions in the literature simultaneously rank technologies and the firms that produce them, whereas we believe that once firms are informed about which firms produce which emerging technologies, both the information transparency about technologically leading firms as well as the efficiency of both inter-firm acquisition and research and development activities should increase significantly.

However, all of these studies focus on a specific set of technologies which is subjectively chosen before the analysis begins (e.g., [10, 17, 19]). As a consequence, extant recommender systems are 'heavy', in that every new case requires extensive

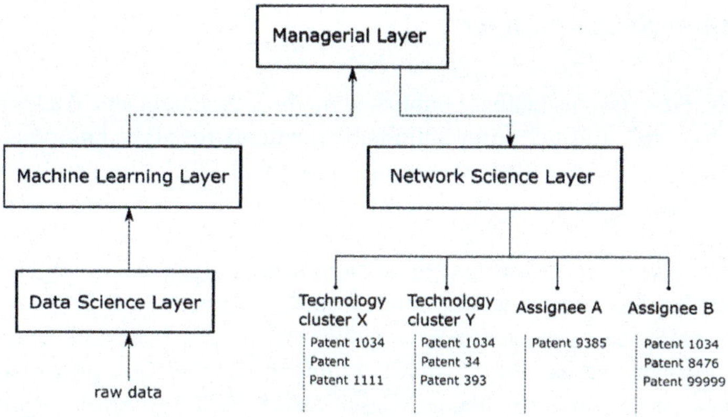

Fig. 7.1 Flowchart depicting data layers and flow

calibration and a long process of selecting the appropriate machine learning model. This calibration can require the full-time attention of a small team of data scientists.

Our approach describes and illustrates a lightweight system that can easily switch between different user queries and provide results with short processing times. It can deal with resource constraints and incomplete data sets by using probabilistic models in machine learning to simplify the research problem and thus its computational complexity. Inspired by financial analysis methods [4, 14], we use multiple indicators and data sources to triangulate our computational analysis and improve the confidence in our results.

7.2 Structure of the Recommender System

Our recommender system[1] uses patent data to generate predictions and recommendations about future technological developments. Patents provide essential, open source, and free information that captures both the growth trajectory and the novelty of a technology [1, 8, 16]. The system is organized in four layers (viz. Fig. 7.1). The *data science layer* is the interface between the external patent database and the recommender system. It inspects raw patent data for inconsistencies and cleans them where necessary. In the *machine learning* layer, the descriptive features of each patent are used to train machine learning classifiers. Thus obtained classifications are transferred to the *managerial layer* which interacts with the user. It records individual queries, matches related patents, and transfers these to the *network science layer* which generates graphs of query-relevant patent clusters and assignees. The layer then constructs several indicators on the basis of these graphs.

[1] For the sake of brevity, the terms 'recommender system' and 'system' are used interchangeably.

7.2.1 Data Science Layer

We used the *Patentsview* database published by the U.S. Patent and Trademark Office (USPTO) to obtain full-text information about patents for all technological applications since 1976. At the time of writing in October 2021, the data set contained 7,101,932 entries. Table 7.1 provides an overview of the specific source files we accessed.

In the following, p designates patents and a its assignees, i.e., organizations or individuals that have an ownership interest in the patent claims. Information about their relationships and association with patents is also retrieved from the *Patentsview* database. Further, we use the *cooperative patent classification* in this database to assign patents to Cooperative Patent Classification (CPC) subgroups ('clusters') c. Each CPC subgroup represents a specific technology, and hence this classification scheme is crucial as it defines the relevant set of technologies which our system ranks subject to user queries.

Table 7.2 summarizes the data points we used and the related source files. We assigned each data point a data type (e.g., integer, string, or date), and missing values were imputed with commonly used metrics such as the median of the column, a plain zero, or NaN values.

Table 7.1 Description of Patentsview datasets

Name of dataset	Description
assignee.tsv	Disambiguated assignee data for granted patents and pre-granted applications, of which we retain the assignee ID and the company name. It is important to note the geographical diversity of the assignees; many non-American companies have submitted documentation to protect their inventions in the United States, and thus our data source extends beyond the confines of the American technological landscape
cpc_current.tsv	Current Cooperative Patent Classification (CPC) data for all patents, of which we retain the patent ID and CPC subgroup ID
otherreference.tsv	Non-patent citations mentioned in patents (e.g., articles, papers, etc). We only retain the patent ID column in order to count the number of references each patent makes to non-patent literature
patent.tsv	Data on granted patents, of which we retain the patent ID, the grant date, the abstract text, and the number
patent_assignee.tsv	Metadata table for many-to-many relationships between assignees and patents, of which we retain the patent ID and assignee ID
patent_inventor.tsv	Metadata table for many-to-many relationships between patents and inventors, of which we retain only the patent ID information in order to count the number of inventors present on application documents
uspatentcitation.tsv	Citations made to US granted patents by US patents, the cited patent ID, and the citing patent ID

Table 7.2 Summary of patent data points

Data point	Description	Source file
assignee_id	Unique assignee identifier used for cross-examination	assignee.tsv
organization	Organization name tied to a specific assignee identifier	assignee.tsv
patent_id	Unique patent identifier used for cross-examination	patent.tsv
date	Patent grant date	patent.tsv
abstract	Patent application abstract	patent.tsv
num_claims	Number of claims made in a patent application	patent.tsv
cpc_group	Cooperative Patent Classification (CPC) subgroup for a specific patent	cpc_current.tsv
otherreference	Number of non-patent literature references for a given patent	otherreference.tsv
inventors	Inventor count for each patent	patent_inventor.tsv
citation_id	Identifier of the patent which cites another patent	uspatentcitation.tsv

7.2.2 Machine Learning Layer

After patent data inspection and cleaning, 242,050 Cooperative Patent Classifications (CPC) were retained as the population from which significant technologies may emerge in the future. We first proxy the absolute interest in these technologies by recording the number of patents granted by the USPTO in each CPC subgroup per year, $count_{c,n}$.

We posit that an emerging CPC subgroup can be recognized by an increase in patent count per year, an increase in the average patent value of the patents it contains, or both. We derive patent value from the forward citations. Figure 7.2 shows the average annual forward citation count for all major technology fields over time. For instance, in the late 1990s, patents related to physics and electricity were highly cited in the first five years following their publication.

We assign a value indicator to each patent which measures how often a specific patent is cited during the five years following its publication, since the median of forward citations is typically between the 4th and 5th year after publication [13]. We term this indicator the *five-year forward citation* (5YFC).

While a raw patent count can be obtained by summing up how many patents were published in a CPC subgroup in a given year, the calculation of patent values requires citation data which may not be available until several years after publication. Therefore, the 5YFC does not exist for patents published five or less years ago, and

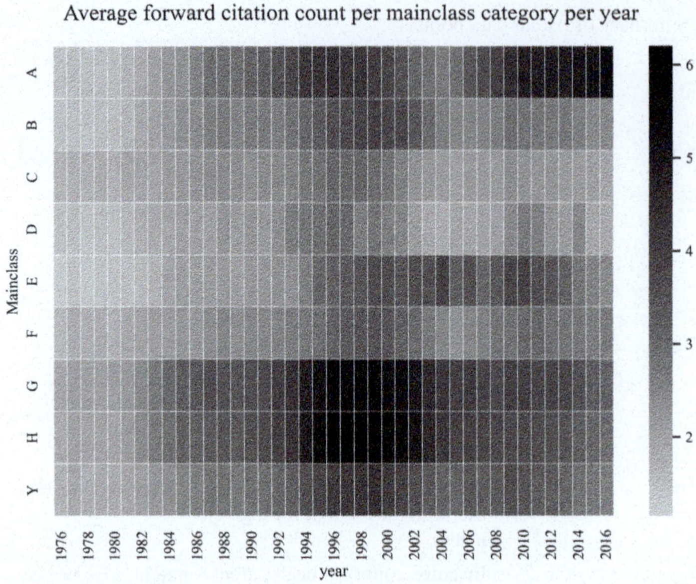

Fig. 7.2 Forward citation of the nine different Cooperative Patent Classification technology sections [a] Key to left-hand axis: A—Human necessities (agriculture, garments,...); B—Performing operations & Transporting; C—Chemistry & Metallurgy; D—Textiles & Paper; E—Fixed constructions; F—Mechanical engineering, lighting, heating, weapons & blasting; G—physics; H—electricity; Y—New technological developments

a CPC subgroup's average patent value cannot be calculated for the most recent five years. Therefore, these values must be predicted with machine learning classifiers. We therefore train the system with extant patent data, with the goal of predicting the 5YFC for patents published in the last five years and queried by the user.

We therefore followed [13] and compiled a shortlist of indicators which objectively capture key information that any patent reveals (viz. Table 7.3). Rather than using a single machine learning algorithm, we opt to search for the best-in-class performance by testing a wide sample of general classifiers on our dataset and comparing their respective performance levels. To accomplish this task, we use the `auto-sklearn` framework, which automatically selects the best possible model and calibrates its hyperparameters to maximize classification scores with patents that already have a 5YFC value.

These indicator data are used as input for a supervised classification algorithm which generates the output value p_i. In studies such as [13], accuracy scores on classification problems using patent data are low, especially for prediction time frames of more than two years. Moreover, the highly unbalanced training datasets of such studies skew the results in favor of the dominant class, and hence the system's overall performance is kept artificially high.

Table 7.3 Summary of patent indicators fed to the machine learning algorithms

Indicator	Description
Five-year forward citation (5YFC)	Number of forward citations over the next five years after a patent is issued
Class-level technological originality (CTO)	Herfindahl index on Cooperative Patent Classification (CPC) groups of cited patents
Prior knowledge (PK)	Number of backward citations
Scientific knowledge (SK)	Number of non-patent literature references
Technology cycle time (TCT)	Median age of cited patents
Main field (MF)	Main class to which a patent belongs
Technological scope (TS)	Number of classes to which a patent belongs
Protection coverage (PCD)	Number of claims
Collaboration (COL)	1 if a patent has more than one assignee, else 0
Inventors (INV)	Number of inventors
Total know-how (TKH)	Total number of patents issued by an assignee
Core area know-how (CKH)	Number of patents in a CPC subgroup of interest issued by an assignee
Total technological strength (TTS)	Number of forward citations of patents issued by an assignee
Core technological strength (CTS)	Number of forward citations of patents in a CPC subgroup of interest issued by an assignee

We therefore propose a more robust approach by reducing the problem to a binary classification system with value p_i of 0 for low-value patents and 1 for high-value patents. In order to label each patent, we first measure the distribution of the 5YFC values of patents older than 5 years. We then define high-value patents as those with a 5YFC above the third quartile of the distribution. We then train the machine learning algorithms on an identical number of low- and high-value patents.

We also considered computational issues to generate a lightweight and fast system which can compute patent clusters and networks faster and with less memory overhead. Compared to the common practice of loading all patent data sets as data frames in random-access memory (RAM), the method is parsimonious in terms of RAM consumption, and thus the system can run on consumer-grade computers with 16- or 32GB RAM space. While running the initial machine learning algorithms can use up to 100GB of RAM, the widespread availability of Azure and AWS makes even this higher computing power affordable. Further, running the graphs requires much less RAM capacity.

Moreover, since we considered creating an external SQL database as too time-consuming, and since the sequential reading of data sets is prone to errors, we stored the data using *tensors*, i.e., multi-dimensional dictionaries which are saved locally using by pickle file formatting rather than the heavier comma-separated-value (csv) format.

In order to improve the applicability and robustness of our system, we let it run on a randomized selection of patents from all 242,050 CPC subgroups. Finally, we simplified the input indicators fed to the system, and we tested our training set on a wide selection of classification algorithms. Once this training phase is completed, the algorithm predicts the binary value of recently granted patents. Finally, for each cluster c in year n, we measure for every year the average value of the patents it contains as well as the yearly patent count, formally:

$$size_{c,n} = |c_n| \tag{7.1}$$

$$value_{c,n} = \frac{1}{size_{c,n}} \sum_{p_i \in c_n} p_i \tag{7.2}$$

where c_n is a technology cluster belonging to C which contains patents issued in time n, and p_i is the binary patent value (0 or 1) for patent i.

7.2.3 Managerial Layer

The managerial layer provides a CLI user interface and generates jobs which process user input. These jobs contain settings to adjust job duration and to specify job content. By providing the system with a list of lone or concatenated keywords related to a search topic, the user designates a particular area of interest. The managerial layer receives these keywords and scans all 7,101,932 patent abstracts for occurrences of these words. The patents in which these keywords appear verbatim are saved in a list of *topical patents*. Each job thus produces a list of patents strongly or weakly connected to the user query, and it uses the list of topical patents to generate a network that maps technologies and companies related to these topical patents.

Although our approach to identifying patents related to specific queries can be deemed elementary, we believe this approach results in a more comprehensive view of the patent population. By specifying a keyword list that is both precise—i.e., bearing little overlap with unrelated queries—and complete—i.e., capturing all essential traits of the search—, the CLI captures statistically significant associations between the search query and the patent population without the need for complex mechanisms which may render false-positive results.

7.2.4 Network Science Layer

The network science layer generates many-to-many tables which group patents p with their respective assignees a and CPC subgroups c. Based on the queries entered and jobs generated in the managerial layer, the network science layer selects relevant CPC subgroups associated with the topical patents (also known as topical clusters). First, all patents belonging to these selected topical clusters are retrieved, then, all assignees that sponsored these patents (*topical assignees*) are recorded. The more topical patents link to a specific CPC subgroup, the more weight the systems give to that subgroup. Further, different jobs can run successively, with each job having a time complexity of $O(\log n)$, since topical patents most likely share topical clusters.

The system finally constructs a graph of bipartite relationships between the selected topical clusters c and the related assignees a, so that each topical cluster and each assignee is depicted as a node. The resulting bipartite network comprises two disjoint sets of topical clusters C and assignees A, with all edges E between the sets only joining one node of each set and never two entities of the same set.

This step considerably reduces the complexity of the computational problem, since no complex time-series of graphs are required, but merely a four-year observation period. Each CPC subgroup node c is weighted by its value $value_{c,n}$ and labeled with its patent count $count_{c,n}$. All edges $e \in E$ between nodes are weighted by the amount of patents that a tuple $c \in C$ and $a \in A$ have in common.

On this basis, the system computes several indices which inform the user about both the emergence of a technology and the firms associated with it. First, it renders a *technology index* by calculating two discrete growth factors between the years $argmax N - 3$ and $argmax N$, namely cluster value growth and cluster size growth, where n is one year between $argmax\ N - 3$ and $argmax\ N$, formally:

$$value\ growth_{c,n} = \frac{value_{c,n}}{value_{c,n-1}} \tag{7.3}$$

$$cluster\ growth_{c,n} = \frac{size_{c,n}}{size_{c,n-1}} \times \sqrt[m]{size_{c,n-1}} \tag{7.4}$$

where m is a penalty for small patent clusters (in our subsequent illustration, a value of $m = 5$ is applied). Both measures are combined into a technology index:

$$tech\ index_c = \frac{1}{3} \sum_{n \in N} value\ growth_{c,n} \times cluster\ growth_{c,n} \tag{7.5}$$

Whereas the technology growth index refers to technologies, the remainder of the indices we calculate refers to assignees (i.e., firms or individuals). The *assignee value index* measures the average value of the patents assigned to a topical assignee a in year $argmax N$. It thus highlights organizations which produce highly impactful research in technological domains the user is interested in. Formally,

$$value_a = \frac{1}{size_a} \sum_{p_i \in a_z} p_i \tag{7.6}$$

The more specific *impact index* measures the value an assignee contributes to a user query and thus rewards assignees whose patents are highly relevant for said query. It is defined as the sum of the relationships each assignee has with the topical clusters. Given an assignee a and a CPC subgroup node c, the strength of this relationship is defined as the product of the $value_a$ of the assignee node, the $tech\ index_c$ of the CPC subgroup node, and the weight of the edge between the two entities $weight_{c,a}$. This index captures the overall contribution a specific assignee makes to a technological field, formally:

$$weight_{c,a} = |\{(c, a) \mid c \in C,\ a \in A\}| \tag{7.7}$$

$$impact_a = \sum_{e \in E_a} value_a \times value_{c,\arg\max N} \times weight_{c,a} \tag{7.8}$$

where E_a is the set of all edges e connected to assignee a.

Further, the *normalized impact index* is a proportionally weighted version of the above impact index. Since smaller assignees could be less influential as they lack the resources to produce a large number of patents, the normalized impact index corrects for this oversight. In particular, this index allows us to highlight small yet influential start-ups. Formally,

$$normindex_a = \frac{impact_a}{|E_a|} \tag{7.9}$$

Finally, we define an eigenvector centrality measure which determines the influence an assignee has in the bipartite network. Eigenvector centrality computes the centrality of a node in the network subject to the centrality of its neighboring nodes [20]. Formally, the eigenvector centrality for node i is the i-th element of the vector x defined by

$$Ax = \lambda x \tag{7.10}$$

where A is the adjacency matrix of the Graph G with eigenvalue λ. The analysis renders two values—the influence of an assignee node $influence_a$ and the influence of CPC subgroup nodes $influence_c$—of which only the first measure is retained to inform the user.

7.3 Illustration

To illustrate the performance of our system, we defined a query with a manually curated list of keywords from the cybersecurity glossary published by the National Initiative for Cybersecurity Careers and Studies (NICCS), namely *'allowlist'*, *'anti-*

malware', *'antispyware'*, *'antivirus'*, *'asymmetric key'*, *'attack signature'*, *'blocklist'*, *'blue team'*, *'bot'*, *'botnet'*, *'bug'*, *'ciphertext'*, *'computer forensics'*, *'computer security incident'*, *'computer virus'*, *'computer worm'*, *'cryptanalysis'*, *'cryptography'*, *'cryptographic'*, *'cryptology'*, *'cyber incident'*, *'cybersecurity'*, *'cyber security'*, *'cyberspace'*, *'cyber threat intelligence'*, *'data breach'*, *'data leakage'*, *'data theft'*, *'decrypt'*, *'decrypted'*, *'decryption'*, *'denial of service'*, *'digital forensics'*, *'digital signature'*, *'encrypt'*, *'encrypted'*, *'encryption'*, *'firewall'*, *'hacker'*, *'hashing'*, *'keylogger'*, *'malware'*, *'malicious code'*, *'network resilience'*, *'password'*, *'pen test'*, *'pentest'*, *'phishing'*, *'private key'*, *'public key'*, *'red team'*, *'rootkit'*, *'spoofing'*, *'spyware'*, *'symmetric key'*, *'systems security analysis'*, *'threat actor'*, *'trojan'*, and *'white team'*.

The training set consisted of 15,000 low-value patents (binary value 0) and 15,000 high-value patents (binary value 1), so that the random guess accuracy rate was 50%. Since execution time is highly correlated with the machine learning step size, we ran a best-model search using the `auto-sklearn` framework, capped at 0.6 h testing time per model and 6 h in total. The framework ran 37 different target algorithms. One algorithm crashed, three exceeded the set time limit, and five exceeded the memory limit. A mix of differently hyperparameterized random forest models predicted the data best, yielding a validation score on accuracy of 0.6737, i.e., about two in three patents were classified correctly.

These models were then used to predict the output values of the 1,740,613 patents granted in the latest five-year period in the Patentsview dataset we used. We ran our job on a specialized high-performance computer (HPC) node with 128 AMD EPYC 7742 CPUs. On this machine, prediction results took just over 11 h, and all steps in the data science and machine learning layers required approximately 26 h to run. Still, we estimate that 16 CPUs should be sufficient for a job of the size in this illustration, since maximum concurrent RAM usage never exceeded 100GB, half of which was occupied by the ten different tensors loaded with Patentsview data and the rest was occupied intermittently by the machine learning dataframes.

Figure 7.3 presents the cumulative distribution function for cluster size. It shows that in most of the clusters related to our query, there are less than 500 relevant patents since the inception of the respective cluster.

However, the cumulative distribution function for cluster value, shown in Fig. 7.4, suggests that there are highly-valued patents among these few.

The 'violin plots' in Figs. 7.5 and 7.6 which describe the probability density functions for cluster size and cluster value capture this result in a more intuitive form. For cluster size, the contrast between the values for CPC clusters related to the query compared to all 242,050 clusters is striking, suggesting that technology related to the query has drawn much attention among researchers. Further, technologies related to the query have an average patent value of above 0.5 for the timespan from 2018 to 2021, implying that the average cluster related to the query has more high-value than low-value patents.

Table 7.4 gives the values for our technology index as defined in Eq. (7.5). It ranks relevant CPC subgroups based on their emergence and growth values. There is a strong interest in privacy-preserving technologies, communication systems, and

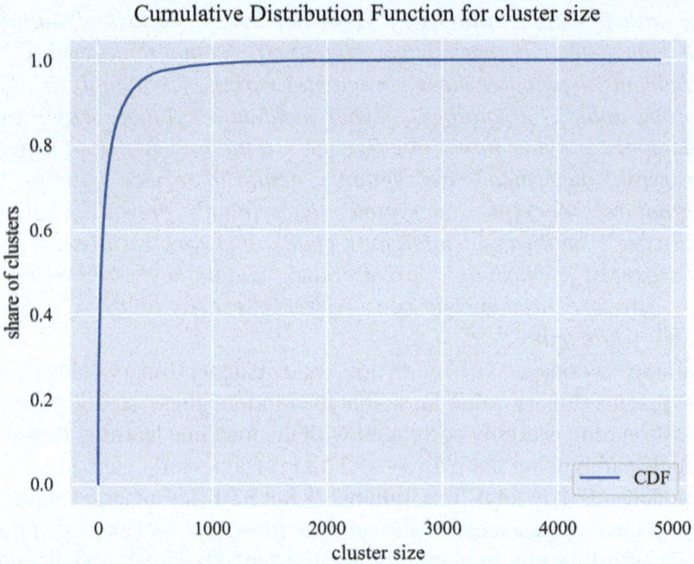

Fig. 7.3 Cumulative distribution function for cluster size

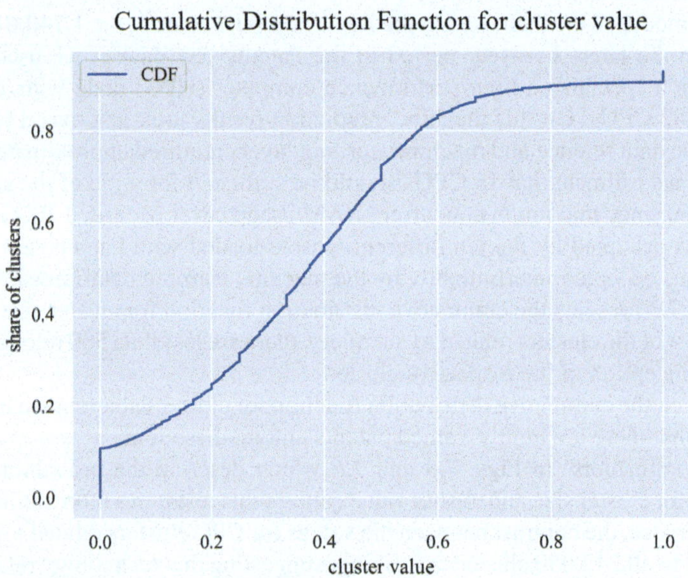

Fig. 7.4 Cumulative distribution function for cluster value

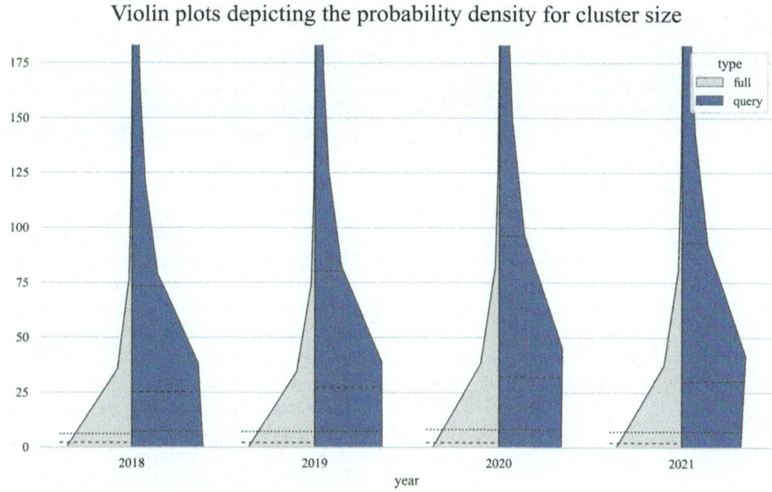

Fig. 7.5 Violin plots for cluster size, from 2018 to 2021

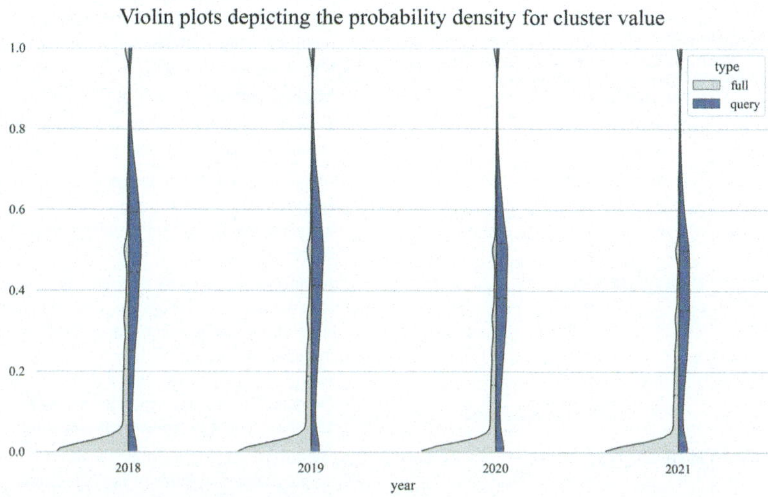

Fig. 7.6 Violin plots for cluster value, from 2018 to 2021

database security, which suggests that these technologies will likely emerge strongly in the future, and they would be of key interest to users who submit a query similar or identical to ours.

Table 7.5 presents the top 10 assignees related to the query, ordered by the impact index as defined in Eq. (7.9). Unsurprisingly, as a result of their large patent counts, major software and hardware companies top the list.

Table 7.6 presents the ranking obtained by the normalized impact index as defined in Eq. (7.9). Since this index qualifies the impact index by patent output size, it high-

Table 7.4 Technologies ranked according to technology index

Score	CPC subgroup	Patent count	Citation count	Description
8.02	G06N3/08	6519	251.6	Computer systems based on biological models-using neural network models-Learning methods
8.02	G06F7/50	163	13.7	Methods or arrangements for processing data by operating upon the order or content of the data handled—Methods or arrangements for performing computations using exclusively denominational number representation, e.g., using binary, ternary, decimal representation-using non-contact-making devices, e.g., tube, solid state device; using unspecified devices-Adding; Subtracting
7.92	G06Q20/3558	132	81.4	Payment architectures, schemes or protocols—characterized by the use of specific devices; or networks-using cards, e.g., integrated circuit [IC] cards or magnetic cards-Personalization of cards for use-Preliminary personalization for transfer to user
7.90	G06N3/0454	5458	141.3	Computer systems based on biological models-using neural network models-Architectures, e.g., interconnection topology-using a combination of multiple neural nets
7.55	G06N20/00	13947	747.4	Machine learning
7.48	H04W80/08	279	14.6	Wireless network protocols or protocol adaptations to wireless operation-Upper layer protocols
7.15	G11C8/20	243	53.7	Arrangements for selecting an address in a digital store—Address safety or protection circuits, i.e., arrangements for preventing unauthorized or accidental access
7.06	G06F9/3818	66	61.4	Arrangements for program control, e.g., control units—using stored programs, i.e., using an internal store of processing equipment to receive or retain programs-Arrangements for executing machine instructions, e.g., instruction decode—Concurrent instruction execution, e.g., pipeline, look ahead-Decoding for concurrent execution
7.05	H04L2209/38	2858	2728.0	Additional information or applications relating to cryptographic mechanisms or cryptographic arrangements for secret or secure communication H04L9/00-Chaining, e.g., hash chain or certificate chain
6.91	G06N3/0472	977	51.0	Computer systems based on biological models-using neural network models-Architectures, e.g., interconnection topology-using probabilistic elements, e.g., p-rams, stochastic processors

Table 7.5 Assignees ranked according to impact index

Rank	Assignee	Patent count	Value	Impact
1	International Business Machines Corporation	7314	0.4793	3,488,180
2	Microsoft Technology Licensing, LLC	2644	0.8150	3,157,710
3	Amazon Technologies, Inc	2133	0.4871	1,632,140
4	Cisco Technology, Inc	1040	0.7798	1,532,470
5	Advanced New Technologies Co, Ltd	518	0.4864	1,453,670
6	Intel Corporation	2788	0.4573	1,283,470
7	EMC IP Holding Company LLC	1235	0.7336	1,265,040
8	Apple Inc	2568	0.5459	1,132,630
9	AS America, Inc	496	0.5987	941,869
10	Google LLC	1621	0.6761	921,388

Table 7.6 Assignees ranked according to normalized impact index

Rank	Assignee	Value	Patent count	Norm. impact
1	CyberArk Software Ltd	0.7567	37	833.551
2	Intertrust Technologies Corporation	0.8571	14	771.041
3	Shape Security, Inc	0.9090	11	769.185
4	F5 Networks, Inc	0.9230	26	765.03
5	Sophos Limited	0.8695	46	744.879
6	McAfee, LLC	0.8924	93	730.186
7	Sonicwall Inc	0.8571	14	726.287
8	MX Technologies, Inc	0.875	16	717.432
9	FireEye, Inc	0.9787	47	683.293
10	Netskope, Inc	0.75	20	632.204

Table 7.7 Assignees ranked by influence in the bipartite network

Rank	Assignee	Patent count	Value	Influence
1	International Business Machines Corporation	7314	0.4793	0.3573
2	Samsung Electronics Co., Ltd	5415	0.3566	0.2811
3	Qualcomm Incorporated	2129	0.5758	0.1948
4	Huawei Technologies Co., Ltd	2765	0.0239	0.1787
5	LG Electronics, Inc	2094	0.1905	0.1763
6	Apple Inc	2568	0.5459	0.1668
7	Microsoft Technology Licensing, LLC	2644	0.8150	0.1608
8	Intel Corporation	2788	0.4573	0.1599
9	Amazon Technologies, Inc	2133	0.4871	0.106
10	Facebook, Inc	1317	0.2498	0.1025

lights smaller, lesser known assignees which nevertheless are of significant relevance in the technological fields relevant to the query. Note the table only shows assignees which have been granted at least five patents in the last year of the timespan we analyzed. By applying this restriction, we can filter outlier assignees which produced very few patents if in highly valuable domains.

Table 7.7 ranks the most influential assignees in the bipartite network of technologies and assignees as defined in Eq. (7.10). Again, technologically dominant assignees top out the list, yet hardware manufacturers have the upper hand.

We finally cross-plot some of the indicators we developed to generate additional insights. Figure 7.7 plots, for each assignee and all topical clusters, the respective patent count (x axis) against the normalized impact index (y axis). The dot plot distribution suggests a negative correlation with an approximate relationship of $y = 1/x, x > 0$. This result supports the economic theory of decreasing marginal return of innovation in large companies; the larger the patent output of an assignee, the less valuable a particular patent seems to be.

Figure 7.8 plots, for all topical clusters, assignee influence (x axis) against assignee impact (y axis). The dot plot suggests no statistically significant trend, hence horizontal integration or investments into many technology areas does not seem to improve an assignee's impact in the respective technological field.

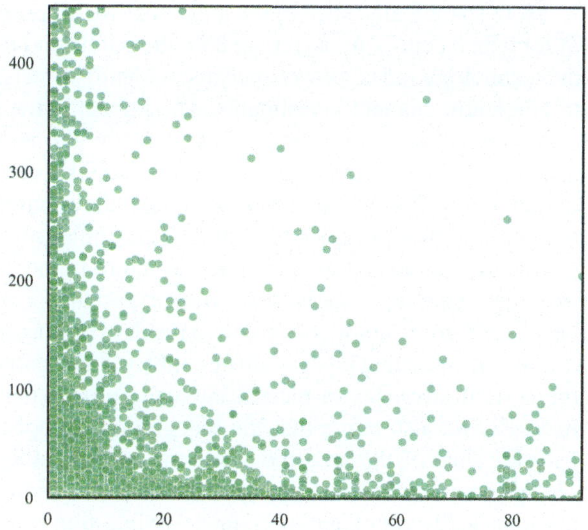

Fig. 7.7 Plot of assignee patent count (x-axis) against normalized impact index (y-axis) by assignee

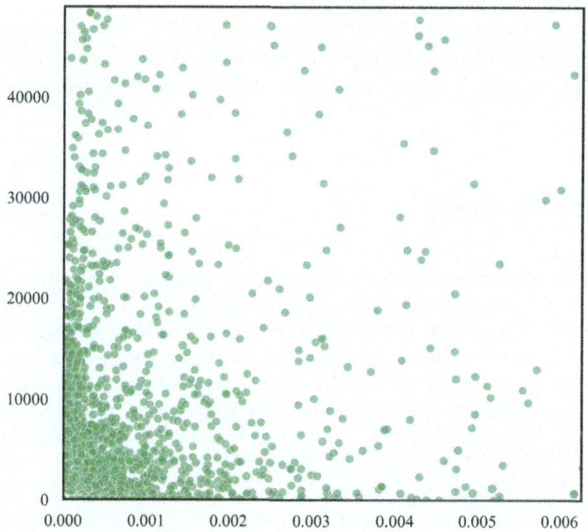

Fig. 7.8 Plot of assignee influence (x axis) against assignee impact (y axis)

7.4 Discussion

In this chapter, we have described a recommender system which predicts emerging technologies by a sequential blend of machine learning and network analytics methods. In so doing, we contribute to both the technical and the economic discussion of cybersecurity in a number of ways. We illustrated the capabilities of the system using data from the United States Patent Office (USPTO).

More specifically, each of the indicators we proposed has a direct economic benefit for cybersecurity managers in both the public and the private sector. For example, the technology index allows analysts to identify emerging technology early and thus to efficiently channel investments. The impact index identifies leading firms in the technological areas of interest. Additionally, the normalized impact index allows analysts to identify opportunities for early-stage investments into promising technology fields. Finally, the influence index allows clients to identify well-connected assignees; it thus provides opportunities for alliances or joint development projects.

The system could still be refined in future rounds of development. For example, in some technology fields, firms may experience a higher pressure to patent, e.g., because of strong competition or as a result of international market structures. Hence, the machine learning layer could be calibrated to incorporate this effect. Further, given the current advances in natural language processing and computational Bayesian methods, we also argue that the recognition of topical clusters could be enhanced by using state-of-the-art topic extraction and modeling methods. Overall, we believe our system to be a first stepping stone toward a prediction tool which is lightweight, accurate and free and replaces subjective intuition or arbitrary choice with systematic and objective analysis.

Ultimately, this improvement in information transparency and investment efficiency should translate into a more effective cyberdefense. We therefore encourage the reader to let our system compete against extant models and consultancy advice.

References

1. Andersen, B. (1999). The hunt for S-shaped growth paths in technological innovation: A patent study. *Journal of Evolutionary Economics, 9*(4), 487–526.
2. Bengisu, M., & Nekhili, R. (2006). Forecasting emerging technologies with the aid of science and technology databases. *Technological Forecasting and Social Change, 73*(7), 835–844.
3. Boon, W., & Moors, E. (2008). Exploring emerging technologies using metaphors: A study of orphan drugs and pharmacogenomics. *Social Science & Medicine, 66*(9), 1915–1927.
4. Clemen, R. (1989). Combining forecasts: A review and annotated bibliography. *International Journal of Forecasting, 5*(4), 559–583.
5. Corrocher, N., Malerba, F., & Montobbio, F. (2003). The emergence of new technologies in the ICT field: Main actors, geographical distribution and knowledge sources. Department of Economics, University of Insubria. https://EconPapers.repec.org/RePEc:ins:quaeco:qf0317.
6. Daim, T., Rueda, G., Martin, H., & Gerdsri, P. (2006). Forecasting emerging technologies: Use of bibliometrics and patent analysis. *Technological Forecasting and Social Change, 73*(8), 981–1012.
7. Halaweh, M. (2013). Emerging technology: What is it? *Journal of Technology Management, 8*(3), 108–115.
8. Haupt, R., Kloyer, M., & Lange, M. (2007). Patent indicators for the technology life cycle development. *Research Policy, 36*(3), 387–398.
9. Hung, S.-C., & Chu, Y.-Y. (2006). Stimulating new industries from emerging technologies: Challenges for the public sector. *Technovation, 26*(1), 104–110.
10. Intepe, G., & Koc, T. (2012). The use of S curves in technology forecasting and its application on 3D TV technology. *International Journal of Industrial and Manufacturing Engineering, 6*(11), 2491–2495.

11. Kucharavy, D., Schenk, E., & De Guio, R. (2009). Long-run forecasting of emerging technologies with logistic models and growth of knowledge. In *Proceedings of the 19th CIRP Design Conference* (p. 277).
12. Kyebambe, M., Cheng, G., Huang, Y., He, C., & Zhang, Z. (2017). Forecasting emerging technologies: A supervised learning approach through patent analysis. *Technological Forecasting and Social Change, 125*, 236–244.
13. Lee, C., Kwon, O., Kim, M., & Kwon, D. (2018). Early identification of emerging technologies: A machine learning approach using multiple patent indicators. *Technological Forecasting and Social Change, 127*(3), 291–303.
14. Makridakis, S., & Winkler, R. L. (1983). Averages of forecasts: Some empirical results. *Management Science, 29*(9), 987–996.
15. Martin, B. (1995). Foresight in science and technology. *Technology Analysis & Strategic Management, 7*(2), 139–168.
16. Meyer, M. (2001). Patent citation analysis in a novel field of technology: An exploration of nano-science and nano-technology. *Scientometrics, 51*(1), 163–183.
17. Nieto, M., Lopéz, F., & Cruz, F. (1998). Performance analysis of technology using the S curve model: The case of digital signal processing (DSP) technologies. *Technovation, 18*(6), 439–457.
18. Porter, A. L., Roessner, J. D., Jin, X. Y., & Newman, N. C. (2002). Measuring national 'emerging technology' capabilities. *Science and Public Policy, 29*(3), 189–200.
19. Ranaei, S., Karvonen, M., Suominen, A., & Kässi, T. (2014). Forecasting emerging technologies of low emission vehicle. In *Proceedings of the PICMET 2014 Conference* (pp. 2924–2937).
20. Ruhnau, B. (2000). Eigenvector-centrality - a node-centrality? *Social Networks, 22*(4), 357–365.
21. Small, H., Boyack, K., & Klavans, R. (2014). Identifying emerging topics in science and technology. *Research Policy, 43*(8), 1450–1467.
22. Wang, Z., Porter, A. L., Wang, X., & Carley, S. (2019). An approach to identify emergent topics of technological convergence: A case study for 3D printing. *Technological Forecasting and Social Change, 146*, 723–732.
23. Zhou, Y., Dong, F., Li, Z., Du, J., Liu, Y., & Zhang, L. (2020). Forecasting emerging technologies with deep learning and data augmentation. *Scientometrics, 123*, 1–29.

Michael Tsesmelis is an MSc student in Computational Science and Engineering at Imperial College London. Before, he was a researcher at the Cyber Defence Campus of armasuisse Science and Technology, and he also served as a cybersecurity expert in the Cyber Battalion of the Swiss Armed Forces. His research focuses on economic data science, cybersecurity and computational physics.

Ljiljana Dolamic is a Scientific Project Manager at the Cyber Defence Campus of armasuisse Science and Technology in Lausanne (Switzerland). Her research interests span computational linguistics, multilingual and cross-lingual information retrieval, machine translation and language modelling. After finalising her Ph.D. at the University of Neuchâtel, she co-developed domain-specific search engines and linguistics projects.

Marcus M. Keupp is the editor of this volume. He chairs the Department of Defense Economics at the Military Academy of the Swiss Federal Institute of Technology (ETH) Zurich. He was educated at the University of Mannheim (Germany) and Warwick Business School (UK) and obtained his Ph.D. and habilitation from the University of St. Gallen (Switzerland). He has authored, co-authored, and edited twelve books and more than 30 peer-reviewed journal articles and received numerous awards for his academic achievements.

Dimitri Percia David is an Assistant Professor of Data Science and Econometrics at the University of Applied Sciences Valais (Switzerland) where he applies data science and machine learning to the field of technology mining. Prior to this position, he was a postdoctoral researcher at the Information Science Institute of the University of Geneva, and the first recipient of the Distinguished CYD Postdoctoral Fellowship. He earned his Ph.D. in Information Systems from the Faculty of Business and Economics (HEC) at the University of Lausanne, and he has more than eight years of professional experience in the commodities trading industry and as a scientific collaborator at the Military Academy at Swiss Federal Institute of Technology (ETH) Zurich.

Alain Mermoud is the Head of Technology Monitoring and Forecasting at the Cyber Defence Campus of armasuisse Science and Technology. He obtained his Ph.D. in Information Systems from the University of Lausanne (Switzerland). He has more than five years of professional experience in the banking industry. His research interests span emerging technologies, disruptive innovations, threat intelligence and the economics of security.

Chapter 8
Cybersecurity Ecosystems: A Network Study from Switzerland

Cédric Aeschlimann, Kilian Cuche, and Alain Mermoud

8.1 Capability Dispersion

In order to produce effective cyberdefense, organizations require capabilities, i.e., organizational routines that purposefully combine human (e.g., trained IT specialists), material (e.g., computer hardware), and knowledge resources (e.g., professional knowledge) to produce a desired outcome [26]. Hence, any organization which lacks the required capabilities must produce them or absorb them from beyond the organizational boundary. None of these options is easy to implement, since the creation of novel capabilities requires considerable time and resources, and the organization may lack the resources to build it. In particular, human and knowledge resources are a scarce commodity in contemporary cyberdefense. There currently is a severe lack of capable specialists available to organizations around the world. Each year, up to 3.5 million cybersecurity job openings cannot be filled [4, 11].

An alternative is to absorb the required capabilities from other organizations in the industry. Scholars predict that the performance of an organization will increase with the number of connections to other organizations in the network since such link-

Supplementary Information The online version contains supplementary material available at https://doi.org/10.1007/978-3-031-30191-9_8.

C. Aeschlimann (✉)
Department of Defense Economics, Military Academy at ETH Zurich, Birmensdorf ZH, Switzerland
e-mail: cedric.aeschlimann@vtg.admin.ch

K. Cuche
Swiss Armed Forces Command Support Organization, Berne, Switzerland
e-mail: kilian.cuche@vtg.admin.ch

A. Mermoud
Cyber-Defence Campus, Armasuisse Science and Technology, Thun, Switzerland
e-mail: alain.mermoud@ar.admin.ch

M. M. Keupp (ed.), *Cyberdefense*, International Series in Operations Research & Management Science 342,
https://doi.org/10.1007/978-3-031-30191-9_8

ages facilitate access to relevant information [3, 13, 15, 24]. However, the promise that capabilities can be 'leveraged' by building inter-organizational networks does not always seem to materialize [29]. Some studies find that network centrality has a negative impact on efficiency since a high number of relationships increases coordination cost and impedes innovation since network management competes with product development for scarce resources. Moreover, organizations may be unwilling to share capabilities for a variety of reasons [1, 14, 27].

We examine this tension in the context of cyberdefense in Switzerland. Since this country is both small and technology-intensive, the network of organizations which offer and demand capabilities for cyberdefense can be captured efficiently. We attempted to identify all public, academic, and private organizations in Switzerland whose business or mission requires significant cyberdefense capabilities (in the following, the 'ecosystem'). We designed and implemented a survey among these organizations that captured different types of capabilities and the extent to which the respective organization possesses or requires these. We analyzed the distribution of these capabilities in the ecosystem and identified net supply and demand. Finally, we used the data to study the links that organizations established (or refused to establish) with each other as they attempted to procure missing capabilities.

We adopted the list of capabilities in the questionnaire from the NICE and the UCCF frameworks. The NICE framework was developed by NIST [21], and it has been adopted on a global scale to gauge the extent to which cyberdefense capabilities exist in both private, public, government, and military organizations (e.g., [5, 12, 19, 25]). In contrast to more context-specific approaches (e.g., [6, 9, 23]), it focuses directly on organizational capabilities and specializes in the analysis of cyberdefense. However, focus group interviews conducted before the launch of our survey suggested that it is not exhaustive for all types of organizations in the ecosystem. Since it was primarily written for private sector firms, it lacks particular capabilities, such as preventive measure-taking and intelligence gathering, all of which are relevant to public institutions, particularly so in the defense sector. We therefore added capabilities from NATO's *Unified Cyber Competence Framework* (UCCF), which is based on NICE but extends it to the above context [8]. The survey captured the following eight dimensions of cyberdefense capabilities which were operationalized by 57 variables:

- *Securely Provision*: Conceptualizing and building secure IT systems;
- *Operate and Maintain*: Providing the support and administrative tasks to ensure secure continued usage of IT systems;
- *Oversee and Govern*: Providing leadership and management allowing for an effective cybersecurity work;
- *Protect and Defend*: Identifying, analyzing, and fighting threats to IT systems;
- *Analyze*: Performing reviews and analyses of incoming information;
- *Collect and Operate*: Providing deception operations to collect information in order to develop cybersecurity;
- *Investigate*: Investigating events or crimes linked to IT systems and handling digital intelligence;

- *Cyber offense*: Strategizing and implementing offensive actions designed to exfiltrate data from or neutralize a target.

Each of the 57 variables was coded on a four-point multinomial scale with four mutually exclusive evaluations; 'we have the respective capability and offer it to other organizations' (in the following, coded as 'offered' for short), 'we have the capability, but do not offer it' (coded as 'used'), 'we do not have it but require it' (coded as 'required') and 'we neither have nor require it' (coded as 'not needed').[1]

To capture organizations in the private sector, we queried the Technology and Market Monitoring (TMM) database which was created by the science and technology division of the Swiss Federal Office for Defense Procurement *armasuisse*.[2] Further, we queried public databases that captured and described startup firms.[3]

Information about organizations in the academic sector was obtained from the Swiss Academy of Engineering Sciences (SATW) which maintains a database of research institutes and academic spin-offs in the cyberdefense domain, and from the member list of the Swiss Informatics Research Association (SIRA).[4] Information on public organizations, the government, and the military sector was obtained from the General Secretariat of the Swiss Federal Department of Defense, Civil Protection and Sport.

Following [18], all databases were queried with a list of keywords specifically relevant to cybersecurity. The raw list of organizations from all three sectors was inspected for double entries and cross-validated with annual reports, trade association documents, entries in the commercial register, and public market intelligence. We used the software *SelectSurvey* to administer the survey. Data were recorded with a secure and non-commercial server architecture hosted at the Swiss Federal Institute of Technology Zurich, and respondents were guaranteed complete anonymity and confidentiality. For the purpose of analysis, the data were aggregated and anonymized.

The final survey population comprised 712 organizations to which the questionnaire was sent. After two reminders were sent, the survey was closed, six weeks after the questionnaire was first sent. 186 organizations had responded, for a response rate of 26.12%. 55 replies were not considered because of too much missing data, so that 131 questionnaires remained for analysis. Among these remaining questionnaires, 76 came from the private, 30 from the academic, 21 from the public sector, and 4 categorized themselves as *other*. Those four were organizations that resulted from a public-private partnership, or independent organizations with a public mandate granted by the government. They were included in the calculation of general averages but not in the sector-specific analysis.

---

[1] The full questionnaire is available on request from the corresponding author.

[2] See https://tmm.dslab.ch/#/home.

[3] These comprised the Swiss Cyber Startup Map (https://cysecmap.swiss/), the Top 100 Startup Ranking (https://www.top100startups.swiss/) and the Startup Directory (https://www.startup.ch/startup-directory).

[4] For the SATW, see https://www.satw.ch/en/topics/cybersecurity; for the SIRA, see https://sira.swissinformatics.org/sira-members/.

8.2 Analysis

Data in all tables in this section is calculated from the responses of the 131 questionnaires in the final sample. Table 8.1 shows how cyberdefense capabilities are used or required on average across all three sectors and among all 131 firms. On average, the private sector is a large supplier of capabilities since 40.14% of all capabilities among organizations in this sector are also offered to other private firms and organizations in the other two sectors. Note that on average, capability requirements in the public and academic sectors are almost twice as large as in the private sector. The academic sector has the highest share of capabilities marked as 'not needed', which probably reflects its role as a creator, rather than a user, of the knowledge and technology from which the respective capability results.

Table 8.2 groups the capability distribution across all three sectors by dimension. On average, organizations seem to have a good mastery of cyberdefense, since more than 70% use or offer to others the capabilities in the dimensions *Securely Provision*, *Operate and Maintain*, *Oversee and Govern* and *Protect and Defend*. However, the ecosystem as a whole also has high net requirements in the capability dimensions *Protect and Defend*, *Analyze*, and *Investigate*.

Table 8.1 Average distribution (%) of capabilities across sectors

	Offered	Used	Required	Not needed
Public sector	24.40	33.48	6.47	35.65
Academic sector	22.90	24.98	5.73	46.39
Private sector	39.46	24.76	3.69	32.09

Table 8.2 Average distribution of capabilities (%) by dimension

	Offered	Used	Required	Not needed	Total
Securely provision	46.39	26.00	8.62	18.99	100
Operate and maintain	42.48	31.97	5.78	19.77	100
Oversee and govern	35.18	38.63	6.78	19.41	100
Protect and defend	38.70	32.30	13.51	15.49	100
Analyze	25.45	19.38	14.15	41.02	100
Collect and Operate	17.78	12.01	4.91	65.30	100
Investigate	34.87	22.13	15.37	27.63	100
Cyber Offense	15.16	4.49	3.40	76.95	100

The dispersion is highest for the dimension *Analyze*, which 14.15% of all organizations require, whereas 41.02% of all organizations mark it as 'not needed', probably because few professional applications for the automated cyberintelligence analysis exist [7]. The more aggressive capability dimensions *Collect and Operate* and *Cyber Offense* have the lowest rate of adoption among all organizations, with 65.30% and 76.95% noting they do not require these. While most organizations may not want to directly attack those who threaten their cybersecurity, those 4.91% (3.4%) which do note they require such capabilities would still have to find a way to procure them.

8.2.1 Sector-Specific Analysis

Table 8.3 shows the data for the subsample of public sector organizations only. They least require capabilities in the dimensions *Cyber Offense* and *Collect and Operate*, whereas the *Protect and Defend* and *Oversee and Govern* dimensions are used most. This probably reflects the fact that Switzerland's government institutions have no offensive cyber doctrine. The public sector also supplies capabilities to other organizations at a below-average yet significant rate. Public sector organizations most require capabilities in the *Investigate* dimension, which reflects a demand for professional forensics operations.

Table 8.4 details the subsample of academic organizations. Overall, this sector is a significant provider of cyber capabilities. More than 50% of all organizations use or provide to others capabilities from five of the eight dimensions. This effect is unsurprising, given that Switzerland has one of the best national higher education systems [30] and its universities rank highly in the field of Computer Science [22]. Just like the public sector, the demand for the capabilities *Collect and Operate* and

Table 8.3 Capability distribution (%) in the public sector by dimension

	Offered	Used	Required	Not needed	Total
Securely provision	33.96	41.86	7.44	16.74	100
Operate and maintain	30.00	44.17	7.50	18.33	100
Oversee and govern	27.73	50.00	5.47	16.80	100
Protect and defend	28.75	50.00	5.00	16.25	100
Analyze	19.42	26.62	7.91	46.04	100
Collect and Operate	19.17	11.67	3.33	65.83	100
Investigate	21.67	35.00	10.00	33.33	100
Cyber Offense	14.53	8.55	5.13	71.79	100

Table 8.4 Capability distribution (%) in the academic sector by dimension

	Offered	Used	Required	Not needed	Total
Securely provision	41.59	28.05	4.62	25.74	100
Operate and maintain	24.85	38.79	4.85	31.51	100
Oversee and govern	22.70	34.59	7.03	35.68	100
Protect and defend	26.73	36.21	6.03	31.03	100
Analyze	21.03	16.41	12.82	49.74	100
Collect and Operate	12.49	11.88	3.13	72.50	100
Investigate	24.69	30.86	4.94	39.51	100
Cyber Offense	9.15	3.05	2.44	85.36	100

Table 8.5 Capability distribution (%) in the private sector by dimension

	Offered	Used	Required	Not needed	Total
Securely provision	50.92	29.55	1.95	17.58	100
Operate and maintain	40.09	40.76	2.45	16.70	100
Oversee and govern	42.19	37.23	3.10	17.48	100
Protect and defend	52.67	29.67	2.99	14.67	100
Analyze	39.92	16.63	3.72	39.73	100
Collect and operate	26.96	7.83	4.84	60.37	100
Investigate	43.11	22.67	4.89	29.33	100
Cyber offense	24.47	6.36	1.88	67.29	100

Cyber Offense is low, which probably reflects the role of the academic sector as a provider of education and knowledge.

Finally, Table 8.5 details the private sector data. Overall, this sector both uses cyber capabilities to greater extent, and it makes them available to other organizations at a significantly higher rate. Average capability requirements across all organizations are a mere 4.06%, which indicates that private firms are capable to produce cyberdefense. Compared to the public and academic sectors, the dimension *Collect and Operate* is used more intensively, while the dimension *Securely provision* has a higher level of demand which probably reflects the lack of IT specialists in that job market. As in the public sector, there is a clear demand for forensic capabilities, since the

Table 8.6 Capability demand (%) by sector and dimension

Capability	Public sector	Academic sector	Private sector
Conduct security tests on your information systems	12.00	13.79	6.67
Provide you with information on cyber legal issues	20.00	24.14	9.33
Implement IT recruitment and training strategies	12.00	6.90	9.33
Conduct operations to enter your own networks (...)	20.00	13.79	4.11
Aggregate and synthesize (...) evidence	20.00	7.14	4.00
Identify (...) targets to conduct offensive cyber operations	0.00	7.69	4.17
Average	6.47	5.73	3.23

Table 8.7 Capability supply (%) by sector and dimension

Capability	Public sector	Academic sector	Private sector
Conduct security tests on your information systems	30.00	13.79	37.33
Provide you with information on cyber legal issues	10.00	6.90	24.00
Implement IT recruitment and training strategies	12.00	6.90	9.33
Conduct operations to enter your own networks (...)	10.00	24.14	50.68
Aggregate and synthesize (...) evidence	20.00	17.86	34.67
Identify (...) targets to conduct offensive cyber operations	10.00	7.69	23.61
Average	24.40	22.90	40.04

dimension *Investigate* ranks second highest among those organizations which require capabilities.

Table 8.6 stratifies by sector those six specific capabilities the demand for which most exceeds the respective sector average, implying there is a net demand. Among these six, supply for the capabilities *Implement IT recruitment and training strategies* and *Identify and create a list of potential targets to conduct offensive cyber operations* is significantly below the respective sector average, implying there is too little supply among organization to fulfill these needs (viz. Table 8.7). Together, both tables show promising fields for inter-organizational capability trades.

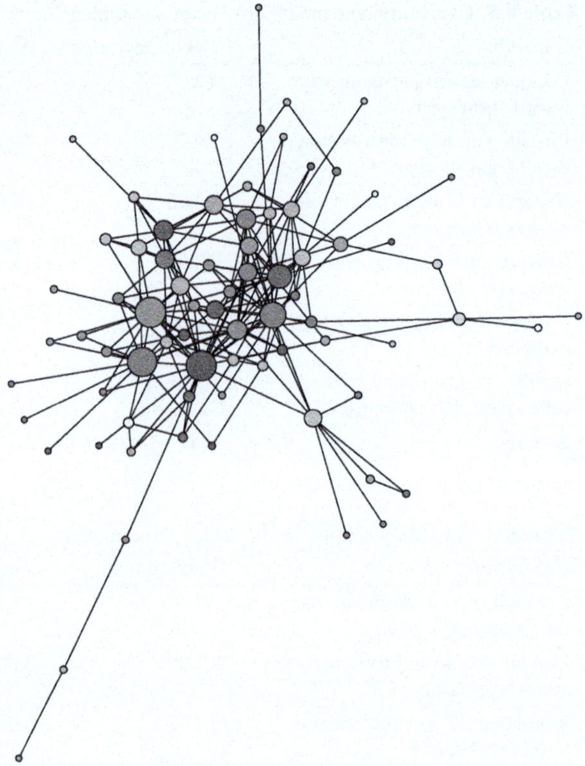

Fig. 8.1 Relations and transfer links between organizations

8.2.2 Network Analysis

Our questionnaire also asked respondents to self-declare the organizations from or to with it procured or supplied capabilities. Two organizations are considered to have a dyadic relationship in the network if one of them provides one or more cyberdefense capabilities that it possesses to the other organization. Given that 65 firms in our final sample either refused to disclose their ties to other organizations or reported they had none such ties, only a subsample of 76 firms remained for the network analysis.

Following the procedural recommendations in [28], we captured these relationships in a worksheet matrix. Then, we fed these data into the open source software tool *Gephi* which plotted the relationships. Links to or from nonrespondents were omitted. Figure 8.1 provides the anonymized structure of the inter-organizational network. The diameter of the node visualizes its degree, such that larger nodes represent organizations which have more relationships with other organizations. The darker the shade of the respective node, the more cyber capabilities the organization uses.

Figure 8.2 differentiates this network by sectors. The public (private, academic) sector is represented in black (white, gray). Interestingly, with only few exceptions,

Fig. 8.2 Interorganizational links by sector

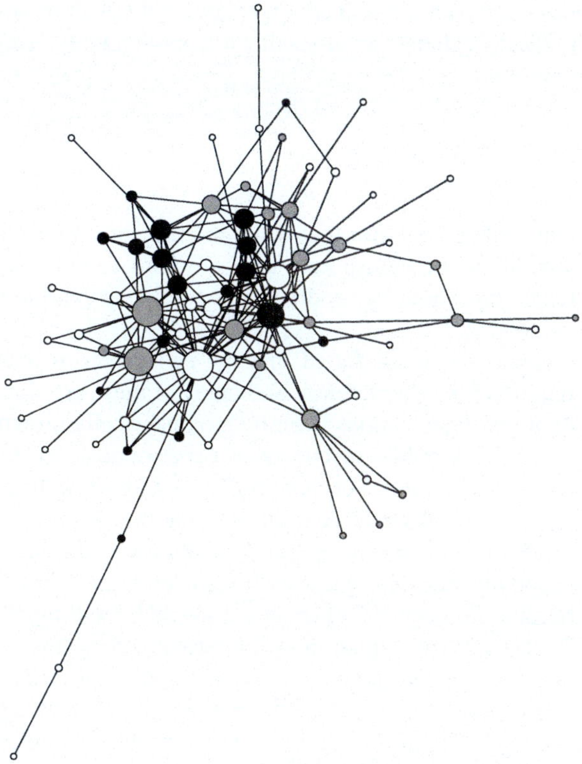

the nodes with the greatest centrality are organizations from the academic and public sector. Further, there is an 'outside network' of mostly private sector firms which have strong bilateral ties but are only weakly integrated in the ecosystem. It appears to be a scale-free network, with a few highly and many loosely connected nodes. A goodness-of-fit test for a power law distribution [10] confirmed this presumption. The degree density fits a power law distribution with $x_{min} = 12$ and $\alpha = 4.46$.

All in all, organizations tend to have more within than between-sector links, whereas the particular capabilities an organization has does not govern its networking behavior. Moreover, the survey identified 50 highly capable but isolated organizations. As these did not report *any* link with other organizations, they are excluded from the visual representation of the graph. Nevertheless, we contacted their representatives and asked if they were willing to disclose the reasons for this isolation in a confidential interview. Those who consented disclosed three types of reasons. Some refused to share or require capabilities since they were concerned this information may reveal vulnerabilities. Others, particularly start-ups and small and medium-sized firms, do want to participate in inter-organizational exchange but are unable to find organizations with which to collaborate. Older and more established organizations also displayed a lack of trust toward those new entrants. Finally, some organizations were sympathetic to inter-organizational collaboration, but they were not at liberty to disclose their operations due to confidentiality requirements.

8.3 Conclusion

Our findings confirm that while the theoretical benefits of inter-organizational collaboration are undisputed, they are hard to reap in organizational practice. As a result, there are three sources of inefficiency that future cyberdefense would have to overcome:

First, while we found that the ecosystem as a whole hosts many capabilities required for cyberdefense, and many of these are shared, cooperation and exchange between organizations is limited to historically grown networks. In particular, there is neither a public inventory of cyber-related capabilities nor an institutionalized inter-organizational exchange that would allow firms to broker capabilities in an open marketplace. Hence, information transparency is low, and the transaction cost of identifying and 'leveraging' capabilities is high. As a result, inter-organizational capability transfers that would strengthen the network as a whole are not executed because no singular organization would be willing to incur the transaction cost.

Second, this situation is co-determined by the requirement for confidentiality and secrecy that many firms expressed when asked why they would voluntarily self-isolate. Any capabilities that are shielded by such motives will likely not be transferred even if such transfers would be beneficial to particular organizations or the ecosystem as a whole. As long as trust is not established between organizations by appropriate institutional design, this problem (and hence the inefficiency of contemporary cyberdefense) likely persists [16, 20].

Third, given that the ecosystem is a scale-free network, i.e., characterized by a small number of highly connected nodes whereas most other nodes have few connections, it is relatively robust to random but highly vulnerable to intentionally induced failure [2]. As a result, the ecosystem can collapse once highly central organizations exit the industry. Classical security research takes such scenarios into account by identifying nodes whose removal would interdict network flows most (e.g., [17]). Future research could run such analyses on inter-organizational networks to identify those whose removal poses the greatest risks for the ecosystem as a whole. In addition, link prediction analysis could reveal which novel links between organizations would be required to strengthen the ecosystem. Then, economic policy could target the respective organizations and provide appropriate institutions which could foster the development of such links.

References

1. Ahuja, G. (2000). Collaboration networks, structural holes, and innovation: A longitudinal study. *Administrative Science Quarterly, 45*(3), 425–455.
2. Albert, R., Jeong, H., & Barabási, A. L. (2000). Error and attack tolerance of complex networks. *Nature, 406,* 378–382.
3. Bonacich, P. (1987). Power and centrality: A family of measures. *American Journal of Sociology, 92*(5), 1170–1182.
4. Burrell, D. N. (2020). An exploration of the cybersecurity workforce shortage. In Information Resources Management Association (ed.), *Cyber warfare and terrorism: Concepts, methodologies, tools, and applications* (pp. 1072–1081). IGI Global.
5. Canadian Centre for Cybersecurity. (2020). Role-based framework. https://cyber.gc.ca/en/guidance/role-based-framework
6. CEN. (2019). *ICT Professionalism and digital competences (CEN/TC 428).* Brussels: European Committee for Standardization.
7. Coulter, R., Han, Q. L., Pan, L., Zhang, J., & Xiang, Y. (2019). Data-driven cyber security in perspective–Intelligent traffic analysis. *IEEE Transactions on Cybernetics, 50*(7), 3081–3093.
8. de Carvalho, L. S. (2019). Education and training towards innovation and capability building. In Gaycken, S. (Ed.) *Cyber defense-policies, operations and capacity building 2018 (NATO science for peace and security series - E: Human and societal dynamics* (Vol. 147, pp. 107–112). IOS Press.
9. ENISA. (2017). *Stock taking of information security training needs in critical sectors.* Brussels: European Union Agency for Cybersecurity.
10. Gillespie, C. S. (2014). Fitting heavy tailed distributions: The poweRlaw package. arXiv:1407.3492
11. Herjavec Group. (2017). *Cybersecurity jobs report.* Toronto: Herjavec Group.
12. Japanese Cross-Industry Cyber Security Study Group. (2016). Human resources definition. https://cyber-risk.or.jp/cric-csf/jinzai_reference_2016.html
13. Koka, B., & Prescott, J. E. (2008). Designing alliance networks: The influence of network position, environmental change, and strategy on firm performance. *Strategic Management Journal, 29*(6), 639–661.
14. Mariotti, F., & Delbridge, R. (2012). Overcoming network overload and redundancy in interorganizational networks: The roles of potential and latent ties. *Organization Science, 23*(2), 511–528.
15. Mentzas, G., Apostolou, D., Kafentzis, K., & Georgolios, P. (2006). Inter-organizational networks for knowledge sharing and trading. *Information Technology and Management, 7*(4), 259–276.
16. Mermoud, A., Keupp, M. M., Huguenin, K., Palmié, M., & Percia David, D. (2019). To share or not to share: A behavioral perspective on human participation in security information sharing. *Journal of Cybersecurity, 5*(1), tyz006.
17. Metzger, J. C., Parad, S., Ravizza, S., & Keupp, M. M. (2020). Vulnerability and resilience of national power grids: A graph-theoretical optimization approach and empirical simulation. In M. M. Keupp (Ed.), *The Security of Critical Infrastructures* (pp. 77–94). Cham: Springer.
18. Nai-Fovino, I., Neisse, R., Hernandez-Ramos, J. L., Polemi, N., Ruzzante, G., Figwer, M., & Lazari, A. (2019). *A proposal for a European cybersecurity taxonomy. Joint Research Center Technical Report JRC118089.* Luxembourg: Publications Office of the European Union.
19. NICE, (2021). Navy COOL and MilGears, U.S. Navy Credentialing Programs Naval Education and Training Command. Gaithersburg MD: National Institute of Standards and Technology.
20. Percia David, D., Keupp, M. M., & Mermoud, A. (2020). Knowledge absorption for cybersecurity: The role of human beliefs. *Computers in Human Behavior, 106,* 106255.
21. Petersen, R., Santos, D., Smith, M. C., Wetzel, K. A., & Witte, G. (2020). *Workforce framework for cybersecurity (NICE Framework). NIST Special Publication 800-181.* Gathersburg MD: National Institute of Standards and Technology.

22. QS. (2021). QS World University Rankings by computer science and information technology. https://www.topuniversities.com/university-rankings
23. Rashid, A., Chivers, H., Danezis, G., Lupu, E., & Martin, A. (2019). *CyBok: The cyber security body of knowledge*. London: National Cyber Security Centre.
24. Sorenson, O., & Stuart, T. E. (2001). Syndication networks and the spatial distribution of venture capital investments. *American Journal of Sociology, 106*(6), 1546–1588.
25. SPARTA Project. (2021). Cybersecurity training and awareness. https://www.sparta.eu/training/
26. Teece, D. J. (2019). A capability theory of the firm: An economics and (strategic) management perspective. *New Zealand Economic Papers, 53,* 1–43.
27. Trkman, P., & Desouza, K. C. (2012). Knowledge risks in organizational networks: An exploratory framework. *Journal of Strategic Information Systems, 21*(1), 1–17.
28. Valente, T. W. (2005). Network models and methods for studying the diffusion of innovations. *Models and Methods in Social Network Analysis, 28,* 98–116.
29. Wang, H., Zhao, J., Li, Y., & Li, C. (2015). Network centrality, organizational innovation, and performance: A meta-analysis. *Canadian Journal of Administrative Sciences/Revue Canadienne des Sciences de l'Administration, 32*(3), 146–159.
30. Williams, R., & Leahy, A. (2020). *U21 ranking of national higher education systems 2020.* The Melbourne Institute of Applied Economic and Social Research: University of Melbourne.

Cédric Aeschlimann is a researcher at the Department of Defense Economics at the Military Academy of the Swiss Federal Institute of Technology (ETH) Zurich. Before returning to academia, he worked for the Swiss Federal Department of Foreign Affairs and the United Nations Development Fund. His research topics focus on the application of social networks for policy-making. He holds an MA in public management from the University of Geneva.

Kilian Cuche holds a BSc in Information Science and an MSc in Business Administration (Information Systems Management) from the University of Applied Sciences Western Switzerland. He worked as a scientific assistent at the Military Academy at the Swiss Federal Institute of Technology (ETH) Zurich where he mapped and modeled the Swiss cyber ecosystem. Today he is in charge of the cybersecurity awareness and training in the Swiss Armed Forces.

Alain Mermoud is the Head of Technology Monitoring and Forecasting at the Cyber Defence Campus of armasuisse Science and Technology. He obtained his Ph.D. in Information Systems from the University of Lausanne (Switzerland). He has more than five years of professional experience in the banking industry. His research interests span emerging technologies, disruptive innovations, threat intelligence and the economics of security.

Chapter 9
Anticipating Cyberdefense Capability Requirements by Link Prediction Analysis

Santiago Anton Moreno, Dimitri Percia David, Alain Mermoud, Thomas Maillart, and Anita Mezzetti

9.1 Predicting Technology Requirements From Job Openings

Firms must continuously learn about novel technologies that are relevant to cyberdefense, and they must forego those which are no longer effective against contemporary threats. The better they master this transformation, the more efficiently they spend their technology budget. However, developing technology in the right direction is fraught with uncertainly, since the technology landscape evolves continuously [28].

Supplementary Information The online version contains supplementary material available at https://doi.org/10.1007/978-3-031-30191-9_9.

D. Percia David (✉)
Institute of Entrepreneurship and Management, University of Applied Sciences Valais, Sierre, Switzerland
e-mail: dimitri.perciadavid@hevs.ch

T. Maillart
Information Science Institute, Geneva School of Economics and Management, University of Geneva, Geneva, Switzerland
e-mail: thomas.maillart@unige.ch

S. A. Moreno
Section of Applied Mathematics, Swiss Federal Institute of Technology Lausanne, Lausanne, Switzerland
e-mail: santiago.antonmoreno@epfl.ch

A. Mezzetti
Swiss Federal Institute of Technology Lausanne, Section of Financial Engineering, Lausanne, Switzerland

A. Mermoud
Cyber-Defence Campus, armasuisse Science and Technology, Thun, Switzerland
e-mail: alain.mermoud@ar.admin.ch

M. M. Keupp (ed.), *Cyberdefense*, International Series in Operations Research & Management Science 342,
https://doi.org/10.1007/978-3-031-30191-9_9

We propose that job openings data can reveal how firms manage this adaptation, since it reflects a process of creative destruction. Economically speaking, job openings reveal employers' preferences since they uncover technological requirements [14]. Likewise, a significant decline of job openings for a particular skill signals that it is becoming increasingly irrelevant. As opposed to patents, whose information remains even if they are technologically outdated, job openings data are dynamic. They follow distribution patterns over time, and such patterns can be exploited for predictive purposes [20].

Link prediction can inform observers about how this distribution will develop in the future, both regarding the emergence of future and the disappearance of contemporary job offers. It is widely used to forecast change in social and business networks (e.g., [1, 3, 22]). It has also informed more specific studies of technological evolution and convergence [15, 16, 18]. We extend this analysis to the context of cyberdefense by proposing a bipartite network of firms which adapt and forego technologies, and we use job openings data to capture these dynamics.

9.2 Link Prediction Model

We define a graph $G = (V, E)$, wherein V is a finite set of companies and technologies, and $E \subseteq V \times V$ is the set of links between them.[1] Then, for any subset $x, y \in V$,

- the neighborhood of x is $\Gamma(x) = \{y \in V s.t. (x, y) \in E\}$;
- the degree of x is $\delta_x = |\Gamma(x)|$;
- there is a path between x and y if there exists $(x_0, x_1, ..., x_n)$ such that $x_0 = x$; $x_n = y$ and $(x_i, x_{i+1}) \in E \; \forall \, 0 \leq i \leq n - 1$;
- a graph G is said to be bipartite if there exists a subject $(A, B) \subset V$ such that if $(x, y) \in E$ then x and y are not in this subset (A, B).
- with $|V| = n$, $A \in \mathbf{R}^{n \times n}$ is an adjacency matrix of G if and only if $\forall x, y \in V A_{x,y} = 1$ implies $(x, y) \in E$ and $A_{x,y} = 0$ otherwise.

Since we are interested in predicting the adaptation of a single organization to changing technology landscapes, we only consider relationships between firms and technologies, but not between different firms. We therefore consider all graphs that link companies and technologies as bipartite, such that a company can only form links with technologies and vice versa.

Link prediction relies on similarity measures which assign a similarity score s_{xy} to each pair of nodes (x, y). The larger s_{xy} is, the higher is the likelihood that a link exists between x and y. While many measures exist by which these scores can be computed, only a subset of them is eligible for the analysis of bipartite networks [17, 20]. We opted to calculate preferential attachment (PA), Katz, and hyperbolic sine (HS)

[1] In the following discussion, we use the neutral term 'nodes' for methodological discussions in which the distinction between companies and technologies is irrelevant.

scores, both because all three measures are eligible, they only require information about neighboring nodes, and they can be calculated in reasonable computing time [2, 13, 17].

Further, we used the predictions from these three static measures to train a support vector machine (SVM), i.e., a supervised machine-learning model [11] which dynamically updates its predictions as the bipartite network changes. We used the radial basis function as kernel.[2]

Since our link prediction setting is highly unbalanced, we evaluated the accuracy of our predictions, i.e., the extent to which predicted matched actual links in the bipartite network, by analyzing the area under the receiver operating characteristic curve (AUC). This curve plots the true positive rate *tpr* against the false positive rate *fpr*. We applied blocked cross-validation to receive robust estimates [4, 6, 18–20, 27]. Further, we computed precision-recall curves, specifying $Precision = \frac{tp}{tp+fp}$ and $Recall = tpr$. From these estimates, we computed average precision (AP) measures, which give the weighted mean of precision accuracy achieved at each threshold, and the increase in recall from the previous threshold is used as the weight.

The model was implemented in Python, with the packages networkX [9], scikit-learn [23], and statsmodel [25]. To create the bipartite network of companies and technologies, we used data from the Technology and Market Monitoring (TMM) database. It is hosted by the science and technology branch of *armasuisse*, the Swiss Federal Office for Defence Procurement. It crawls open online repositories, such as the commercial register, industry databases, Wikipedia, and arXiv, in order to aggregate and link data about firms and technologies.[3]

The database also crawls job openings data from *Indeed*, one of the world's largest virtual labor markets.[4] We therefore queried the job openings the firms in the TMM database had posted there, and we recorded which technologies they sought.

We used automated document analysis to identify technologies related to cybersecurity (e.g., [7, 8, 12, 18]). Using the Python library difflib, we computed word similarity indices and removed irrelevant matches. This procedure yielded a list of 124 keywords by which firms, technologies, and job offers were linked.[5] The resulting bipartite graph had 1805 nodes.

Our model builds on prior work that has used supervised learning with link prediction [10, 12, 30]. In order to maximize the accuracy of our predictions, we observed the development of this network on a monthly basis between March 2018 and December 2020 and used these data to train the prediction algorithm. Thus, we created 33 graphs, each of which describes the bipartite network for the respective month in this interval. We define $\mathbf{G}$ as the set that contains all 33 graphs, ordered by time, such that $G_0 \in \mathbf{G}$ and $G_{33} \in \mathbf{G}$ correspond to the graphs for March 2018 and December 2020, respectively. We also define $\mathbf{G_{i-j}}$ with $i < j \in 0, 1, ..., 32$ to be the subset of

[2] Detailed technical information about the machine and its recursive prediction procedure is available from the corresponding author.

[3] The database can be accessed by registered users, see https://tmm.dslab.ch.

[4] See https://indeed.com.

[5] The full set of these keywords is available from the corresponding author.

Table 9.1 Confusion matrix

	Predicted	
Actual	Link exists	Link absent
Link exists	tp	fn
Link absent	fp	tn

G that contains all graphs between G_i and G_j (including the interval boundaries). Further, we used all possible links in the graphs of $\mathbf{G}_{i-j}$ as training sets for the SVM predictions.

The prediction algorithm considers the dynamic development of the bipartite network by recursive time series analysis. Rather than predicting a static set of links, it considers the present and past states of the network in order to predict both extant and yet absent links that will exist *t* months in the future [21]. Such time-dependent recursion yields results which are significantly more accurate, if at the expense of computing time [5, 26].[6]

The prediction algorithm uses the set of graphs $\mathbf{G_{i-j}}$ to predict which links will (not) exist in the bipartite network t months ahead, subject to $j + t < 33$ and $1 < t < 6$. It computes the similarity scores s_{xy} for $x, y \in V$ for each graph in $\mathbf{G}_{i-j}$ and uses them to predict those in each graph G_{j+t}. Starting from the set of graphs $\mathbf{G_{i-j}}$, it predicts that *t* months from now, a link either will or will not exist between every company and every technology in G_{j+t}.

These predictions are subject to a threshold θ. A link is predicted to exist if $s_{xy} \geq \theta$, else, the link is predicted to not exist. This threshold maximizes a simple function of *tpr* and *fpr*. Both rates are obtained from the confusion matrix shown in Table 9.1. It gives the number of true positives (tp), false positives (fp), false negatives (fn) and true negatives (tn). The total number of positives P is equal to $(tp + fn)$, and the total number of negatives F is equal to $(fp + tn)$.

We optimized the difference between tpr and fpr by Youden's J statistic [29]. Robustness tests with the geometric mean of sensitivity and specificity and F scores of precision and recall yielded identical thresholds values [24].

9.3 Results

Table 9.2 details all simulation results and their respective mean AUCs, the standard deviation of which is between 0.03 and 0.07. The best predictions are highlighted in bold.

There is no straightforward influence of the intensity with which the model is trained. When we predicted the state of the bipartite network between one and four months in the future, we observed that AUC and accuracy improve with the number

[6] Detailed technical information on the recursive steps is available from the corresponding author.

of graphs used to train the model, whereas for a prediction interval of five and six months, the smallest number of training graphs gave the best AUC but not the best accuracy. The best accuracy was always obtained by the SVM method with a training period of six months. Further, for all but one forecast rage, among the four different measures we used, the SVM method best predicted the actual links.

Figure 9.1 compares the performance of the four methods, the mean AUC of which is plotted over different forecast periods. These means were calculated by

Table 9.2 Accuracy of predicted versus actual links in the bipartite network

			Forecast range					
Method	Training size	Metric	1 month	2 month	3 month	4 month	5 month	6 month
Katz Index	2 months	AUC	0.831	0.737	0.668	0.642	0.628	0.626
		Accuracy	0.852	0.768	0.707	0.683	0.671	0.665
	3 months	AUC	0.836	0.734	0.664	0.632	0.626	0.619
		Accuracy	0.859	0.772	0.711	0.685	0.676	0.669
	4 months	AUC	0.844	0.727	0.652	0.623	0.615	0.606
		Accuracy	0.864	0.772	0.71	0.686	0.676	0.667
	6 months	AUC	0.853	0.759	0.689	0.626	0.622	0.612
		Accuracy	0.871	0.792	0.735	0.693	0.684	0.676
PA Index	2 months	AUC	0.818	0.709	0.643	0.61	0.586	0.574
		Accuracy	0.826	0.743	0.687	0.659	0.646	0.634
	3 months	AUC	0.837	0.733	0.652	0.616	0.599	0.589
		Accuracy	0.837	0.757	0.692	0.668	0.657	0.647
	4 months	AUC	0.844	0.736	0.658	0.62	0.602	0.594
		Accuracy	0.842	0.761	0.703	0.675	0.661	0.653
	6 months	AUC	0.849	0.754	0.683	**0.65**	0.633	0.619
		Accuracy	0.841	0.77	0.718	0.694	0.681	0.672
HS Index	2 months	AUC	0.832	0.737	0.669	0.642	0.628	0.626
		Accuracy	0.853	0.768	0.707	0.683	0.671	0.665
	3 months	AUC	0.837	0.734	0.664	0.632	0.625	0.619
		Accuracy	0.859	0.772	0.711	0.685	0.676	0.669
	4 months	AUC	0.844	0.727	0.652	0.624	0.615	0.605
		Accuracy	0.865	0.772	0.71	0.686	0.676	0.667
	6 months	AUC	0.853	0.759	0.689	0.626	0.621	0.612
		Accuracy	0.871	0.792	0.735	0.693	0.684	0.676
SVM	2 months	AUC	0.836	0.742	0.676	0.648	**0.635**	**0.629**
		Accuracy	0.856	0.773	0.712	0.688	0.678	0.671
	3 months	AUC	0.838	0.741	0.667	0.638	0.63	0.624
		Accuracy	0.863	0.777	0.715	0.69	0.68	0.673
	4 months	AUC	0.852	0.734	0.658	0.628	0.619	0.613
		Accuracy	0.867	0.777	0.715	0.69	0.682	0.673
	6 months	AUC	**0.856**	**0.762**	**0.695**	0.641	0.631	0.621
		Accuracy	**0.874**	**0.794**	**0.74**	**0.702**	**0.692**	**0.684**

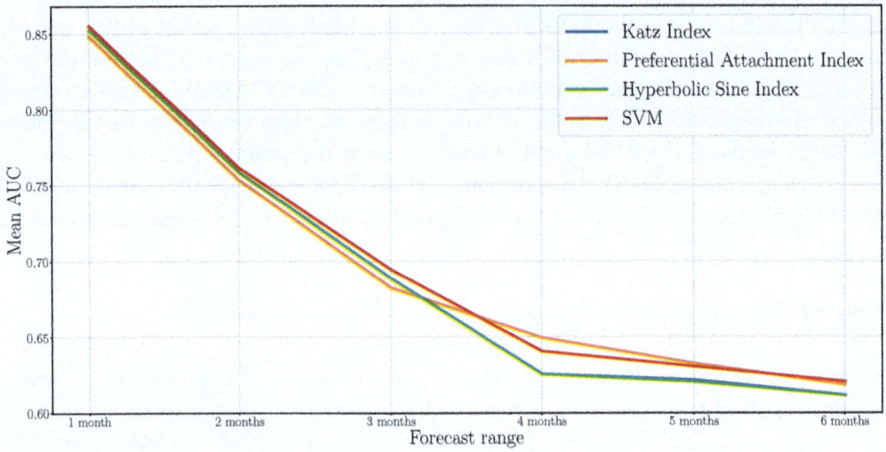

Fig. 9.1 Mean AUC over forecast range

blocked cross-validation for a prediction model trained with six months of training graphs. Their standard deviation is between 0.03 and 0.07.

Figure 9.2 provides the receiver operating curves (ROC) for a prediction that was trained with the full set of all 32 training graphs. They show the model reliably predicts the actual links in the bipartite network; in this setting, the best accuracy is 0.965. When we reran the model with a set of 28 training graphs, AUC was between 0.743 and 0.753 for all four prediction methods, and accuracy was between 0.75 and 0.77 which, for each forecast period, far exceeded the mean AUC and accuracy obtained from all settings with a different number of training graphs. This effect illustrates that link prediction results strongly vary with the extent to which the prediction model is trained with data that describes the historical development of the bipartite network over time.

The precision-recall curves in Fig. 9.3 confirm that the SVM method best predicts the links in the bipartite network. They are plotted over a random classifier, the AP of which is less than 0.01. We calculated all curves with the full set of all 32 training graphs. AP values for the SVM predictions were always superior, no matter how we varied the number of training graphs and forecast periods. The Katz and HS index curves are almost congruent in this chart, whereas there is some variation between them when these parameters are altered. As measured by the AP metric, the PA index performs worst.

Figure 9.4 shows a final robustness test in which we used only the seven training graphs between months 21 and 27 to predict the network. The SVM method still predicts the actual links best, whereas all four methods are clearly superior to a random classifier.

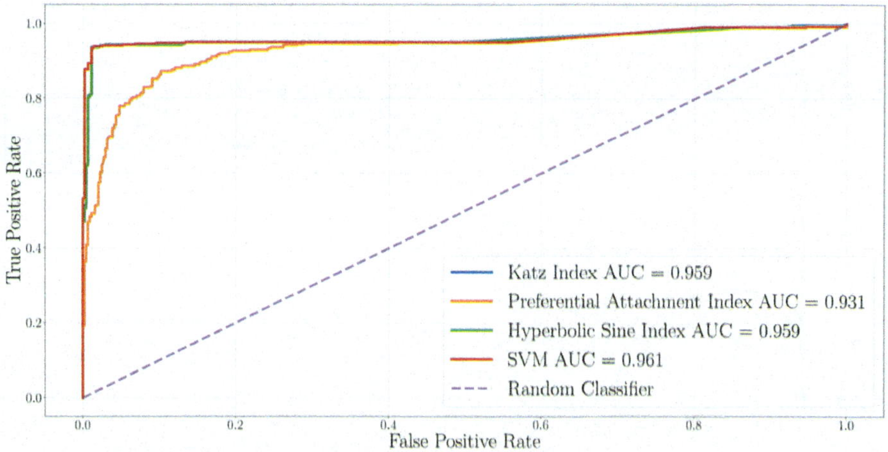

Fig. 9.2 ROC curves by metric

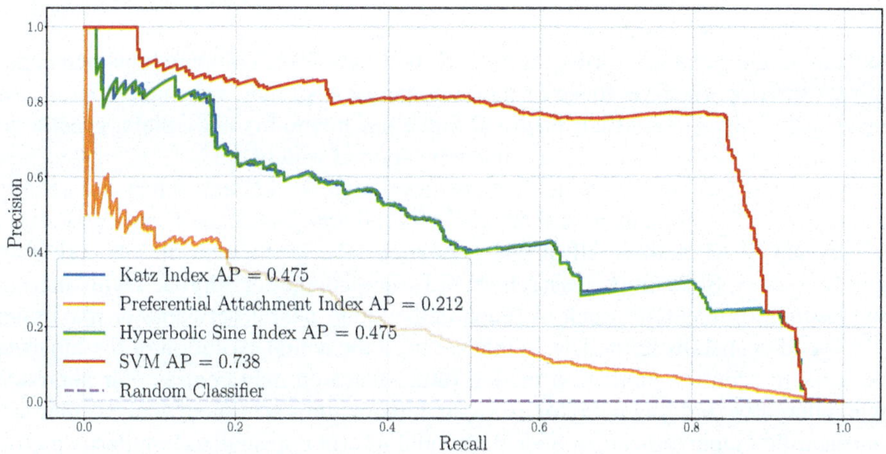

Fig. 9.3 Precision recall curves calculated with the full training set

9.4 Discussion

In this work we applied extant research on link prediction to a bipartite network of firms and technologies, and we considered that this network dynamically changes with the technology landscape. We posit that job offers can be used as a tool by which firms' preferences about technologies are revealed.

We therefore propose that our analysis helps any particular firm in the network to make more informed decisions about future technologies. By using our link prediction method to anticipate future skill demand, firms can anticipate the development of the bipartite network and thus spend their budgets more efficiently as they adapt

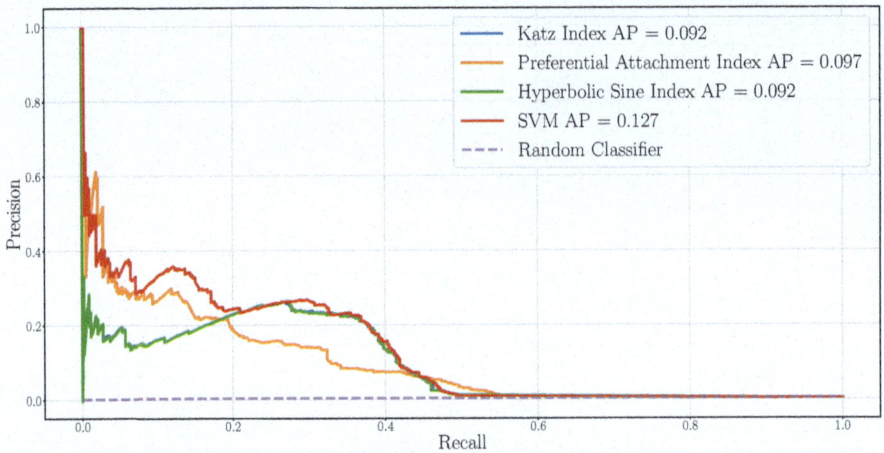

Fig. 9.4 Precision recall curves with reduced training set

to technological change. Firms can also use our methods to compare how their capabilities develop vis-á-vis those of their competitors, so they can make appropriate investments to maintain their position. Since our method is not context-specific to any particular network or industry, it can be applied widely.

All in all, the prediction method we developed works well when it forecasts the network. We implemented three classic similarity-based algorithms and also a supervised SVM method, all of which predict links in the bipartite network with good accuracy. Still, future research should complement our approach with alternative estimation methods, such as graph embedding, neural networks or maximum likelihood probabilistic models. While we used the actual evolution of the bipartite network to train the prediction model, future research may contrast our approach with alternative training data, for example, job openings sentiment analysis metrics, or scientific output indicators. Such data could inform a specialized similarity metric which could be used to construct an unsupervised model.

While we believe our approach is productive, it could be strengthened further in a number of ways. Future research may employ more general and broader text-mining approaches. We selected a single virtual job market (if one of the largest in the world), so future research may also consider job markets that exist by virtue of social networks. Quantitative methods of keyword generation would produce more consistent lists of keywords with specialized category matching, so that network analyses could be customized to specific industries and fields. Further, researchers may strive to create a balanced dataset in order to maximize the accuracy of our SVM method, such that even longer forecast ranges would be possible.

Our analysis is restricted to the context of Switzerland because our goal was to show the feasibility and effectiveness of the analytical method we proposed. Future research should therefore corroborate our method with different national contexts since the technology landscape in Switzerland represents but a fraction of the global technological environment. A global crawling protocol with multi-language keyword extraction and a clear disambiguation framework for companies present in multiple countries could extend our method to a global context.

References

1. Akcora, C. G., Carminati, B., & Ferrari, E. (2011). Network and profile based measures for user similarities on social networks. In *Proceedings of the 2011 IEEE international conference on information reuse integration* (pp. 292–298).
2. Barabási, A. L., & Réka, A. (1999). Emergence of scaling in random networks. *Science, 286*(5439), 509–512.
3. Benchettara, N., Kanawati, R., & Rouveirol, C. (2010). Supervised machine learning applied to link prediction in bipartite social networks. In *Proceedings of the 2010 international conference on advances in social networks analysis and mining* (pp. 326–330).
4. Bergmeir, C., & Benítez, J. M. (2012). On the use of cross-validation for time series predictor evaluation. *Information Sciences, 191*, 192–213.
5. da Silva Soares, P. R., & Prudêncio, R. B. C. (2012). Time series based link prediction. In *Proceedings of the 2012 international joint conference on neural networks (IJCNN)* (pp. 1–7).
6. Fawcett, T. (2006). An introduction to ROC analysis. *Pattern Recognition Letters, 27*(8), 861–874.
7. Gerken, J. M., & Moehrle, M. (2012). A new instrument for technology monitoring: Novelty in patents measured by semantic patent analysis. *Scientometrics, 91*, 645–670.
8. Geum, Y., Kim, C., Lee, S., & Kim, M. S. (2012). Technological convergence of IT and BT: Evidence from patent analysis. *ETRI Journal, 34*(3), 439–449.
9. Hagberg, A., Schult, D., & Swart, P. (2008). Exploring network structure, dynamics, and function using NetworkX. In Varoquaux, G., Vaught, T., & Millman, J. (Eds.), *Proceedings of 7th python in science conference* (pp. 11–15).
10. Hasan, M. A., Chaoji, V., Salem, S., & Zaki, M. (2006). Link prediction using supervised learning. In *Proceedings of the SDM workshop on link analysis, counterterrorism and security*.
11. Hearst, M. A., Dumais, S. T., Osuna, E., Platt, J., & Scholkopf, B. (1998). Support vector machines. *IEEE Intelligent Systems and their Applications, 13*(4), 18–28.
12. Huang, L., Chen, X., Ni, X., Liu, J., Cao, X., & Wang, C. (2021). Tracking the dynamics of co-word networks for emerging topic identification. *Technological Forecasting and Social Change, 170*(4), 120944.
13. Katz, L. (1953). A new status index derived from sociometric analysis. *Psychometrika, 18*, 39–43.
14. Kim, J., & Angnakoon, P. (2016). Research using job advertisements: A methodological assessment. *Library & Information Science Research, 38*(4), 327–335.
15. Kim, J., & Geum, Y. (2021). How to develop data-driven technology roadmaps: The integration of topic modeling and link prediction. *Technological Forecasting and Social Change, 171*, 120972.
16. Kim, J., Kim, S., & Lee, C. (2019). Anticipating technological convergence: Link prediction using Wikipedia hyperlinks. *Technovation, 79*, 25–34.
17. Kunegis, J., De Luca, E. M., & Albayrak, S. (2010). The link prediction problem in bipartite networks. In E. Hüllermeier, R. Kruse, & F. Hoffmann (Eds.), *Computational intelligence for knowledge-based systems design* (pp. 380–389). Heidelberg: Springer.
18. Lee, J., Ko, N., Yoon, J., & Son, C. (2021). An approach for discovering firm-specific technology opportunities: Application of link prediction to F-term networks. *Technological Forecasting and Social Change, 168*, 120746.

19. Lichtenwalter, R. N., Lussier, J. T., & Chawla, N. (2010). New perspectives and methods in link prediction. In *Proceedings of the 16th ACM SIGKDD international conference on knowledge discovery and data mining* (pp. 243–252).
20. Lü, L., & Zhou, T. (2011). Link prediction in complex networks: A survey. *Physica A: Statistical Mechanics and its Applications, 390*(6), 1150–1170.
21. Montgomery, D. C., Jennings, C. L., & Kulahci, M. (Eds.). (2015). *Introduction to time series analysis and forecasting* (2nd ed.). Hoboken: Wiley.
22. Mori, J., Kajikawa, Y., Kashima, H., & Sakata, I. (2012). Machine learning approach for finding business partners and building reciprocal relationships. *Expert Systems with Applications, 39*(12), 10402–10407.
23. Pedregosa, F., et al. (2011). scikit-learn: Machine learning in Python. *Journal of Machine Learning Research, 12*, 2825–2830.
24. Powers, D. M. W. (2011). Evaluation: From precision, recall and F-measure to ROC, informedness, markedness and correlation. *International Journal of Machine Learning Technology, 2*(1), 37–63.
25. Seabold, S., & Perktold, J. (2010) Statsmodels: Econometric and statistical modeling with Python. In *Proceedings of the 9th python in science conference* (pp. 92–96).
26. Tylenda, T., Angelova, R., & Bedathur, S. (2009). Towards time-aware link prediction in evolving social networks. In *Proceedings of the 3rd workshop on social network mining and analysis* (pp. 1–10).
27. Yang, Y., Lichtenwalter, R. N., & Chawla, N. (2015). Evaluating link prediction methods. *Knowledge and Information Systems, 45*, 751–782.
28. Yoon, J., Park, H., Seo, W., Lee, J. M., Coh, B. Y., & Kim, J. (2015). Technology opportunity discovery (TOD) from existing technologies and products: A function-based TOD framework. *Technological Forecasting and Social Change, 100*, 153–167.
29. Youden, W. J. (1950). Index for rating diagnostic tests. *Cancer, 3*(1), 32–35.
30. Zhang, M., & Chen, Y. (2018). Link prediction based on graph neural networks. arXiv:1802.09691

Santiago Anton Moreno is a M.Sc. student at the Swiss Federal Institute of Technology (EPFL) Lausanne and holds a Bachelor's degree in Mathematics and Statistics from EPFL. He has professional experience as an assistant and intern in different international companies and worked as a researcher at the Cyber Defence Campus of armasuisse Science and Technology.

Dimitri Percia David is an Assistant Professor of Data Science and Econometrics at the University of Applied Sciences Valais (Switzerland) where he applies data science and machine learning to the field of technology mining. Prior to this position, he was a postdoctoral researcher at the Information Science Institute of the University of Geneva, and the first recipient of the Distinguished CYD Postdoctoral Fellowship. He earned his Ph.D. in Information Systems from the Faculty of Business and Economics (HEC) at the University of Lausanne, and he has more than eight years of professional experience in the commodities trading industry and as a scientific collaborator at the Military Academy at Swiss Federal Institute of Technology (ETH) Zurich.

Alain Mermoud is the Head of Technology Monitoring and Forecasting at the Cyber Defence Campus of armasuisse Science and Technology. He obtained his Ph.D. in Information Systems from the University of Lausanne (Switzerland). He has more than five years of professional experience in the banking industry. His research interests span emerging technologies, disruptive innovations, threat intelligence and the economics of security.

Thomas Maillart holds a Master degree from the Swiss Federal Institute of Technology (EPFL) Lausanne (2005) and a Ph.D. from the Swiss Federal Institute of Technology (ETH) Zurich (2011). He received the 2012 Zurich Dissertation Prize for his pioneering work on cyber risks. Before joining the University of Geneva, he worked as a researcher at the Center for Law and Economics at ETH and as a post-doctoral researcher at the University of California at Berkeley. His research focuses on modeling and improving human collective intelligence, particularly in a context of a fast-expanding cyberspace.

Anita Mezzetti currently works as a quant engineer, modelling the price of structured products at Credit Suisse. She holds a Bachelor in Mathematics for Engineering from Polytechnic of Turin, where she was supported by a full scholarship for the top students, and she earned a Master in Financial Engineering at the Swiss Federal Institute of Technology (EPFL) in 2020. She completed her Master Thesis, supported by a CYD fellowship, at the Cyber Defence Campus of armasuisse Science and Technology.

Part III
Effectiveness

Chapter 10
Drawing with Limited Resources: Statistical Modeling of Computer Network Exploitation and Prevention

Philipp Fischer, Fabian Muhly, and Marcus M. Keupp

10.1 Introduction

The technological capabilities of computer hardware and IT infrastructure have grown exponentially over the last 40 years, and intelligence agencies have fueled this growth [4, 5, 11, 23]. Today, computer networks can be attacked remotely at little cost, and the speed of technological innovation gives attackers the initiative to which defenders must constantly adapt.

We focus on a particular type of attack where the goal is not to physically destroy a computer network or to extort ransom, but to exfiltrate valuable information from a computer network [12, 19, 21, 22]. In this case, attackers prefer to operate discreetly and remain unnoticed. Specialized branches of national armed forces, but also intelligence agencies and state-sponsored proxy actors can perform such operations [2, 3, 6–8, 14, 16].

For any attacker, only a fraction of all documents stored in a computer network has actual operational or informational value in regard to the mission [13, 15]. Attackers who infiltrate a computer network therefore continuously face a ballot sampling

---

Supplementary Information The online version contains supplementary material available at https://doi.org/10.1007/978-3-031-30191-9_10.

P. Fischer (✉)
Department of Computer Science, Swiss Federal Institute of Technology Zurich, Zurich, Switzerland
e-mail: fischphi@student.ethz.ch

F. Muhly · M. M. Keupp
Department of Defense Economics, Military Academy at the Swiss Federal Institute of Technology Zurich, Birmensdorf, Switzerland
e-mail: fabian.muhly@vtg.admin.ch

M. M. Keupp
e-mail: mkeupp@ethz.ch

M. M. Keupp (ed.), *Cyberdefense*, International Series in Operations Research & Management Science 342,
https://doi.org/10.1007/978-3-031-30191-9_10

problem: They must sample each information unit once and decide whether to exfiltrate or discard it. We explore how such an attack can be systematically modeled, and how an attacker would decide about the length and intensity of an attack under time and resource constraints. We also study how defenders may react as they attempt to neutralize the attack. We hence view the problem from the attacker's side, and we assume that a security breach has already taken place.

We propose to formally model the exfiltration process as a repeated urn draw under uncertainty and budget constraints, and we illustrate the model with some simple examples. Finally, we propose some implications for effective defense. The model was programmed in `R`, and all plots were generated using the `ggplot2` package.

10.2 Theoretical Model

We posit that the information stored in a computer network can be described by a quantity of discrete information units (e.g., computers in a network that can be compromised, or files or binary objects stored on a single machine). We denote the set of all information units available in the attacked network by Ω. While this set may be numerically large, it is finite since information storage is restrained by the physical boundaries of the network's capacity, hence $|\Omega| = N \in \mathbb{N}$.

The attack proceeds in discrete time steps $i \in \mathbb{N}$, the total number of which is subject to the termination date of the attack. During each time step i, attackers draw an information unit $\omega_i \in \Omega$ and assess its value in the context of their objectives. This draw can happen at random or according to a pre-set sequence; our model explores both options. During the same time step, defenders survey the network for security breaches. Note that our model is independent of the reason why the attack terminates (attackers could voluntarily withdraw, or they may be ousted by the defenders).

10.2.1 Drawing and Evaluation of Information Units

We posit that attackers face budget constraints in terms of time (detection becomes more likely the longer they operate in the network) and information processing capacity (they can only evaluate a finite number of information units per time step). Whenever attackers exfiltrate a particular information unit, we refer to this as a 'draw'.

Let x denote the number of information units they can successfully exfiltrate from the network while the attack is undetected for a duration d. Then $S = \frac{x}{d}$ gives the average exfiltration rate for the campaign, and attackers who want to exfiltrate as many units as possible with a minimum of time spent in the system would be interested in maximizing S. At the same time, such a massive exfiltration will probably catch the attention of the systems operators, so that attackers may alternatively wish to remain unnoticed as long as possible or to extract as little information as possible in order not to be noted. In this case, they would seek to optimize the inverse of the above ratio $Q = 1/S = d/x$. Since attackers cannot maximize both ratios simultaneously, they can be thought of as two competing quasi-goods g_S and g_Q,

Both quasi-goods are associated with transaction costs t_S and t_Q since exfiltration requires attackers to invest time and personnel. We posit that $t_Q < t_S$ since significant extraction requires more resources, if to mask the attack in order to avoid detection. The joint two-good production can be modeled by a Cobb-Douglas utility maximization:

$$maxf(g_S, g_Q) = g_S^{\rho} g_Q^{1-\rho} \tag{10.1}$$

subject to the budget constraint

$$g(g_S, g_Q) = t_S g_S + t_Q g_Q \leq b \tag{10.2}$$

where b is the maximum number of draws the attacker can make while staying undetected. The Lagrangian for this optimization problem is

$$L = f(g_S, g_Q) - \lambda g(g_S, g_Q) = g_S^{\rho} g_Q^{1-\rho} - \lambda(b - t_S g_S - t_Q g_Q) \tag{10.3}$$

which, after partial differentiation, yields the optimum combination

$$g_S^* = \frac{1}{\rho} \frac{\frac{t_S}{t_Q}}{(1-\rho) g_Q} \quad g_Q^* = \rho g_S \frac{\frac{t_S}{t_Q}}{(1-\rho)} \tag{10.4}$$

By inserting the optimal amounts of the two quasi-goods into the budget constraint equation (10.3), attackers can calculate the optimal number of draws.

However, in a real computer network, attackers likely have a mission to exfiltrate but a fraction n of all information units N stored in the network, hence $n \ll N$. Let the proportion of relevant units be denoted by $\alpha := \frac{n}{N}$. Attackers now draw discrete information units and evaluate them, and they draw each unit only once. Thus, the exfiltration process resembles a covered draw in an urn lottery where there is a very high probability $1 - \alpha$ of drawing an irrelevant unit and a small probability α of drawing a valuable one.

Assuming that draws are independent and that the drawing procedure is identical at each time step i, the number of possible combinations of information units summing up to exactly $k < m$ valuable information units after m draws is given by the binomial coefficient

$$\binom{m}{k} = \frac{m!}{k!(m-k)!} \tag{10.5}$$

so that the probability of identifying k valuable units is

$$\mathbb{P}[V = k] = \binom{m}{k} \cdot \alpha^k \cdot (1-\alpha)^{m-k} \tag{10.6}$$

Still, draws need not be independent. Attackers may well adapt their operation according to the value of the information units they have already drawn, e.g., by investing more resources in the pursuit of promising tracks, or by abandoning futile searches. In this case, attackers would still face a probability of $\alpha = \frac{n}{N}$ that the first draw identifies a valuable information unit. Yet, in all subsequent draws, this probability would decrease to $\frac{n-1}{N-1}$ if the drawn information unit was indeed valuable, else it would increase to $\frac{n}{N-1}$.

In this setting, the probability of finding k relevant information units after m draws without replacement can be derived through combinatorial arguments. There are $\binom{n}{k}$ ways of drawing exactly k valuable information units out of n available units, and there are $\binom{N-n}{m-k}$ ways of drawing exactly $m-k$ irrelevant information units from $N-n$ available units. Since there are $\binom{N}{m}$ ways of drawing a sample of size m from the set of all units the probability of identifying k valuable units is

$$\mathbb{P}[V = k] = \frac{\binom{n}{k}\binom{N-n}{m-k}}{\binom{N}{m}} \tag{10.7}$$

which has a hypergeometric distribution. Since the probability mass function of this distribution only depends on N, and since it requires the calculation of large binomial coefficients as N grows, an approximation is desirable for large N. Under the assumption that $m \ll N$, the variances of the two distributions converge:

$$\frac{\mathrm{Var}_{\mathrm{HG}}[V]}{\mathrm{Var}_{\mathrm{Bin}}[V]} = \frac{\mathbb{E}_{\mathrm{HG}}\left[\left(V - \frac{mn}{N}\right)^2\right]}{\mathbb{E}_{\mathrm{Bin}}\left[\left(V - \frac{mn}{N}\right)^2\right]} = \frac{m\frac{n(N-n)(N-m)}{N^2(N-1)}}{m\frac{n(N-n)}{N^2}} = \frac{N-m}{N-1} \tag{10.8}$$

Figure 10.1 plots this convergence for a success probability of $\alpha = \frac{1}{4}$, $m = 20$ draws and a 10-fold increase of N across the panels.

Relevant information units in the network likely differ with respect to how valuable they are to the attackers. Highly sensitive information should be much more relevant to the goals of their operation, hence the model should consider different categories of information value. We let $\ell \in 1, \ldots, L$ denote a number of mutually exclusive cardinal categories of value, where higher numeric values are associated with greater value.

We assume that there are n_ℓ information units of category ℓ among all information units, hence $N = \sum_{\ell=1}^{L} n_\ell$. The probability of drawing an information unit of category ℓ therefore is $\alpha_\ell = \frac{n_\ell}{N}$. Then, the random vector $\mathbf{X}_i := [X_i^{(1)} \cdots X_i^{(L)}] \in \{0,1\}^L$ has a categorical distribution with probabilities $\boldsymbol{\alpha} = [\alpha_1 \cdots \alpha_L]$.

Attackers therefore exfiltrate a total number of information units in each category of $\mathbf{V} = \sum_{i=1}^{m} \mathbf{X}_i$ where each component $V^{(\ell)} = \sum_{i=1}^{m} X_i^{(\ell)}$ corresponds to the num-

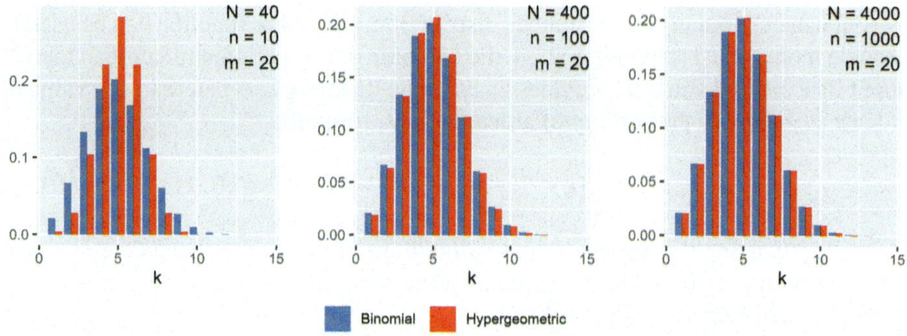

Fig. 10.1 Convergence of binomial and hypergeometric distribution

ber of information units drawn from the ℓ-th category. This number has a multinomial distribution with the probability mass function

$$\mathbb{P}\left[V^{(1)} = k_1, \ldots, V^{(L)} = k_L\right] = \frac{m!}{k_1! \cdots k_L!} \alpha_1^{k_1} \cdots \alpha_L^{k_L} \tag{10.9}$$

To facilitate a scalar expression of this value, we introduce a vector of weights $\mathbf{w} \in \mathbb{R}^L$ that assigns a cardinal number to each category. For example, one could choose $\mathbf{w} = [0\ 1\ 100]$ for the categories *unclassified*, *classified* and *top-secret* to model a setting where unclassified information is useless, whereas top-secret information is 100-fold more valuable to the attackers than classified information.

With these weights, the total value the attackers can realize is the dot product $V = \mathbf{w} \cdot \mathbf{V} = \sum_{\ell=1}^{L} w_\ell V^{(\ell)}$ which has the expected value

$$\mathbb{E}[V] = \mathbf{w} \cdot \mathbb{E}[\mathbf{V}] = m \sum_{\ell=1}^{L} w_\ell \alpha_\ell \tag{10.10}$$

We now extend the model to a setting where a categorical value comparison is unfeasible. For example, attackers who intend to exfiltrate personal user data may find it difficult to rank the relevance and value of demographic characteristics or usage statistics. We discuss a simple and a more advanced case.

First, if the pattern of the attack suggests that X_i follows a Gaussian distribution $X_i \sim \mathcal{N}(\mu, \sigma^2)$, the expected value of a single draw simply corresponds to its first parameter $\mathbb{E}[X_i] = \mu$. One can show with probability generating functions that the total value attackers can expect from the operation is[1]

$$V = \sum_{i=1}^{m} X_i \sim \mathcal{N}(m\mu, m\sigma^2) \tag{10.11}$$

[1] Formal proof is available on request from the corresponding author.

Since the Gaussian is a continuous distribution, a quantile function can be used to provide more robust statements about the outcome of an operation rather than merely about its expected value. It provides an estimate that attackers can realize a value of at least $q(\gamma)$ with a probability of at least $1-\gamma$, formally:

$$q(\gamma) := \min\left[k \in \mathbb{N} \mid \mathbb{P}[V \leq k] \geq \gamma\right], \quad \gamma \in [0, 1] \tag{10.12}$$

Implicitly using the distribution function $\Phi(x)$ of the standardized Gaussian distribution with $\mu = 0$ and $\sigma^2 = 1$, the quantile function that gives the variability of the value as specified in Eq. (10.11) is

$$q(\gamma) = m\mu + \Phi^{-1}(\gamma)\sqrt{m}\sigma \tag{10.13}$$

Even if X_i follows a binomial distribution, quantile functions can still be used [18]. In this case, $\mathbb{E}[V] = m\alpha$ and $\mathrm{Var}[V] = m\alpha(1-\alpha)$. The lower bound of the quantile function then is

$$q(\gamma) \geq m\alpha + \Phi^{-1}(\gamma)\sqrt{m\alpha(1-\alpha)} - \frac{1}{3}\Phi^{-1}(\gamma)^2 - 1 \tag{10.14}$$

A specification of $\gamma = 0.01$ suggests that attackers want to obtain a particular value with a probability of at least 99%. Since $\Phi^{-1}(0.01) = -2.326$, the lower quantile bound is

$$q(0.01) \geq m\alpha - 2.326 \cdot \sqrt{m\alpha(1-\alpha)} - 0.804 \tag{10.15}$$

Figure 10.2 plots the respective quantiles for different specifications of m and α, together with their respective lower bounds.

Finally, prospect theory suggests that humans overvalue realized losses and undervalue the opportunity to realize future but uncertain gains [10]. Hence, whenever attackers learn that they have exfiltrated an irrelevant information unit, they realize a loss in terms of the time and resources they spent to draw this particular unit. Hence,

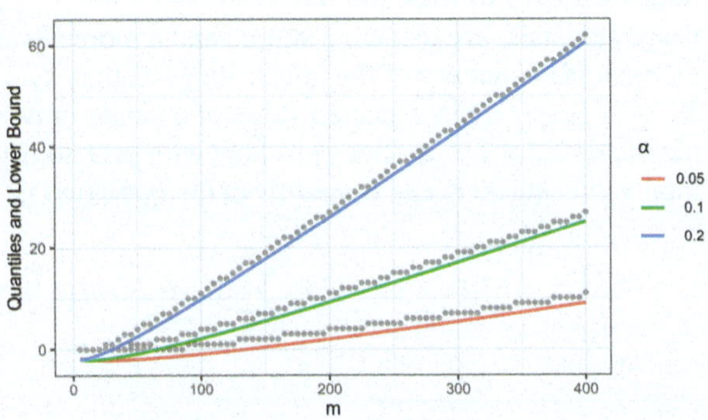

Fig. 10.2 Quantile plots for a binomial distribution with $\gamma = 0.01$

the experience of repeated exfiltrations of information irrelevant to their operational goals may motivate attackers to terminate the attack prematurely.

Prospect theory posits that the expected value of a discrete decision under uncertainty and K alternatives is the sum of the value of all k=1, …, K outcomes v_k multiplied with their respective likelihood of occurrence p_k:

$$\mathbb{E}[V] = \sum_{k=1}^{K} p_k v_k \tag{10.16}$$

This expected value is qualified with a re-weighting function which takes into account loss aversion [9]:

$$\eta(v) = \begin{cases} v^{\beta}, & v \geq 0 \\ -\lambda |v|^{\beta}, & v < 0 \end{cases} \tag{10.17}$$

Takemura and Murakami [20] experimentally found $\beta = 0.88$ and $\lambda = 2.55$. Finally, following prospect theory, we correct the probability for human overreaction to events with small probabilities. The corrected probability $\pi(p)$ is given by

$$\pi(p) = \frac{p^{\delta}}{\left(p^{\delta} + (1-p)^{\delta}\right)^{\frac{1}{\delta}}} \tag{10.18}$$

where δ is an ancillary parameter that captures the asymmetric perception of probabilities by human agents [9]. We use these two corrections to construct a pseudo-probability measure $\mathbb{P}_{\pi}[V = v_k] = \pi(p_k)$ and to calculate the revised values of $\eta(v_k)$. Attackers thus realize an expected perceived value per draw of

$$\mathbb{E}_{\pi}[\eta(V)] = \sum_{k=1}^{K} \pi(p_k)\eta(v_k) \tag{10.19}$$

While this modification works well with discrete distributions, further modifications as suggested by [17] are required for continuous distributions.

10.2.2 Interaction with Defenders

We assume that those who operate and maintain the computer network (the 'defenders') will attempt to protect the data from exfiltration. Attackers therefore operate under the risk of being monitored or detected. At the same time, defenders can falsely conclude there is an attack when in fact there is none (false positives), or they may be ignorant of an actual attack (false negatives).

Let the random variable $Y \in \{0, 1\}$ objectively indicate whether the system is compromised during a specific time step. Defenders can only imperfectly observe the extent to which this is the case. Let the random variable $Z \in \{0, 1\}$ capture their (if erroneous) assessment. We assign a total probability to both variables:

$$\mathbb{P}[Y = 1] =: q \quad \text{and} \quad \mathbb{P}[Z = 1] =: p \tag{10.20}$$

We assume that the probability of an actual cyber network exploitation occurring at present is small, hence $q \ll 1$. Defenders strive to realize almost-perfect prediction, formally, the set $\{Z = 1 \wedge Y = 1\}$ the probability of which we denote as $\xi \in [0, 1]$. Assuming that there are only positive associations of Y and Z, its lower bound is given by the multiple of p and q, and its upper bound is given by the Fréchet bound:

$$pq \leq \xi \leq \min\{p, q\} \tag{10.21}$$

Then, the true positive rate that captures correct predictions (and thus the effectiveness of defense operations) is

$$\mathbb{P}[Z = 1 | Y = 1] = \frac{\mathbb{P}[Z = 1 \wedge Y = 1]}{\mathbb{P}[Y = 1]} = \frac{\xi}{q} \tag{10.22}$$

and the false positive rate that captures erroneous predictions (and thus the inverse of the efficiency of defense operations) is

$$\mathbb{P}[Z = 1 | Y = 0] = \frac{\mathbb{P}[Z = 1 \wedge Y = 0]}{\mathbb{P}[Y = 0]} = \frac{p - \xi}{1 - q} \tag{10.23}$$

Defenders therefore face a basic trade-off: With $q \ll p$, the true positive rate can be maximized by maximizing p toward 1. However, this also implies to maximize the false positive rate, so that highly sensitive monitoring systems (i.e., those with a high true positive rate) also generate many false alarms. This trade-off can be expressed by the false discovery rate:

$$\mathbb{P}[Y = 0 | Z = 1] = \frac{\mathbb{P}[Z = 1 \wedge Y = 0]}{\mathbb{P}[Z = 1]} = \frac{p - \xi}{p} = 1 - \frac{\xi}{p} \tag{10.24}$$

Since, by the Fréchet bound, $\xi \leq q$, and assuming $q \ll p$, the false discovery rate is close to unity, implying that almost all alarms are false alarms. This effect may discourage defenders from investigating every incident, and hence attackers have a chance to remain in the network not only for a negligible number of time steps.

As they monitor the network, defenders sample indicators of compromise during each time step, assuming attackers exfiltrate information units at random. With probability $p \in [0, 1]$, they discover that the network has been compromised. Therefore, each time step can be considered as an independent Bernoulli trial whose outcome is captured by the indicator random variable $Z_i \in \{0, 1\}$ which is Bernoulli distributed with probability p.

We assume that defenders can terminate the attackers' operation as soon as they have collected $r \in \mathbb{N}$ indicators of compromise. The time by which this collection is complete is captured by the random variable $T \in \mathbb{N}$. Hence, the sum of all indicators of compromise up to time step T is

$$r = \sum_{i=1}^{T} Z_i \tag{10.25}$$

which implies that T has a negative binomial distribution whose probability mass function is

$$\mathbb{P}[T = k] = \binom{k-1}{r-1} p^r (1-p)^{k-r}, \quad \text{for}\, k = r, r+1, r+2, \ldots \tag{10.26}$$

Thus, the number of draws the attackers can expect to make before the defenders terminate the attack is

$$m := \mathbb{E}[T] = \sum_{k=r}^{\infty} k \binom{k-1}{r-1} p^r (1-p)^{k-r} = \frac{r}{p} \tag{10.27}$$

We argued before that during a real attack, the exfiltration process resembles a covered draw in an urn lottery, whereby attackers do not evaluate the same information unit twice. In this case, T has a negative hypergeometric distribution, and the probability of defenders terminating the attack after k time steps is

$$\mathbb{P}[T = k] = \frac{\binom{k-1}{k-r}\binom{N-k}{pN-k+r}}{\binom{N}{pN}} \tag{10.28}$$

and hence the expected number of information units that the attackers can draw before the defenders terminate the attack is

$$m = \mathbb{E}[T] = r \frac{N+1}{(1-p)N+1} \tag{10.29}$$

Finally, intelligent defenders likely learn incrementally about the attack with every confirmation that an information unit was exfiltrated. With such a learning mechanism in place, an observed is also a confirmed incident, and the probability of detection during each time step t should be proportional to the number of information units drawn. Therefore, the probability of detection p_t is

$$p_t := \mathbb{P}[Z_t = 1] = \frac{t}{N} \tag{10.30}$$

and the probability that defenders can terminate the attack by time step k is

$$\mathbb{P}[T=k]=p_k\prod_{t=0}^{k-1}(1-p_t)=\frac{k}{N}\prod_{t=0}^{k-1}\left(1-\frac{t}{N}\right)=\frac{k}{N^k}\frac{(N-1)!}{(N-k)!}=\frac{k!}{N^k}\binom{N-1}{k-1} \tag{10.31}$$

While the expectation value of this distribution does not have a closed-form solution, it can be computed by fitting a power function to it. For $1 < N < 40,000$, we found

$$m=\mathbb{E}[T]=\sum_{k=1}^{N}k\mathbb{P}[T=k]=\sum_{k=1}^{N}k\frac{k!}{N^k}\binom{N-1}{k-1}\approx 1.236\cdot N^{0.501}\approx 1.236\cdot\sqrt{N} \tag{10.32}$$

Once defenders can react in this way, the attackers must qualify the total value their operation can attain with the possibility that the defenders terminate it. The true value of the operation is therefore given by the compound distribution of X_t and T:

$$V=\sum_{t=1}^{T}X_t \tag{10.33}$$

Let again α denote the share of valuable information units in the network, and let $\mathbb{E}[T]=m$ denote the number of draws the attackers can make before the defenders terminate the attack. Assuming that T and X_t are independent, we can exploit the tower property of the expectation value to obtain

$$\mathbb{E}[V]=\mathbb{E}\left[\sum_{t=1}^{T}X_t\right]=\mathbb{E}\left[\mathbb{E}\left[\sum_{t=1}^{T}X_t\middle|T\right]\right]=\mathbb{E}[T\mathbb{E}[X|T]]=\mathbb{E}[T\alpha]=\alpha m \tag{10.34}$$

10.3 Illustrations

Suppose the attackers have obtained access to a client management server of an industrial firm with $N = 10,000$ clients, of which only $n = 100$ have highly valuable strategy documents on them, whereas the rest does not store any data worth exfiltrating. Thus, $\alpha = \frac{n}{N} = 0.01$. Under pure random choice, valuable clients are binomially distributed, so the expected value is $\mathbb{E}[V] = \alpha m = 0.01 \cdot m$, implying the attackers would have to conduct at least 100 discrete exfiltrations to identify at least one valuable client. If they are following a promising track, the number of valuable clients would be hypergeometrically distributed. Still, under both distributional assumptions, the chance to have exfiltrated at least one valuable client after

100 draws is only 26.4%. Using the quantile function, and assuming a binomial distribution, attackers can calculate that they would need to exfiltrate at least $m = 299$ (459) clients to find a valuable one among these with a probability of at least 95% (99%). If the attackers do not draw at random, but evaluate each client only once—implying a hypergeometric distribution—they would require 294 (448) draws for a success probability of at least 95% (99%). The defenders can expect to observe at least $m = \mathbb{E}[T] = 1.236 \cdot \sqrt{N} \approx 124$ draws before they can terminate the attack.

Say the attackers have identified a way to exfiltrate user data from the database of a social network. Since individual user data sets are independent from another and each set can be potentially valuable, the drawing sequence is irrelevant. Assuming the value of user data sets has a Gaussian distribution with mean μ and standard deviation σ, the expected value for the operation after m draws is $V = \sum_{j=1}^{m} X_j$ with expectation value $\mathbb{E}[V] = m\mathbb{E}[X] = m\mu$. The value of the operation therefore crucially depends on the average value of a user data set. For $\mu = 0.1\$$ - a relatively low value which implies there are many users in the network who do not have any particularly valuable data associated with their profile, or that the evaluation of such data is costly - there is only a 54% probability that the value of the whole operation is greater than zero. The attackers would have to draw at least 271 (542) user data sets to be 95% (99%) sure this is the case. Therefore, they are likely to compensate the low expected value with a high attack frequency. After drawing 100,000 user data sets, the attackers can be at least 99% sure that the value of their operation will exceed \$9,264.

Finally, consider a case where the attackers have breached the firewall that protects the main file server of a government organization. They can now download any file stored on it, but only learn about its information value upon inspection, hence the draw is a random event. Suppose the files are classified under *unclassified*, *internal*, *confidential*, *secret* and *top-secret*. The expected value of a randomly chosen file then is $\mathbb{E}[X] = \sum_{\ell=1}^{5} p_\ell v_\ell$, and the expected value of all m files that the attackers draw before the defenders can stop them has a multinomial distribution with $\mathbb{E}[V] = m \sum_{\ell=1}^{5} p_\ell v_\ell$. Say the vector of the respective value of a file per classification is $\mathbf{v} = [0\ 1\ 5\ 10\ 100]$ monetary units, implying that unclassified files are worthless, whereas top-secret files are highly valuable. Say the vector for the respective probabilities that a randomly chosen document pertains to one of the five categories is $\mathbf{p} = [0.9\ 0.05\ 0.04\ 0.009\ 0.001]$, implying that there is a very high chance of finding irrelevant files and a minute chance of finding very valuable ones. A single random draw therefore has an expected value of $\mathbb{E}[X] = \mathbf{p} \cdot \mathbf{v} = 0.44$, and the total expected value after m draw is $\mathbb{E}[V] = m\mathbf{p} \cdot \mathbf{v}$. If the file server stores $N = 10,000$ files, we would expect the attackers to draw $m = 1.236 \cdot \sqrt{N} \approx 124$ files with an expected value of 54.6 monetary units.

Applying prospect theory to this case, we skew the value vector elementwise, using the function from Eq. (10.17), which gives $\eta(v) = v^{0.88}$. We do so to reflect the fact that, according to prospect theory, humans prefer to avoid losses over betting on risky gains. Hence, the vector of perceived values is $\boldsymbol{\eta} \approx [0.0\ 1.0\ 4.1\ 7.6\ 57.5]$. We calculate the perceived probabilities with $\delta = 0.5$ as suggested by [9], so that $\pi(p) =$

$\frac{\sqrt{p}}{(\sqrt{p}+\sqrt{1-p})^2}$, which replaces the probability vector $\mathbf{p}$, can be computed elementwise to get $\boldsymbol{\pi} \approx [0.59\ 0.16\ 0.14\ 0.08\ 0.03]$.

The perceived expected value that the attackers hope to realize per draw is now much higher, since $\mathbb{E}_\pi[\eta(X)] = \boldsymbol{\pi} \cdot \boldsymbol{\eta} = 3.1$ monetary units. Accordingly, the perceived expected value of the whole operation after $m = 124$ files are exfiltrated is $\mathbb{E}_\pi\left[\sum_{j=1}^{124} \eta(X_j)\right] = 380$ monetary units. Hence, if the attackers overreact to events with small probabilities, they may engage in an exfiltration operation although, from a purely rational point of view, this operation is unlikely to yield much value.

10.4 Conclusion

We intended to put ourselves in the position of attackers who are interested in exfiltrating valuable information from a computer network. The formal model we developed not only considers different methods by which attackers would proceed with or terminate the attack, but it also attempts to show how they might operate under a situation of asymmetric information, budget constraints, and typical fallacies of human judgment.

It is true that defenders cannot prevent attacks from happening—there is no zero-day, all-hazard protection level, or if there is, excessive investments or total system isolation are required to realize it. While strong encryption is an option to render exfiltrated information units useless to attackers, it does not dissuade them from continuing the operation.

Our model suggests that defenders can deceive attackers by conveying a credible message that the network stores no valuable information, or that an excessive number of draws may be required to exfiltrate valuable information units. As a result, attackers are motivated to terminate their operation. Defenders have two options to convey such messages.

First, defenders can decrease the probability that attackers exfiltrate valuable information units by increasing the total number N of all units, e.g., by flooding the network with irrelevant information. While this idea is counter-intuitive to the principle of clean data management, the repeated exfiltration of worthless information units likely deters attackers from continuing the operation. This situation resembles the famous 'market for lemons' problem [1]. Just like buyers of used cars, attackers are faced with information asymmetry about the quality of the good to be obtained, and they must incur transaction costs to resolve this asymmetry. These 'hidden characteristics' of information units—attackers do not and cannot know the true value prior to exfiltration—make the attack costly and may motivate attackers to abandon it early. Ideally, such intentionally worthless information units could be equipped with false flags or conspicuously strong encryption, so that they would serve as honeypots which attract attackers and enable defenders to monitor and analyze their behavior.

Second, defenders may minimize the number of draws m attackers can make before they are detected. In all variants of our model, the value attackers can realize depends on m. Hence, defenders should not wait until an attack has occurred and then analyze it with ex-post forensics, but they should strive to build early detection system and fast incident response.

References

1. Akerlof, G. (1970). The market for lemons: Quality uncertainty and the market mechanism. *Quarterly Journal of Economics, 84*, 488–500.
2. Barnes, J. E. (2020). US accuses hackers of trying to steal coronavirus vaccine data for China. The New York Times, July 21, 2020.
3. Cunliffe, K. S. (2021). Hard target espionage in the information era: New challenges for the second oldest profession. *Intelligence and National Security, 36*(7), 1018–1034.
4. Davies, D. W. (1995). The Lorenz cipher machine SZ42. *Cryptologia, 19*(1), 39–61.
5. Denning, P. J., & Lewis, T. G. (2016). Exponential laws of computing growth. *Communications of the ACM, 60*(1), 54–65.
6. Eastwood, J. (2019). Enabling militarism? The inclusion of soldiers with disabilities in the Israeli military. *International Political Sociology, 13*(4), 430–446.
7. Hurley-Hanson, A. E., Giannantonio, C. M., & Griffiths, A. J. (2020). Organizations with autism initiatives. In A. Hurley-Hanson, C. Giannantonio, & A. J. Griffiths (Eds.), *Autism in the Workplace* (pp. 179–214). Cham: Palgrave Macmillan.
8. Iasiello, E. J. (2017). Russia's improved information operations: From Georgia to Crimea. *The US Army War College Quarterly: Parameters, 47*(2), 51–63.
9. Kahneman, D., & Tversky, A. (1992). Advances in prospect theory: Cumulative representation of uncertainty. *Journal of Risk and Uncertainty, 5*, 297–323.
10. Kahneman, D., & Tversky, A. (1979). Prospect Theory: An analysis of decision under risk. *Econometrica, 47*(2), 263–291.
11. Koomey, J., Berard, S., Sanchez, M., & Wong, H. (2010). Implications of historical trends in the electrical efficiency of computing. *IEEE Annals of the History of Computing, 33*(3), 46–54.
12. Lin, H. S. (2010). Offensive cyber operations and the use of force. *Journal of National Security Law & Policy, 4*(1), 63–86.
13. Lindsay, J. R. (2017). Cyber espionage. In P. Cornish (Ed.), *Handbook of cyber security* (pp. 223–238). Oxford: Oxford University Press.
14. Mickolus, E. (2015). *The Counterintelligence chronology: Spying by and against the United States from the 1700s through 2014*. McFarland.
15. Moore, D. (2018). Targeting technology: Mapping military offensive network operations. In *IEEE 2018 10th international conference on cyber conflict (CyCon)* (pp. 89–108).
16. Nowrasteh, A. (2021). Espionage, espionage-related crimes, and immigration: A risk analysis, 1990–2019. Cato Institute Policy Analysis No. 909.
17. Rieger, M. O., & Wang, M. (2008). Prospect theory for continuous distributions. *Journal of Risk and Uncertainty, 36*(1), 83–102.
18. Short, M. (2021). On binomial quantile and proportion bounds: With applications in engineering and informatics. *Communication in Statistics - Theory and Methods*, forthcoming.
19. Smeets, M. (2018). The strategic promise of offensive cyber operations. *Strategic Studies Quarterly, 12*(3), 90–113.
20. Takemura, K., & Murakami, H. (2016). Probability weighting functions derived from hyperbolic time discounting: Psychophysical models and their individual level testing. *Frontiers in Psychology, 7*, 778.
21. Weissbrodt, D. (2013). Cyber-conflict, cyber-crime, and cyber-espionage. *Minnesota Journal of International Law, 22*, 347.
22. Wettering, F. L. (2001). The internet and the spy business. *International Journal of Intelligence and Counterintelligence, 14*(3), 342–365.

23. Wilson, R., & Campbell-Kelly, M. (2020). Computing: The 1940s and 1950s. *Math Intelligencer, 42*, 92.

Philipp Fischer received his Bachelor's degree in Computational Science and Engineering in 2019 and is currently completing his Master's degree in Data Science, both at the Swiss Federal Institute of Technology (ETH) Zurich. His professional expertise in data science spans algorithm development, statistical modeling and visualization, specifically for IoT data. His research interests focus on statistical computing and the development of data analytics tools and software.

Fabian Muhly holds a MA in Economics from the University of Fribourg (Switzerland) and is currently finishing his PhD in Criminology at the University of Lausanne (Switzerland). He is the co-founder of a cyber advisory start-up firm that consults on strategic aspects of cyber risks. He is also a member of EUROPOL's expert etwork in data protection and cybercrime and an affiliated lecturer for he International Master in Security, Intelligence and Strategic Studies at the University of Glasgow.

Marcus M. Keupp is the editor of this volume. He chairs the Department of Defense Economics at the Military Academy of the Swiss Federal Institute of Technology (ETH) Zurich. He was educated at the University of Mannheim (Germany) and Warwick Business School (UK) and obtained his PhD and habilitation from the University of St. Gallen (Switzerland). He has authored, co-authored, and edited twelve books and more than 30 peer-reviewed journal articles and received numerous awards for his academic achievements.

Chapter 11
Individual Career Versus Corporate Security: A Simulation of CSO Investment Choices

David Baschung, Sébastien Gillard, Jean-Claude Metzger, and Marcus M. Keupp

11.1 Introduction

Although global cybersecurity expenditures have increased with a compound annual growth rate of about 8% over the last years, and although governments and industry organizations have introduced regulatory requirements and certification processes such as ISO 27001, organizations still suffer from security breaches and struggle to defend themselves against cyber attacks. Reports abound with case studies of business interruption caused by cyberattacks [1, 12, 30]. Further, certifications and regulatory requirements assess the proper implementation of formal processes, but not how effectively they neutralize or thwart cyberattacks [7, 9]. Often, cyberdefense effectiveness is assessed by tests that verify the existence rather than the effective performance of cyberdefense measures [6, 10, 29].

Although microeconomic theory proposes straightforward solutions to these problems (e.g., [18, 19]), corporate reality is more complicated. It is difficult to quantify losses from cyber incidents in monetary terms since future attacks and the damage

D. Baschung (✉)
D-MTEC, Swiss Federal Institute of Technology Zurich, Zurich, Switzerland
e-mail: dbaschun@student.ethz.ch

S. Gillard · M. M. Keupp
Military Academy at the Swiss Federal Institute of Technology Zurich, Birmensdorf, Switzerland
e-mail: sebastien.gillard@milak.ethz.ch

M. M. Keupp
e-mail: mkeupp@ethz.ch

J.-C. Metzger
Hemotune AG, Zurich, Switzerland
e-mail: jean-claude.metzger@hemotune.ch

M. M. Keupp (ed.), *Cyberdefense*, International Series in Operations Research & Management Science 342,
https://doi.org/10.1007/978-3-031-30191-9_11

they cause are uncertain [8, 11]. Therefore, CSOs can only estimate, but never know the truly (objectively) required values of the parameters of the Gordon-Loeb model, and hence the effectiveness of their investment decisions depends on their ability to accurately predict the vector, scope and extent of future cyberattacks.

Further, the personal career ambitions CSOs have may not always directly align with the interests of the firm [2–4]. Since the average tenure of a CSO typically spans between 24 and 48 months [23], managers whose investment decisions fail to produce effective cyberdefense may already have found employment with another firm before security breaches occur at their original employer. However, the reputation, i.e., the way an agent is perceived by others as a result of past accomplishments and failures [22] is likely negatively affected by such moves. In contrast, CSOs who managed to produce effective cyberdefense should enjoy a good reputation in the industry even if they leave the original firm they worked for.

Hence, CSOs who understand to organize cyberdefense effectively would acquire a good reputation in the industry over time. In turn, this reputation would maximize their employment opportunities in the job market, such that firms which require effective cyberdefense would be willing to hire these CSOs at a premium. By the same token, the inter-firm mobility of CSOs who fail to provide effective cyberdefense should be limited since the loss of reputation associated with such events negatively affects their employment prospects. We would therefore expect that, in the long run, and despite the principal-agent-problem, CSOs with a high (low) reputation in the industry will be found in firms which have effective (ineffective) cyberdefense in place. We therefore propose a recursive multi-round model which simulates the migration of cybersecurity investments by 10,000 CSOs over a period of 40 years.

11.2 Modeling CSO Investment Decisions

11.2.1 Basic Gordon-Loeb Setup

Our approach is based on the Gordon-Loeb model [18], and Table 11.1 details its key parameters and variables. A firm is facing a yearly monetary loss λ_j as a result of a cybersecurity breach which occurs with a probability of t_j, where the subscript j denotes discrete years. In the absence of any investment in information security, the vulnerability of the IT asset stock is noted as $v_j \in [0, 1]$, and the yearly expected loss is given by $\lambda_j t_j v_j$.

By investing an amount z_j in cyberdefense, the firm can reduce this expected loss, subject to a technology productivity parameter $\alpha \in]0, 1]$. As a result of such investments, the yearly expected loss decreases to $\lambda_j t_j S_j(z_j, v_j)$, where S_j is the security breach probability function given by

$$S_j(z_j, v_j) = v_j^{\alpha z_j + 1} \tag{11.1}$$

Table 11.1 Model parameters and variables

Parameter	Definition range	Description
j	$\{1, \ldots, 40\}$	Index for time periods
λ_j	$[1, \infty[$	Expected loss in period j
t_j	$]0, 1[$	Probability of a security breach in period j
v_j	$]0, 1[$	Vulnerability of IT asset stock without cyberdefense
S_j	$[0, v_j]$	Security breach probability function
α	$]0, 1]$	Productivity parameter
z_j	$[0, \infty[$	Accumulated IT asset stock in the current period j
z_{j-1}	$[0, \infty[$	Accumulated IT asset stock carried over from prior period $j-1$
$z_{a,j}$	$[0, \infty[$	Degraded IT asset stock by year j
$\widehat{\lambda}_j$	$[0, \infty[$	CSO's estimate of true but unknown λ_j
$\widehat{t}_j$	$[0, 1]$	CSO estimate of true but unknown t_j
$\widehat{v}_j$	$[0, 1]$	CSO estimate of true but unknown v_j
$z_{j,\text{des}}$	$[0, \infty[$	Desired IT asset stock by CSO's estimates
$\Delta z_{j,\text{des}}$	$[0, \infty[$	Optimal investment required to realize $z_{j,\text{des}}$
$d_{j,\text{CSO}}$	$[0, 10]$	Factor by which CSO qualifies $\Delta z_{j,\text{des}}$ in year j
$z_{j,\text{app}}$	$[0, \infty[$	Investment approved by executive board in time period j
$\varkappa_0$	$[0, 1]$	Scaling factor for CSO's prediction accuracy
$\varkappa_1$	$[0, 1]$	Scaling factor for CSO self-confidence by reputation growth
$\varkappa_2$	$[0, 1]$	Scaling factor for CSO self-confidence by past budget approvals
$\varkappa_3$	$]1, 3]$	Scaling factor for relative size of requested budget
$\varkappa_4$	$[0, 1]$	Scaling factor for arbitrariness of CSO behavior
$d_{\text{EB},j}$	$[0, 3]$	Investment the executive board approves in year j
$\lambda_{B,j}$	$[0, \infty[$	Maximum loss realized loss due to a security breach
$\lambda_{A,j}$	$[0, \infty[$	Maximum loss as a result of failing an audit
R_j	$[0, 1]$	CSO reputation by time period j
R_{j-1}	$[0, 1]$	CSO reputation in the prior time period $(j-1)$
ΔR_A	$\mathbb{R}$	Change in CSO reputation due to executive board approvals
ΔR_B	$\mathbb{R}$	Change in CSO reputation due to security breaches
ΔR_C	$\mathbb{R}$	Change in CSO reputation due to (not) passing audits
$C_{\text{tot},j}$	$[10^7, 10^9]$	Total capitalization of the organization
r_j	$[0, \infty[$	Revenue the firm makes in year j
ρ	$[0, 1]$	Return on investment (ROI) the firm realizes
τ_{typ}	$[0, 1]$	Typical investment rate in cyberdefense in the industry
ζ_{typ}	$[0, 1]$	Typical loss in the industry after a cyberattack

We assume there is one CSO per firm. A rational and fully informed CSO would invest an amount of z_j which maximizes the expected net benefit for information security (ENBIS):

$$ENBIS_j = \lambda_j t_j v_j - \lambda_j t_j S_j\left(z_j, v_j\right) - z_j \tag{11.2}$$

Funds are invested until the marginal cost of the investment z_j is equal to the marginal expected net benefit $\lambda_j t_j v_j - \lambda_j t_j S_j\left(z_j, v_j\right)$, formally:

$$z_{j,\text{opt}}\left(\lambda_j, t_j, v_j\right) = \frac{\ln\left(\frac{1}{-\alpha v_j \lambda_j t_j \ln(v_j)}\right)}{\alpha \ln\left(v_j\right)} \tag{11.3}$$

11.2.2 Dynamic Extension

We suggest that in corporate reality, an investment in cybersecurity is not a one-off event, and neither can CSOs fully control the amount that is spent nor are IT assets exempt from depreciation and obsolescence. Rather, we believe that any investment in cybersecurity is an interactive process which comprises several subsequent steps as shown in Fig. 11.1.

Both technological evolution and depreciation degrade an initial IT asset stock of z_0 made in year $j = 0$ to $z_{a,0}$. Therefore, last years' security breach probability function changes to $S_{a,j-1} = \eta \cdot S_{j-1}$, where $\eta > 1$. The lower bound of $z_{a,j}$ is given by the vulnerability v_{j-1}. Hence,

$$S_{a,j-1} = \eta \cdot S_{j-1} = v_{j-1}^{\alpha z_{a,j-1}+1} \tag{11.4}$$

This equation can be solved for $z_{a,j-1}$, so that the monetary value of the degraded asset stock is

$$z_{a,j-1} = \left(\frac{\ln\left(\eta \cdot S_{j-1}\right)}{\ln\left(v_{j-1}\right)} - 1\right) / \alpha_n \tag{11.5}$$

where α_n is the individual productivity parameter of the n-th CSO (since our model considers a setting of many CSOs who migrate between firms). As they note this degradation, CSOs generate estimates in the subsequent year $j = 1$ for λ_j, t_j and v_j, all of which are based on their personal beliefs and threat assessments, in order to determine how much to invest in order to renew the asset stock. We model these estimates by a symmetric probability function, according to which it is equally likely that a CSO over- or underestimates the actual values of these parameters. Hence, in contrast to [18], we believe that any CSO can only imperfectly estimate the parameter

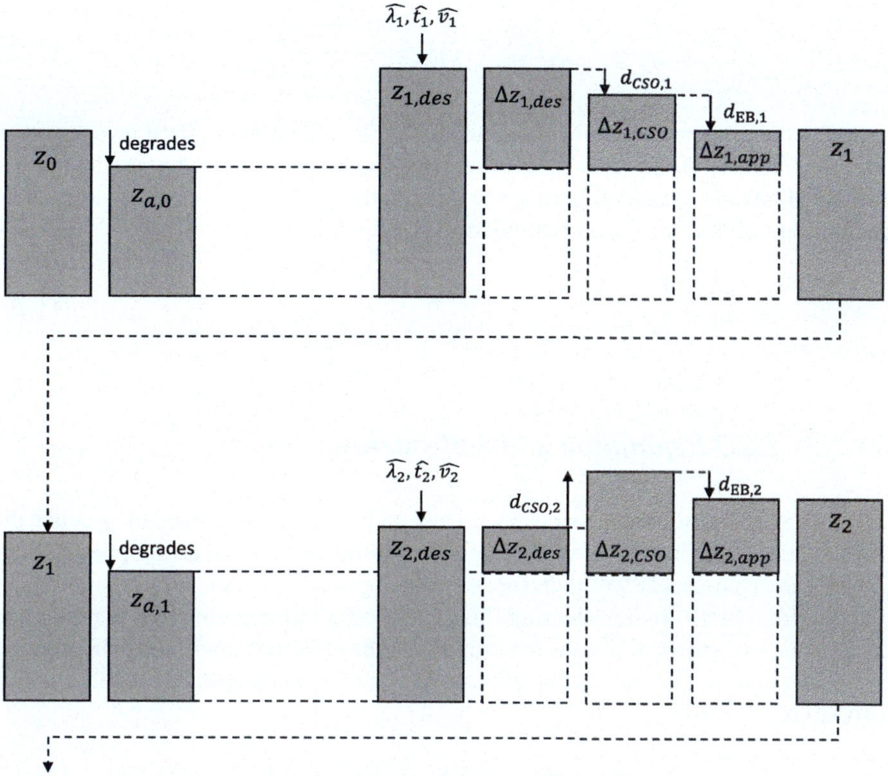

Fig. 11.1 Dynamic interactions before and after investment decision

values which determine the optimal investment in cybersecurity. We use a Gaussian distribution to model these estimates and set the real threat environment of the corresponding year j as expected values:

$$\widehat{\lambda_j} \sim \mathcal{N}\left(\lambda_j, (\varkappa_0 \cdot \lambda_j)^2\right) \tag{11.6}$$

$$\widehat{t_j} \sim \mathcal{N}\left(t_j, (\varkappa_0 \cdot t_j)^2\right) \tag{11.7}$$

$$\widehat{v_j} \sim \mathcal{N}\left(v_j, (\varkappa_0 \cdot v_j)^2\right) \tag{11.8}$$

The variance of the distribution σ^2 is modeled with a scaling factor $\varkappa_0$; the smaller it is, the more accurately CSOs can estimate the true parameters. The scaling factor is always chosen so that the condition that the loss $\widehat{\lambda_j}$ is never smaller than 0 and the attack probability $\widehat{t_j}$ and the breach probability $\widehat{v_j}$ never exceed the bounds [0, 1] during the simulation. As CSOs enter their estimates in Eq. (11.3), they obtain a desired asset stock of $z_{j,\text{des}}$, formally:

$$z_{j,\text{des}} = z_{j,\text{opt}}\left(\widehat{\lambda_j}, \widehat{t_j}, \widehat{v_j}\right) = \frac{\ln\left(\frac{1}{-\alpha \widehat{v_j}\lambda_j t_j \ln(\widehat{v_j})}\right)}{\alpha \ln\left(\widehat{v_j}\right)} \tag{11.9}$$

By deducting the remaining stock of z_a, 0, they obtain the desired investment of $\Delta z_{1,\text{des}}$ which is required to renew the asset stock. In addition, we assume that a CSO will have to exhibit at least some basic activity and hence invest not less than a minimum of 5% of the optimal investment amount. Hence,

$$\Delta z_{j,\text{des}} = \begin{cases} z_{j,\text{des}} - z_{a,j-1} & z_{j,\text{des}} - z_{a,j-1} > 0.05 \cdot z_{j,\text{des}} \\ 0.05 \cdot z_{j,\text{des}} & z_{j,\text{des}} - z_{a,j-1} \leq 0.05 \cdot z_{j,\text{des}} \end{cases} \tag{11.10}$$

11.2.3 CSO Reputation and Self-interest

We model CSOs as managers who do not only request a budget to provide the organizations they work for with effective cyberdefense, but also to optimize their future career prospects. We therefore alter the optimal investment of $\Delta z_{j,\text{des}}$ calculated in Eq. (11.10) by considering this self-interest in reputation. Since reputation is dynamic—it grows or decays over time with the effectiveness of the cyberdefense the CSOs invested in—we define a measure of current reputation $R_j \in [0, 1]$ which evolves recursively:

$$R_j = R_{j-1} + \Delta R_A + \Delta R_B + \Delta R_C \tag{11.11}$$

where R_{j-1} is CSO reputation in the preceding year, ΔR_A is the growth reputation obtained from effective investments, ΔR_B is the reputation obtained from preventing losses from a cyberattack, and ΔR_C is the reputation obtained from passing assessments and audits. Their recursive dynamization is described further below in section 6.2.4. Note that all three terms can be positive or negative, so that CSO reputation can grow or decay over any time period. We delimit $R_j \in [0, 1]$ so that values of $R_j > 1$ or $R_j < 0$ are reset to $R_j = 1$ and $R_j = 0$, respectively. To operationalize and calculate these components of CSO reputation, we introduce four scaling factors which captures different antecedents which we believe influence reputation. The first scaling factor captures the path dependency of reputation over time, formally:

$$d_{\text{CSO}_1}(R_{j-1}) = \varkappa_1 \cdot \frac{R_{j-1} - R_{j-1,min}}{R_{j-1,\max} - R_{j-1,\min}} \tag{11.12}$$

where $\varkappa_1$ is an ancillary parameter whose magnitude reflects how strongly CSO self-confidence changes with a repeated growth or decay over time. Further, we believe the budget CSOs present to the executive board for approval is likely influenced by the extent to which (if any) this board has already approved prior requests [5, 28]. We therefore introduce a second scaling factor of

$$d_{\mathrm{CSO}_2}(d_{\mathrm{EB}}) = \varkappa_2 \cdot \frac{1}{j-1} \cdot \sum_{i=1}^{j-1} d_{i,\mathrm{EB}} \tag{11.13}$$

where $\varkappa_2$ is an ancillary parameter whose magnitude reflects how strongly CSO self-confidence changes as a result of past successful budget requests, and $d_{j,\mathrm{EB}}$ is the extent to which the board is likely to approve the current request. We assume that approval is certain if a cybersecurity breach b_{j-1} has occurred in the previous year, otherwise, the budget approved by the executive board grows with CSO reputation. However, we assume that at least 50% of the request will be granted if there was no breach in period $j-1$ even if CSO reputation is low, hence:

$$d_{j,\mathrm{EB}} = \begin{cases} 1 & b_{j-1} = 1 \\ \frac{1}{2} + \frac{R_{j-1}}{2} & b_{j-1} = 0 \end{cases} \tag{11.14}$$

Newly appointed CSOs likely want to conduct a larger IT security project to prove their competence and increase their reputation in the industry, or they are even expected to implement large projects upon appointment [17]. Hence, we model a third scaling factor which makes larger budget requests more likely between the second and fourth year of CSO tenure (we assume CSOs require the first year on the job to establish themselves and learn about the company). Thus,

$$d_{CSO_3}(j) = \begin{cases} \varkappa_3 & \text{if } j \in \{2,3,4\} \text{ and } X = 1, \text{ where } X \sim \text{Bernoulli}(p = 2/3) \\ 1 & \text{otherwise} \end{cases} \tag{11.15}$$

where $\varkappa_3$ is an ancillary parameter which measures how large the requested budget is in comparison to an average project. Finally, a fourth scaling factor of d_{CSO_4} captures arbitrariness and random behavior among CSOs:

$$d_{\mathrm{CSO}_4}(j) \sim \text{Uniform}[1 - \varkappa_4, 1 + \varkappa_4] \tag{11.16}$$

where $\varkappa_4$ is an ancillary parameter whose magnitude reflects the degree of arbitrariness of CSO behavior. Note that while d_{CSO_1} and d_{CSO_2} are calculated iteratively, d_{CSO_3} and d_{CSO_4} are not. Finally, these four scaling factors are used to qualify the optimal investment of $\Delta z_{j,\mathrm{des}}$ obtained from Eq. (11.10). The resulting amount $z_{j,\mathrm{app}}$ which the executive board approves then is

$$\begin{aligned} z_{j,\mathrm{app}} &= \Delta z_{j,\mathrm{des}} \cdot d_{\mathrm{CSO}} = \\ &\Delta z_{j,\mathrm{des}} \cdot \left[d_{\mathrm{CSO}_1}(R_{j-1}) + d_{\mathrm{CSO}_2}(d_{\mathrm{EB}}) + d_{\mathrm{CSO}_3}(j) \right] \cdot d_{\mathrm{CSO}_4} \end{aligned} \tag{11.17}$$

Note that this final amount can be larger or smaller than the optimal investment obtained in Eq. (11.10) and the CSO's initial budget request. After investment, the IT asset stock increases, and the next round of degradation begins, which in turn is followed by renewed investment. Since any cybersecurity investment cannot exceed the firm's total revenue r_j in the respective budget year, we take the minimum of the computed desired investment $\Delta z_{j,\text{des}} \cdot d_{j,\text{CSO}} \cdot d_{j,\text{EB}}$ and the revenue r_j:

$$\Delta z_{j,\text{app}} = \min\{\Delta z_{j,\text{des}} \cdot d_{j,\text{CSO}} \cdot d_{j,\text{EB}}, r_j\} \tag{11.18}$$

$$z_j = z_{a,j-1} + \Delta z_{j,\text{app}} \tag{11.19}$$

11.2.4 Recursive Modeling of CSO Reputation

Since $y = \tanh(x) \in [-1, 1]$, and since the function is strictly monotonous, we can condition each of the three components of CSO reputation in Eq. (11.11) on the minimum and maximum range of R_j. Further, since $\tanh(\pm 2.65) = \pm 0.99$, we include a factor of ± 2.65 which limits the maximum increase or decrease of reputation per time interval.

To model CSO reputation change over time, we compare the approved amount with what would be a 'typical' investment z_{typ} in the focal firm's industry, given its total capitalization $C_{j,\text{tot}}$, total return on investment (ROI) ρ, and the typical cyberdefense investment rate of τ_{typ}. Since firms typically spend US\$2.84 per US\$1,000 of revenue on IT security [21], we set $\tau = 0.284\%$.

$$z_{\text{typ}} = C_{j,\text{tot}} \cdot \rho \cdot \tau_{\text{typ}} \tag{11.20}$$

We suggest that CSO reputation increases in period j if the investment the executive board approves is larger than this 'typical' investment. Thus,

$$\Delta R_A = \tanh\left(2.65 \cdot \frac{\Delta z_{j,\text{des}} \cdot d_{j,\text{CSO}} \cdot d_{j,\text{EB}}}{z_{\text{typ}}}\right) \tag{11.21}$$

While CSOs cannot prevent a cyberattack from occurring, they can (if erroneously) predict which investment is likely required to minimize future losses. Hence, CSO reputation likely decreases with the magnitude of the loss a firm suffers when a cybersecurity breach occurs. We therefore simulate a randomly occurring breach in year j which occurs with probability t_j and leads to a loss of $\lambda_{B,j} \cdot S_j(z_j, v_j)$. The executive board compares this actual loss to what would be a 'typical' loss $(\lambda \cdot S)_{\text{typ}}$ among other firms in the industry which occurs every $1/t_j$ years. This 'typical' loss can be expressed as

$$(\lambda \cdot S)_{\text{typ}} = \rho \cdot C_{j,\text{tot}} \cdot \zeta_{\text{typ}} \tag{11.22}$$

where ζ_{typ} is the typical loss rate as a result of a cyberattack. Given that the cost of a cyber incident in a firm typically amounts to 0.4% of annual revenues [26], we set $\zeta = 0.4\%$. The resulting change in reputation then is

$$\Delta R_B = \tanh\left(-2.65 \cdot \frac{\lambda_{B,j} \cdot S_j\left(z_j, v_j\right)}{(\lambda \cdot S)_{\text{typ}}} + 1\right) \cdot \frac{1}{t_j} \tag{11.23}$$

Note that the addition of the term (+1) in Eq. (11.23) implies that a loss due to a cybersecurity breach only diminishes CSO reputation if this loss is significant. Note that CSO reputation can decrease significantly as a result of this effect; it decays the stronger the larger the loss is in comparison to a 'typical' loss.

CSO reputation is considered irrevocably destroyed if the firm loses 90% or more of its total capitalization, no matter if this loss is due to a devastating impact of $\lambda_{B,j}$ or insufficient investment $S_j(z_j, v_j)$. Whenever either event occurs, the respective CSO is considered fired and the firm insolvent, and neither is further considered in the simulation.

Our approach follows prior contributions which confirm a log-normal distribution is appropriate to model $\lambda_{B,j}$ [16, 20]. Its probability density function is determined by two ancillary parameters μ and σ^2 which are defined in the probability distribution function [14]:

$$P(X = x) = \frac{1}{x\sigma\sqrt{2\pi}} \exp\left(-\frac{[\ln(x) - \mu]^2}{2\sigma^2}\right), \tag{11.24}$$

Hence,

$$\text{med}(X) = \exp(\mu) \Rightarrow \mu = \ln(\text{med}(X)), \tag{11.25}$$

and

$$E(X) = \exp\left(\mu + \frac{\sigma^2}{2}\right) \Rightarrow \sigma^2 = 2\ln(E(X) - \mu) \tag{11.26}$$

We use the data on actual cyber security breaches and the losses they caused that [26] provides. The $n = 921$ breaches studied caused a median loss of 250,000 US$, while the expected loss is 7.84 million US$. From these values, we obtain rounded ancillary parameters of $\mu = 12.43$ and $\sigma^2 = 6.89$.

Finally, CSO reputation should grow with the extent to which he or she can make the firm successfully pass cybersecurity assessments which audit the security probability breach function S_j.

Since auditors cannot evaluate a complex IT landscape exhaustively within a reasonable time frame, they will likely run a test which simulates a cybersecurity breach. The potential loss from this simulated breach amounts to $\lambda_{A,j} \cdot S_j\left(z_j, v_j\right)$. The higher this loss is in comparison to a typical loss of $(\lambda \cdot S)_{\text{typ}}$ in the firm's industry, the more CSO reputation will decrease. We assume that $\lambda_{A,j}$ follows a log-normal distribution with ancillary parameters of $\mu = 12.43$ and $\sigma^2 = 6.89$, and that over a simulation period of 40 years, an audit is scheduled every three years. Therefore, the associated change in CSO reputation is

$$\Delta R_C = \tanh\left(-2.65 \cdot \frac{\lambda_{A,j} \cdot S_j\left(z_j, v_j\right)}{(\lambda \cdot S)_{\text{typ}}} + 1\right) \cdot \frac{40}{13} \tag{11.27}$$

Like above.

11.3 Simulation Set-Up and Parameter Initialization

We performed four different simulations of this model, the parametric setup of each of which is given in Table 11.2. In each simulations, the time index is set to $j \in [1, 40]$. Each CSO has a productivity parameter α_n which corresponds to the n-th CSO.

The firm faces an (uncertain) monetary loss of $\lambda_j \in \mathbb{R}^*$ with a probability of $t_j \in]0, 1[$. We assume a rather aggressive threat landscape and therefore set $v \in [0.5, 0.9]$. Since by Eq. (11.1), $S_j(z_j, v)$ follows a power law, as the left-hand panel of Fig. 11.2 shows, and since $z_j \geq 0$, each α_n must exceed a lower bound defined by the intersection between the x-axis and the curve in the right-hand panel of Fig. 11.2. The power law distribution entails that the convergence of $S_j(z_j, v)$ toward zero is slow as α_n grows. Hence, a too large α_n would imply that even very small investments of z_j would reduce the firm's vulnerability to 0. We therefore define a range of $\pm 10\%$ around $\alpha_{\max}$ which corresponds to $\max(j, z_{\text{opt}}(\alpha_n))$.

In period $j = 0$, the investment of $z_{j=0}$ is initialized with $z_{j=0} = z_{j=0,\text{opt}}$. Each year, this investment degrades with a rate of η to $z_{a,j}$ as a result of depreciation and technological development (viz., Eq. 11.5). Typically, cybersecurity investments are fully depreciated after four years [25, 27], so the residual of $S_j(z_j, v) - v$ decreases annually by 25%. With Eq. (11.5) and the properties of all other parameters, we obtain $\eta = 1.25$.

We set $\varkappa_0 \in]0.00, 0.05[$, both $\varkappa_1$ and $\varkappa_2 \in [0, 1]$, and $\varkappa_4 \in]0, 1[$. We let $\varkappa_3 in]1, 3]$ follows a Bernoulli distribution, by which a random variable X takes on a value of $X = 1$ with a probability p and of $X = 0$ with a probability $q = 1 - p$. In our case, over the three-year interval $j \in 2, 3, 4$, the CSO has two chances to succeed ($X = 1$)

Table 11.2 Model parameters used in the simulation runs

No.	φ	v	$\varkappa_0$	$\varkappa_1$	$\varkappa_2$	$\varkappa_3$	$\varkappa_4$	C_{tot}
1	$\frac{2}{40}$	0.70	0.02	0.90	0.90	2.00	0.20	10^9\$
2	$\frac{1}{40}$	0.60	0.02	0.10	0.30	3.00	0.30	10^7\$
3	$\frac{5}{40}$	0.50	0.04	0.70	0.30	2.00	0.50	10^8\$
4	$\frac{3}{40}$	0.80	0.03	0.50	0.60	2.00	0.20	10^7\$

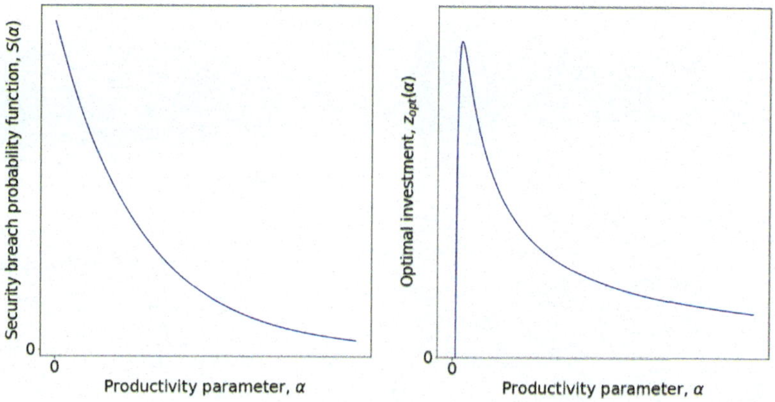

Fig. 11.2 Power law distribution of security breach probability function

and one to fail ($X = 0$) when he or she proposes a major project. Thus, the optimal investment $\Delta z_{j,\text{des}}$ that CSOs request grows with $\varkappa_3$.

To compute the 'typical' investment z_{typ}, we consider larger firms with a total capitalization $C_{\text{tot},j} \in [10^7, 10^9]$, and we follow prior literature on average S&P 500 earnings which assumes an ROI of $\rho = 12\%$ [13, 24].

Finally, we assume that between one and five significant security breaches can occur within a timeframe of 40 years and that the probability of such a breach follows a Bernoulli distribution, hence $\mathcal{B}_{j-1} \sim \text{Bernoulli}(\varphi)$, with $\varphi \in \{\frac{1}{40}, \frac{2}{40}, \frac{3}{40}, \frac{4}{40}, \frac{5}{40}\}$.

11.4 Results

The four panels in Fig. 11.3 show the changes in CSO reputation over 40 years for all 10,000 CSOs and for each of the four simulations specified in Table 11.2. The four panels in Fig. 11.4 show the associated changes in firms' ENBIS. Due to significant overlap between the individual curves in both figures, the respective means (green circles) and medians (indigo crosses) have been redrawn separately.

Using OLS regression, we modeled ENBIS_j as a function of CSO reputation R_j after 10, 20, 30 and 40 years. We assessed the goodness-of-fit of each regression model by Pearson's coefficient of determination R^2 and a Wald test. All computations were performed with the Python library `scipy.stats.linregress`. Table 11.3 documents the results, and Fig. 11.5 plots those for $j = 40$ years.

The results suggest that the OLS parameter estimates are significant. Given that we analyze human behavior which is notoriously hard to model and predict, with one exception we find a relatively high correlation between reputation R_j and ENBIS_j ($0.36 \leq R^2 \leq 0.82$) once the simulation covers a full 40-year time span (viz., Fig. 11.5).

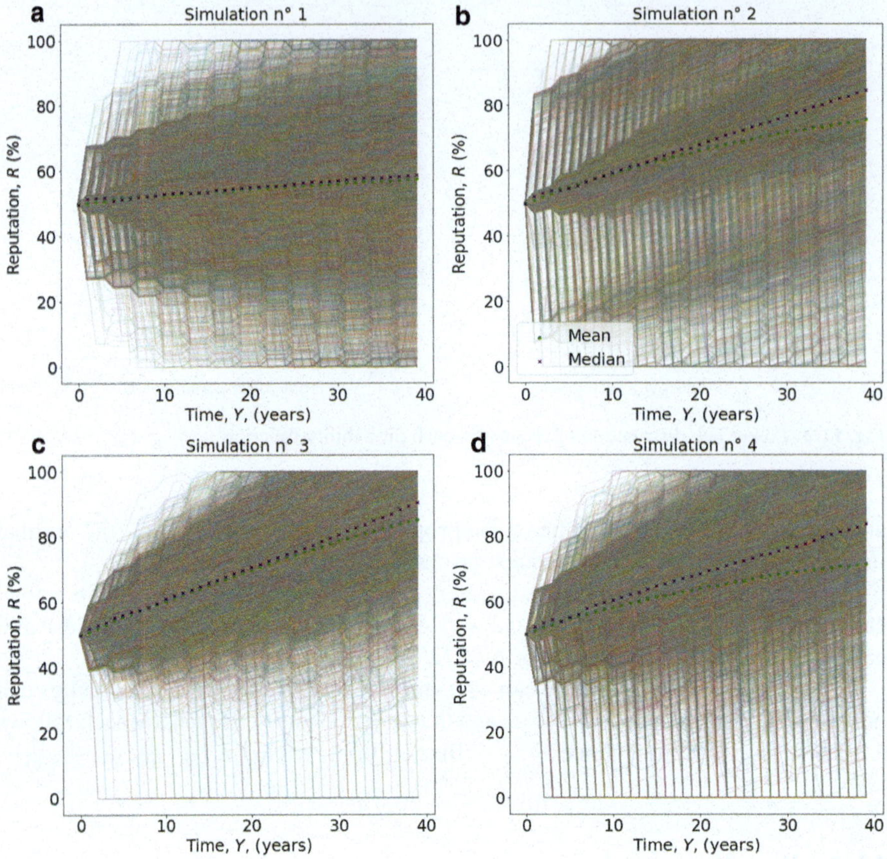

Fig. 11.3 Evolution of CSO reputation over time

Figure 11.6 analyses, for a simulation time of $j = 40$ years, the consequences for CSO reputation when the loss of a specific security breach significantly exceeds the 'typical' range of such a loss, i.e., when $\lambda_{B,j} \cdot S_j(z_j, v_j) > (\lambda \cdot S)_{\text{typ}}$. In each of the four simulations, there is a significant and negative relationship between the number of such security breaches and CSO reputation.

We expect that CSOs with a low reputation would be found in firms which have higher cumulative losses from repeated security breaches $\sum_{j=1}^{40} \lambda_{B,j} \cdot S_j(z_j, v_j)$ over a timespan of $j = 40$ years. Table 11.4 provides the OLS regression parameters we found when we simulated this relationship, and Fig. 11.7 plots the results for all four simulation time spans (note the y-axis in all panels of Fig. 11.7 is on a logarithmic scale).

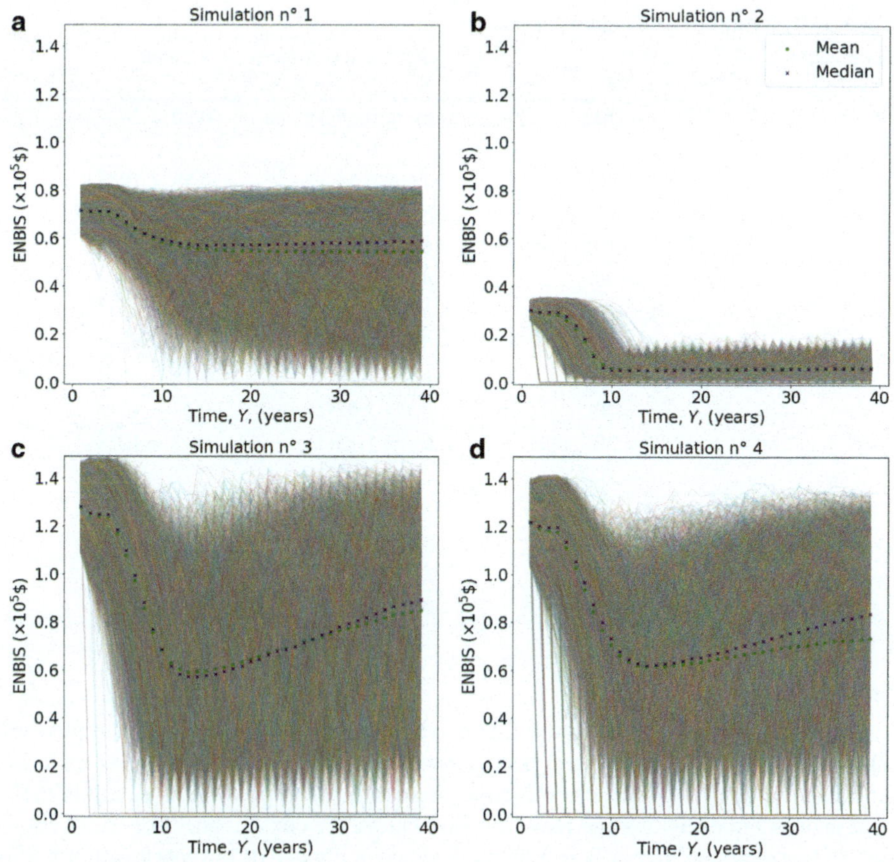

Fig. 11.4 Changes in firms' ENBIS over time

The results suggest that there is no such relationship for simulations 1 and 3 (panels A and C in Fig. 11.7), but the effect exists in simulations 2 and 4 (panels B and D).

11.5 Conclusion

Although the strength of the correlation varies, the simulation illustrates our point that there should be a positive relationship between CSO reputation and the cyberdefense effectiveness. Hence, we posit that in the long term, CSOs with a high (low) reputation will be found in firms with high (low) ENBIS. Therefore, the individual emphasis on maximizing reputation (and thus employability) need not contest the firm's interest in effective cyberdefense.

Table 11.3 Results of OLS regression analysis

Simulation n°	Year	Estimated parameter R^2	p-value
1	$j = 10$	$\beta_E = 0.38(1)$	$0.20 < 10^{-3}$
	$j = 20$	$\beta_E = 0.57(1)$	$0.48 < 10^{-3}$
	$j = 30$	$\beta_E = 0.58(1)$	$0.58 < 10^{-3}$
	$j = 40$	$\beta_E = 0.58(1)$	$0.64 < 10^{-3}$
2	$j = 10$	$\beta_E = 0.06(1)$	$0.08 < 10^{-3}$
	$j = 20$	$\beta_E = 0.06(1)$	$0.23 < 10^{-3}$
	$j = 30$	$\beta_E = 0.07(1)$	$0.32 < 10^{-3}$
	$j = 40$	$\beta_E = 0.07(1)$	$0.36 < 10^{-3}$
3	$j = 10$	$\beta_E = 1.15(2)$	$0.18 < 10^{-3}$
	$j = 20$	$\beta_E = 1.07(2)$	$0.32 < 10^{-3}$
	$j = 30$	$\beta_E = 1.13(1)$	$0.42 < 10^{-3}$
	$j = 40$	$\beta_E = 1.17(1)$	$0.47 < 10^{-3}$
4	$j = 10$	$\beta_E = 1.04(1)$	$0.40 < 10^{-3}$
	$j = 20$	$\beta_E = 0.99(1)$	$0.63 < 10^{-3}$
	$j = 30$	$\beta_E = 1.03(1)$	$0.76 < 10^{-3}$
	$j = 40$	$\beta_E = 1.04(1)$	$0.82 < 10^{-3}$

However, we expect that those CSOs who attempt to maximize their reputation but fail to implement effective cyberdefense will eventually degrade their reputation and end up in firms with less effective protection. It is possible that CSOs make bad investment decisions and leave the firm before the consequences of their actions show. For example, panel B in Fig. 11.5 shows a cluster of low-performing CSOs who enjoy a fairly high reputation (>60%) although ENBIS is low. However, the simulation results for longer time frames also suggest that noncompliant behavior is not rewarded in the long run.

Reputation, in our view, provides firms with a signaling mechanism that allows them to differentiate between CSO candidates. Firms should therefore hire CSOs with a long and proven track record, rather than those who can merely demonstrate short-term success. Moreover, they should provide CSOs with incentives that align with their individual interest in maximizing a positive reputation in the industry.

Future research could further extend our simulation model to gain additional insights. For example, one could additionally distinguish between $\lambda_B > \lambda_{\text{typ}}$ and $\lambda_B \leq \lambda_{\text{typ}}$, and also between $\sum_j \left(\Delta z_{\text{approved},j}\right)$ and $\sum_j \left(\lambda_{B,j} \cdot S_j S_j(z_j, v_j)\right)$.

Further, the response of executive board members to CSO budget proposals could be modeled in greater detail. Since budget decisions are typically an interactive process that involves initiatives and negotiations, members could be modeled as risk-taking or risk-avoiding, and also their reaction to 'small' security breaches which do not threaten the going concern of the firm should be assessed.

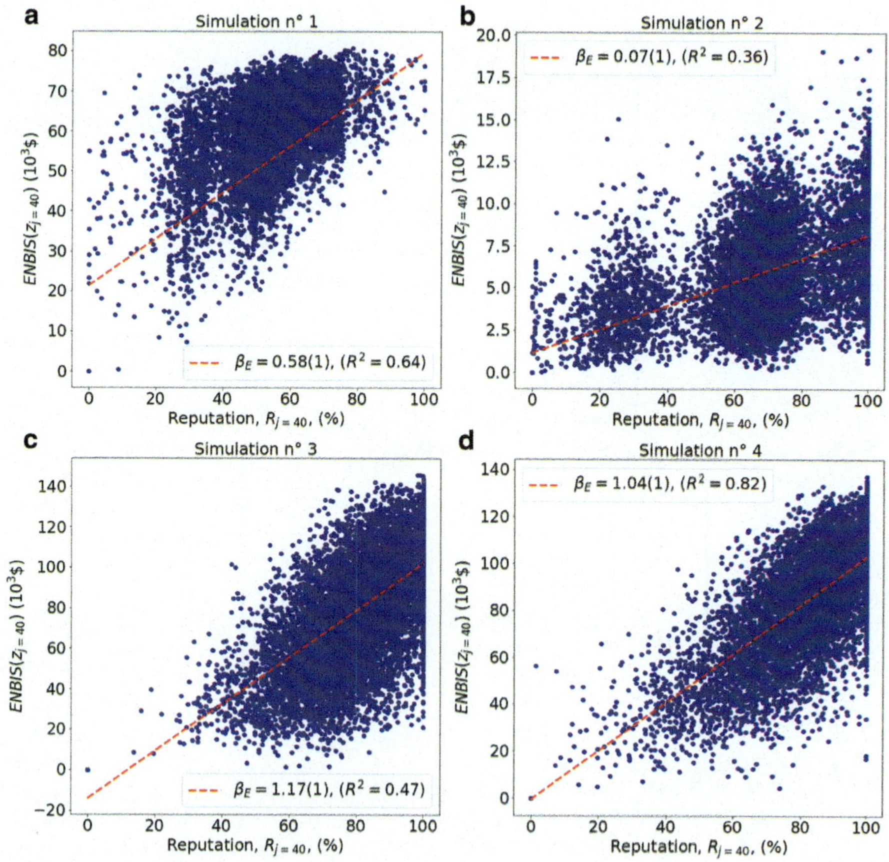

Fig. 11.5 OLS regression results for $j = 40 years$

Even with these incremental improvements, our approach still fundamentally rests on the Gordon-Loeb setting of a single breach probability function and a single parameter set which approximates the totality of all technologies the firm uses in its cyberdefense. Hence, future research could subdivide the simulation into components with different (λ, t, v)-tuples or different probability functions with different productivity factors α. For example, there are established markets for antivirus, firewall and intrusion prevention systems, implying that α is high, whereas it should be lower for smaller and specialized markets such as sandboxing. Finally, threat vectors could be differentiated by 'stealth' (intelligence services, industry espionage) and 'noisy' agents (criminals, script kids) or by technological capabilities such as 'identify', 'protect', 'detect' and 'respond' [15].

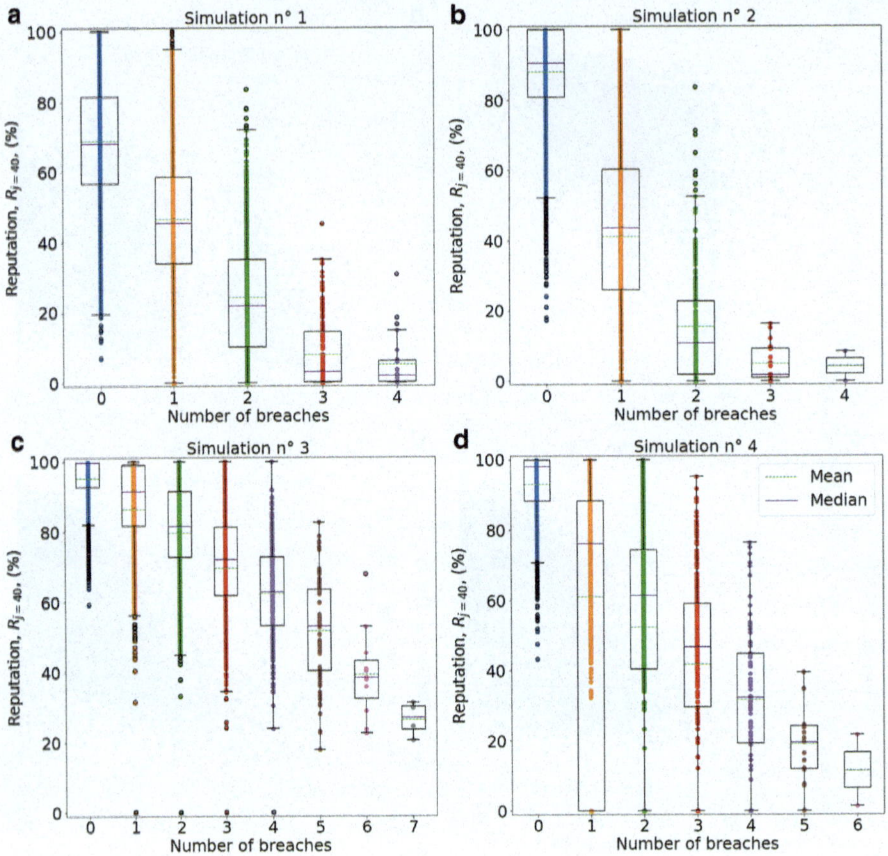

Fig. 11.6 Impact of significant security breaches on CSO reputation

Table 11.4 Estimation results for effect of cumulative loss on CSO reputation

Simulation no.	Estimated parameter	R^2	p-value
1	$\beta_{\lambda,R} = -0.03(1)$	0.39	$<10^{-3}$
2	$\beta_{\lambda,R} = -0.03(1)$	0.67	$<10^{-3}$
3	$\beta_{\lambda,R} = -0.03(1)$	0.30	$<10^{-3}$
4	$\beta_{\lambda,R} = -0.02(1)$	0.54	$<10^{-3}$

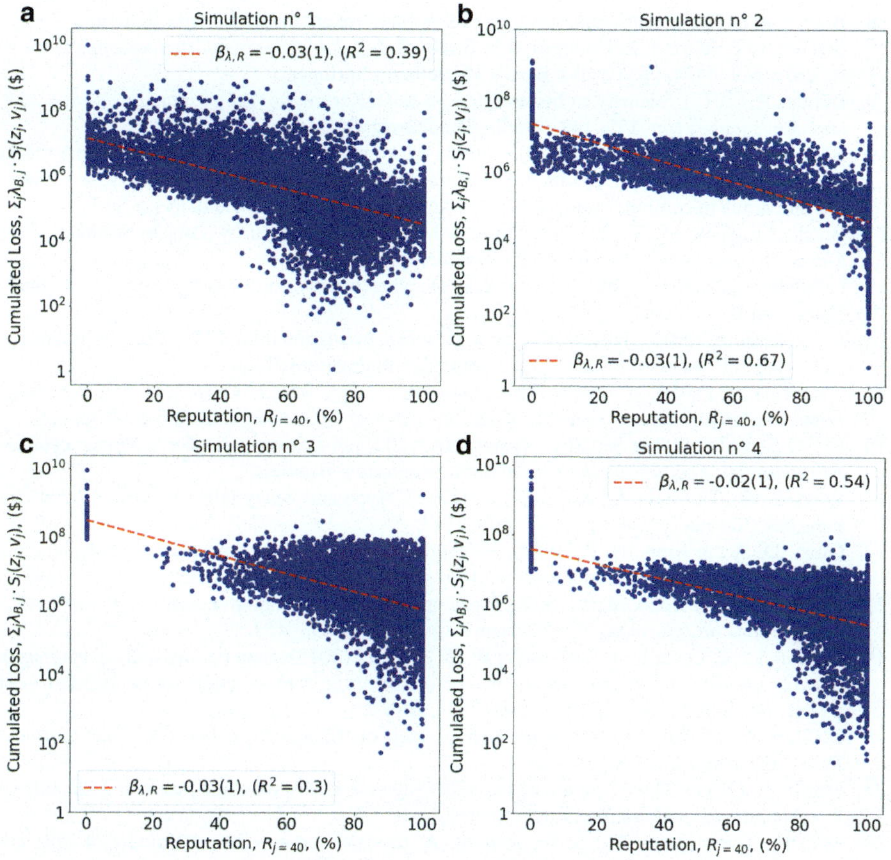

Fig. 11.7 OLS regressions for impact of CSO reputation on cumulative losses

References

1. Allianz Global Corporate and Specialty. (2022). Allianz risk barometer 2022. https://www.agcs.allianz.com/news-and-insights/reports/allianz-risk-barometer.html
2. Anderson, R. (2001). Why information security is hard - an economic perspective. In *IEEE 17th annual computer security applications conference* (pp. 358–365).
3. Anderson, R., & Moore, T. (2006). The economics of information security. *Science, 314*(5799), 610–613.
4. Anderson, R., & Moore, T. (2007). Information security economics - and beyond. In A. Menezes (Ed.), *Lecture notes in computer science* (Vol. 4622, pp. 68–91). Berlin, Heidelberg: Springer.
5. Ashford, S., Rothbard, N., Piderit, S., & Dutton, J. (1998). Out on a limb: The role of context and impression management in selling gender-equity issues. *Administrative Science Quartery, 43*, 23–57.
6. Bishop, M. (2007). About penetration testing. *IEEE Security Privacy, 5*(6), 84–87.
7. Blakley, B., McDermott, E., & Geer, D (2001) Information security is information risk management. In *Proceedings of the 2001 workshop on new security paradigms* (pp. 97–104).

8. Böhme, R. (2010). Security metrics and security investment models. Lecture Notes in Computer Science. In I. Echizen, N. Kunihiro, & R. Sasaki (Eds.), *Advances in information and computer security* (Vol. 6434, pp. 10–24). Berlin, Heidelberg: Springer.
9. Böhme, R. (2012). Security audits revisited. In A. D. Keromytis (Ed.), *Financial cryptography and data security* (pp. 129–147). Berlin, Heidelberg: Springer.
10. Böhme, R., & Félegyházi, M. (2010). Optimal information security investment with penetration testing. In A. Alpcan, L. Buttyán, & J. S. Baras (Eds.), *Decision and game theory for security*. Lecture notes in computer science (Vol. 6442, pp. 21–37). Berlin, Heidelberg: Springer.
11. Brecht, M., & Nowey, T. (2013). A closer look at information security costs. In Böhme R (Ed.), *The economics of information security and privacy* (pp. 3–24).
12. Columbus, L. (2020). The 2020 roundup of cybersecurity forecasts and market estimates. Forbes, April 5, 2020.
13. Damodaran, A. (2015). Historical returns on stocks, bonds and bills: 1928–2021. https://pages.stern.nyu.edu/~adamodar/New_Home_Page/datafile/histretSP.html
14. Dennis, B., & Patil, G. P. (2018). Applications in ecology. In E. L. Crow & K. Shimizu (Eds.), *Lognormal distributions: Theory and applications* (pp. 303–330). Oxfordshire: Routledge.
15. ECSO European Cyber Security Organisation. (2021). *A taxonomy for the European cybersecurity market: Facilitating the market defragmentation*. Brussels.
16. Edwards, B., Hofmeyr, S., & Forrest, S. (2016). Hype and heavy tails: A closer look at data breaches. *Journal of Cybersecurity, 2*(1), 3–14.
17. Gioia, D. A., & Sims, H. P. (1983). Perceptions of managerial power as a consequence of managerial behavior and reputation. *Journal of Management, 9*(1), 7–26.
18. Gordon, L. A., & Loeb, M. P. (2002). The economics of information security investment. *ACM Transactions on Information and System Security, 5*(4), 438–457.
19. Gordon, L. A., Loeb, M. P., Lucyshyn, W., & Zhou, L. (2015). Externalities and the magnitude of cyber security underinvestment by private sector firms: A modification of the Gordon-Loeb model. *Journal of Information Security, 6*(1), 24–30.
20. Maillart, T., & Sornette, D. (2010). Heavy-tailed distribution of cyber-risks. *The European Physical Journal B, 75*(3), 357–364.
21. Martin, B. (2019). Three benchmarks to inform cyber security spending plans for 2020. https://insights.integrity360.com/security-spending
22. Mui, L., Mohtashemi, M., & Halberstadt, A. (2002). A computational model of trust and reputation. In *Proceedings of the 35th annual Hawaii international conference on system sciences* (pp. 2431–2439).
23. Oltsik, J. (2019). The life and times of cybersecurity professionals 2018. Research report, The ESG Group Inc.
24. Ramsey, D. (2022). Can you really get a 12% return on your investments? https://www.ramseysolutions.com/retirement/the-12-reality
25. RMON Networks. (2020). Do you update your firewall every quarter, or ever? Did you know this should be done daily? https://rmonnetworks.com/do-you-update-your-firewall-every-quarter-or-ever-did-you-know-this-should-be-done-daily/
26. Romanosky, S. (2016). Examining the costs and causes of cyber incidents. *Journal of Cybersecurity, 2*(2), 121–135.
27. SonicWall. (2022). Product lifecycle tables. https://www.sonicwall.com/support/product-lifecycle-tables/
28. Watson, A., & Wooldridge, B. (2005). Business unit manager influence on corporate-level strategy formulation. *Journal of Managerial Issues, 17*(2), 147–161.
29. Winkler, S., & Proschinger, C. (2009). Collaborative penetration testing. 9. *Internationale Tagung Wirtschaftsinformatik, 1*, 793–802.
30. Wirth, A. (2019). Reviewing today's cyberthreat landscape. *Biomedical Instrumentation and Technology, 53*(3), 227–231.

David Baschung is a doctoral student at the Chair of Technology and Innovation Management at the Swiss Federal Institute of Technology (ETH) Zurich. He holds an M.Sc. in Mechanical Engineering from this institution and has several years of experience as an information security project manager, consultant and business analyst in the financial and healthcare industry.

Sébastien Gillard received an M.Sc. in Physics from the University of Fribourg (Switzerland) in 2016. He specializes in computational physics and statistics, in particular, data analysis and applied statistical modeling and analytical and numerical resolution methods for differential equations. His current research interest is the application of insights from recommender systems to critical infrastructure defense, including the development of code that can power deep learning algorithms.

Jean-Claude Metzger holds an M.Sc. and Ph.D. in Mechanical Engineering from the Swiss Federal Institute of Technology (ETH) Zurich. He completed his master thesis at the Massachusetts Institute of Technology (MIT). His doctoral thesis focused on the development and clinical evaluation of a hand rehabilitation device for stroke patients. He has several years of professional experience as a project and team leader with Roche Diagnostics. In December 2017, he joined the a medical device start-up company where he leads the development of a blood purification device.

Marcus M. Keupp is the editor of this volume. He chairs the Department of Defense Economics at the Military Academy of the Swiss Federal Institute of Technology (ETH) Zurich. He was educated at the University of Mannheim (Germany) and Warwick Business School (UK) and obtained his Ph.D. and habilitation from the University of St. Gallen (Switzerland). He has authored, co-authored, and edited twelve books and more than 30 peer-reviewed journal articles and received numerous awards for his academic achievements.

Chapter 12
Improving Human Responses to Cyberdefense by Serious Gaming

Fabian Muhly

12.1 Social Engineering and Information Security

Social engineering—a term originally coined in political science [16]—designates a set of psychological influence techniques (PIT) by which attackers exploit social situations or typical human fallacies to gain access to computer systems [3, 5, 11, 18]. In a longitudinal study that spanned five years, researchers applied such manipulation techniques and managed to penetrate 96.4% of the systems they tested [17]. The 2020 Twitter hack also used social engineering methods to access the handles of several politicians and celebrities [6]. However, social engineering is not merely related to cybercrime, on the contrary it creates severe security threats for critical infrastructures, governments, and national defense [8, 9].

This study investigates the extent to which serious gaming may educate people to recognize and neutralize such social engineering attacks. Serious gaming (SG) is an interactive way to convey knowledge in an experiential learning style. Trainers can use interactive, experiential learning tools which are both entertaining and of educational value. To date, only a handful of studies have applied SG approaches to fight social engineering [1, 2, 14, 15].

In an attempt to contribute to this debate, the present study designed and implemented an experiment which studied human participants in a controlled setting. The study is based on and a result of the author's PhD work [13]. Experimental designs are procedures where one or more sample groups are treated in a specific way and where the outcome of different treatment measures among a treatment group and a control group is compared against each other to derive conclusions about the treatment's

F. Muhly (✉)
Department of Defense Economics, Military Academy at the Swiss Federal Institute of Technology Zurich, Birmensdorf, Switzerland
e-mail: fabian.muhly@milak.ethz.ch

M. M. Keupp (ed.), *Cyberdefense*, International Series in Operations Research & Management Science 342,
https://doi.org/10.1007/978-3-031-30191-9_12

effectiveness [7, 10]. In the present study, participation in a serious gaming exercise was used as the 'treatment' that is supposed to 'immunize' human participants against future social engineering attacks.

12.2 Experiment

The study was conducted as a quasi-experiment between February 2022 and May 2022. It comprised a pre-test, treatment, and post-test phase which are detailed in Fig. 12.1. Before the study was carried out, a number of preliminary field observations with three samples collected between December 2019 and February 2020 were performed in order to test and refine the study concept [12].

Study participants were recruited from a technical reserve battalion of the Swiss Armed Forces. The daily tasks of soldiers, NCOs, and officers in this battalion frequently involved operating computer systems and communicating by email and internet applications. Since the study intentionally mimics psychologically abusive behaviors, and since these must appear as realistically as possible, ethical considerations had to be respected. Therefore, to safeguard both research ethics, professional standards, and participants' personal data, the study design was reviewed and approved both by the legal department of the Swiss Armed Forces and by the ethics committee of the School of Criminal Justice of the University of Lausanne (Switzerland).

12.2.1 Pre-test Phase

A survey was administered among all members of the technical reserve battalion to gather knowledge about participants' personality traits, behaviors, and attitudes

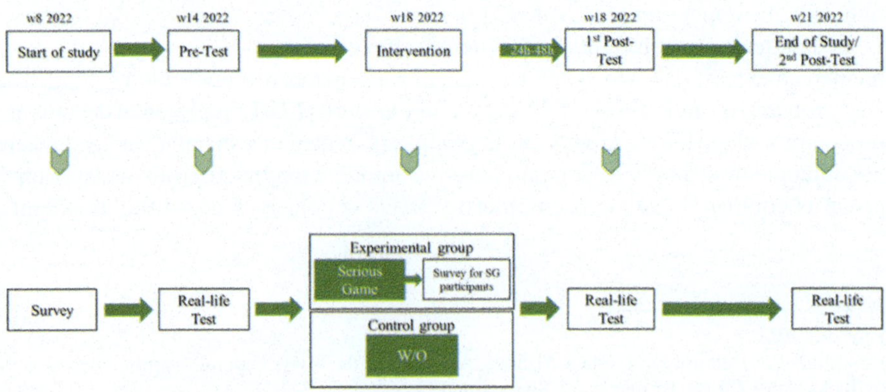

Fig. 12.1 Overview of research design and phases

toward cyber risk. Participation was completely voluntary, and participants had to submit an active declaration of consent. The questionnaire contained 129 questions in 5 sections which did not allow respondents to navigate back once they had completed a section. Table 12.1 summarizes the variables the survey captured. It was implemented between February 25, 2022, and March 27, 2022 with the free and anonymized online survey tool *LimeSurvey*.[1] Before implementation, the questionnaire was pre-tested for clarity and understandability by the study leader and a group of colleagues.

A physical flyer was produced which explained the survey and gave a QR code by which the online questionnaire could be accessed. This code was scanned by 276 unique individuals, 182 of whom fully completed the questionnaire. The arithmetic mean of processing time was 21 minutes and 42 seconds. After the survey was completed, two individuals decided to opt out. In order to provide conservative estimates, imputation was not applied, so all analyses were performed with the remainder of the 180 participants.

On April 8, 2022, these 180 participants received a phishing email in their work account inbox that intended to test participants' proneness to fall for PIT. Four different and intricate variants were designed, each of which asked respondents to click on a link and provide information. The technical implementation and execution of this email was performed by a vendor of the Swiss Armed Force's cybersecurity and awareness team who had no direct relation to the battalion. In order to increase time pressure, the phishing emails were sent on a Friday, and information asymmetry was induced by discouraging escalation or consultation with co-workers. Upon receipt, 57.2% of study participants clicked on the link, and 88.3% of these also disclosed information.

12.2.2 Treatment

Three and a half weeks after the phishing email had been sent, representatives of the Swiss Armed Forces grouped study participants into a treatment group whose 42 members played a serious game, and a in control group whose 138 members carried on with their ordinary work tasks.

Strictly speaking, this allocation process involves some subjectivity, and therefore the experimental design cannot be considered a fully randomized controlled experiment. However, a meta-analysis of social engineering intervention studies shows that the type of participant randomization was not a significant predictor for the effectiveness of the respective intervention under scrutiny [4].

The serious game was played during the whole day of May 4, 2022. In order to control diffusion bias, members of the treatment group were assigned to either a morning (8am to noon) or an afternoon (1:30pm to 5:30pm) session. The game adopted the design by Beckers and Pape [2]. It featured an offline, physical 'tabletop'

---

[1] See https://www.limesurvey.org/.

Table 12.1 Overview of variables in the survey

Variable	Code name	Scale	Question
Clicking on link in phishing email	Link	Binary	–
Inputting requested information on dedicated landing page	Info	Binary	–
Participation in serious game training	PSGpart	Binary	–
Post-test 1	time1post	Binary	Results of post-test1
Post-test 2	time2post	Binary	Results of post-test2
Honesty-Humility	Hone	5-point Likert scale	60-item HEXACO personality inventory
Emotionality	Emot	5-point Likert scale	60-item HEXACO personality inventory
Extraversion	Extr	5-point Likert scale	60-item HEXACO personality inventory
Agreeableness	Agre	5-point Likert scale	60-item HEXACO personality inventory
Conscientiousness	Cons	5-point Likert scale	60-item HEXACO personality inventory
Openness	Open	5-point Likert scale	60-item HEXACO personality inventory
Previous information security training for personal information	PIST_pitrue	Binary	Have you attended any training in the last 12 months that focused on the protection of personal data and information?
Previous online information security training for personal information	PIST_piOtrue	Binary	Was it an online training?
Previous information security training for military information	PIST_mitrue	Binary	Have you attended any training in the last 12 months that focused on protecting military data and information?
Previous online information security training for military information	PIST_miOtrue	Binary	Was it an online training?
Previous individual victimization	PIV_receivetrue	Binary	In the last 12 months, have you ever received an email link from someone asking you to provide sensitive information such as personal identification, bank and credit card details, and passwords?
Individual victimization expectation	IVE	5-point Likert scale	In the next 12 months, how likely are you to provide personal information online to someone who asks you to provide sensitive information (e.g., personal identification, bank and credit card information, and passwords) via email?
Risky cybersecurity behavior	RCsB_Mean	7-point Likert scale	20-item inventory concerning self-reported cybersecurity behavior
Attitudes toward cybersecurity and cybercrime in business	ATCIB_Mean	4-point Likert scale	25-item inventory concerning self-reported attitudes

setting which created a situation plan of a fictitious company and a set of fictitious employees, each of whom was characterized by job position, computer skills, and personal strengths and weaknesses. The game is designed to help people familiarize with the concept of social engineering, so that they are able to understand and detect related attacks. Participants play with two stacks of cards, one of which covers typical PIT, and one of which details how attackers approach their targets using these techniques.

The game is led by a game master and played iteratively by 4–5 teams of 2–3 persons each per game table. In the study, there were three game masters, each of whom led a game table with eight participants grouped in teams of two. The game masters were all male, between 25 and 36 years old, and none of them had any direct relation to the battalion or the Swiss Armed Forces during the period of the study. At the end of the game, each game table has a winning team. During each round, the teams are asked to create a social engineering attack. Each team defines a target asset they want to exfiltrate from the fictitious company, such as financial information, documents, or passwords.

After an initial phase of about 10 minutes during which the teams familiarize with the situation plan and the fictitious employees, each team draws three cards from the PIT and attack technique stacks. The teams now have 10 minutes to formulate a reasonable social engineering attack. Depending on which cards they drew, they must find a combination of PIT and attack technique which, in their opinion, effectively targets one of the fictitious employees. Subsequently, they must script their strategy and detail how they deceived these particular employees. The teams then present these formulated plans to each other. Each team's attack is evaluated by the other teams at the table with a pre-defined point scale. This rating essentially checks whether the team correctly understood and applied the PIT and social engineering techniques in question.

This process is repeated for each team at the table. Once all teams at the table have been evaluated, another round begins. The team which accumulated the most points over all rounds is the winner of the respective game table. Although winning is not the sole purpose of the game, it motivates participants to familiarize with the concepts of social engineering and PIT. When all teams have completed the game, the game master moderates a joint discussion about the opinions and experiences the participants had while playing, in order to let them reflect and learn about the concepts and techniques they were confronted with during the game.

12.2.3 Post-test Phase

On May 6, 2022, all participants again received a phishing email that was generated as described before. This first post-test phase served to test whether participants had realized short-term learning effects immediately after the game. It applied the same PIT as those sent in the pre-test phase. After this first post-test, a second phishing email was sent to all participants on May 27, 2022, i.e., three and a half weeks after the game was played. These two post-tests were independent, and their PIT scenarios were different from those used in the pre-test phase. During the first post-test, 16.7% (–70.1% compared to the pre-test phase) clicked on the link, and 26.7% (–69.7%) of these provided information as requested, suggesting an immediate and significant reduction. During the second post-test, the effect was weaker, but still constituted a significant reduction. Compared to the pre-test phase, 25.6% (–55.2%) clicked on the link, and 43.5% (–50.7%) of these provided information.

12.3 Effect Size and Marginal Analysis

While these descriptive results suggest that serious gaming is, at least in the short term, a tool which sensitizes IT operators against PIT and social engineering techniques, the learning effect could also be correlated to a particular personality type. To investigate this hypothesis, a logistic regression was run, the results of which are shown in Tables 12.2 and 12.3. In this model, victimization was measured by multiple constructs. The variable *Link* measures the victimization of participants who clicked on the link in the phishing email during the first stage of the experiment, and the variable *Info* measures whether those participants also provided information. The variables *participation in serious game, previous phishing victimization, personality traits, previous information security training, previous individual victimization, individual victimization expectation, risky cybersecurity behaviors* and *attitudes toward cybersecurity in business* were all used as instrumental variables which could predict future phishing victimization.

Then, bidirectional stepwise elimination was performed to exclude all variables which did not significantly contribute to effect size. The reduced-form models for both dependent variables are shown in Tables 12.4 and 12.5.

A chi-square test (viz. Table 12.6) confirmed that the estimates in the reduced-form model were not significantly different from those in the original model.

The results suggest that previous completion of a security training related to handling classified information correctly (*PIST_mitrue*), as well as self-reported previous individual victimization (*PIV_receive_mitrue)* almost halve the chance that a participant will fall for social engineering exploits.

Among the predictors in the reduced-form model, *individual victimization expectation* (IVE3) seems to contribute most to effect size, with a coefficient of 4.280 (4.454) for the probability that a participant clicks on the link in the phishing email (provides information as requested). Thus, study participants who reported that they consider themselves neither likely nor unlikely to fall for social engineering techniques during next 12 months are almost four times more likely to do so than those who were more pessimistic and said that they will likely fall for such a scam in the 12 months ahead.

All in all, both confident (IVE2) and indifferent (IVE3) participants seem to have the highest probability of eventually falling for social engineering techniques, whereas those who expect to be victimized by such an attack are less likely to actually

Table 12.2 Logistic regression model for clicking the link in the phishing email

Variable	Coefficient	p-value
Intercept	3.216	0.519
PSGpart	0.962	0.882
time1post	0.129	0.000
time2post	0.229	0.000
Hone	1.093	0.655
Emot	0.787	0.246
Extr	0.951	0.783
Agre	0.860	0.472
Cons	1.027	0.884
Open	1.053	0.764
PIST_pitrue	0.704	0.275
PIST_pi0True	1.024	0.965
PIST_miTrue	0.467	0.296
PIST_mi0True	0.982	0.981
PIV_receivetrue	0.540	0.005
IVE2	1.635	0.089
IVE3	4.494	0.003
IVE4	1.113	0.914
RCsB_Mean	1.199	0.412
ATCIB_Mean	1.040	0.931

become victims, probably because their pessimistic stance cautions them against inappropriate trust and restrains the initiative to immediately respond or comply.

Finally, the extent to which participation in the serious game prevented participants from falling for the attack remains to be determined. Somewhat surprisingly, and contrary to the descriptive findings during the post-test phase, the treatment indicator *PSGpart* which captures whether or not a participant has played the game is not significant in the reduced-form model.

Since this effect may be due to the small sample size, power analysis was used to determine if there truly was no effect size. Power analysis is an alternative way to detect statistically significant effects, since a power level of 80% corresponds to the chance of detecting an effect at a significance level of 5% or less.

The required number of participants depends on the base level, which is the probability that a member of the control group passes the post-test independent of prior training. The desired effect to be measured is expressed as the odds ratio that a participant fails the post-hoc test despite having participated in the game. The effect estimates are transformed from a log to a linear scale in order to represent ratios. Figure 12.2 illustrates the respective ranges.

Under the (somewhat generous) assumption that participation in the game implies a measurable odds ratio of 0.5—in other words, a participant who participated in

Table 12.3 Logistic regression model for providing information after clicking

Variable	Coefficient	p-value
Intercept	0.188	0.447
PSGpart	1.178	0.597
time1post	0.037	0.000
time2post	0.104	0.000
Hone	1.637	0.047
Emot	0.838	0.480
Extr	1.080	0.727
Agre	1.095	0.719
Cons	0.788	0.295
Open	0.811	0.320
PIST_pitrue	0.914	0.811
PIST_pi0True	1.012	0.985
PIST_miTrue	0.660	0.601
PIST_mi0True	0.754	0.740
PIV_receivetrue	0.509	0.012
IVE2	1.653	0.151
IVE3	5.219	0.005
IVE4	0.652	0.737
RCsB_Mean	1.247	0.412
ATCIB_Mean	1.678	0.340

Table 12.4 Final model for *link* after bidirectional stepwise selection

Variable	Coefficient	p-value
Intercept	2.048	0.001
time1post	0.131	0.000
time2post	0.232	0.000
PIST_miTrue	0.429	0.003
PIV_receivetrue	0.530	0.003
IVE2	1.635	0.075
IVE3	4.280	0.002
IVE4	0.954	0.961
Hone	NA	NA

Table 12.5 Final model for *info* after bidirectional stepwise selection

Variable	Coefficient	p-value
Intercept	0.348	0.204
time1post	0.039	0.000
time2post	0.107	0.000
PIST_miTrue	0.505	0.044
PIV_receivetrue	0.519	0.011
IVE2	1.653	0.132
IVE3	4.454	0.007
IVE4	0.574	0.655
Hone	1.496	0.068

Table 12.6 Chi-square test results

Dependent variable	Resid. Df	Resid. Dev	Df	Deviance	$P > \chi)$
Link	539	686.041	NA	NA	NA
Link	532	580.566	7	105.175	0.000
Link	520	576.963	12	3.903	0.985
Info	539	569.566	NA	NA	NA
Info	531	419.126	8	150.440	0.000
Info	520	413.949	11	5.177	0.922

the game has a 50% chance to fail the post-hoc test—a sample of more than 500 participants would be required for a statistically significant result. Moreover, if the post-hoc tests had a base effect of around 50% like the pre-tests had, the number of participants would have been sufficient to measure an odds ratio of up to 0.6.

Finally, an analysis of the discordant probability ratio was run, which is the ratio between the participants that went from failing to passing after participation, and those who changed vice versa. The respective ratios are shown in Fig. 12.3.

The same analysis can be run only for the group that participated in the training. Then, the base effect is the chance that participants change at random from failing the pre-test to passing the post-tests or vice versa randomly. The measured effect is the discordant probability ratio. Figure 12.3 shows that with a probability level of 1%, the size of the training participant group (the black line) was sufficient to return a measured effect of 20 times more participants who improved from the pre-test to the post-test phase than vice versa. Thus, there is statistically significant evidence that the number of participants in the experimental group was sufficient.

Finally, resampling was used to derive a synthetic dataset for marginal analysis, more specifically, to estimate the extent to which the post-test results were influenced by the serious game training. Participants were resampled in a way that an equal number of them passed and failed the first post-test. Moreover, the number of participants was also synthetically oversampled to exaggerate any measured effects and to study

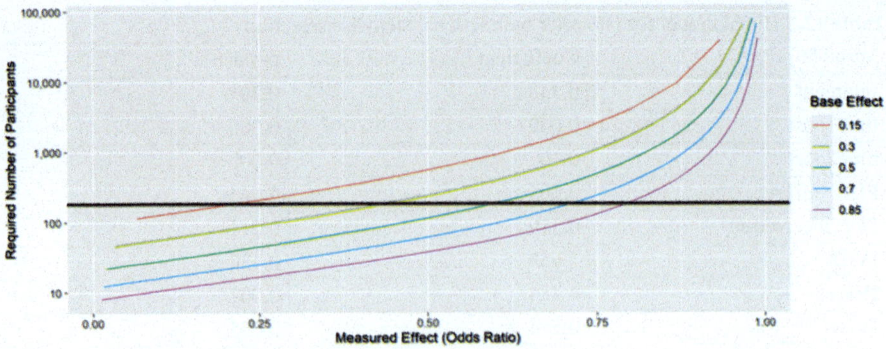

Fig. 12.2 Required number of participants per base effect

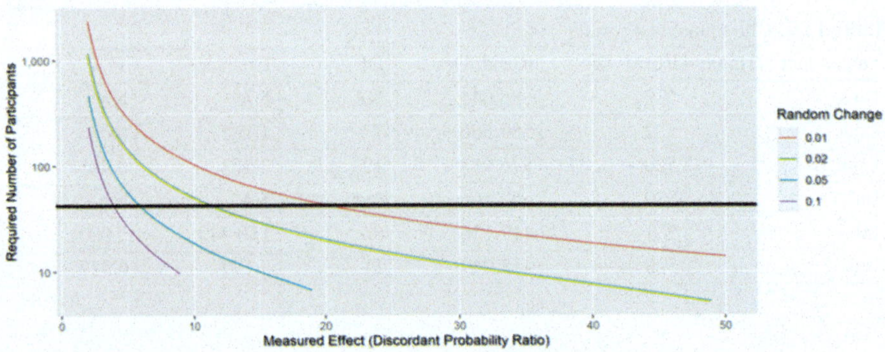

Fig. 12.3 Required number of participants per discordant probability ratio

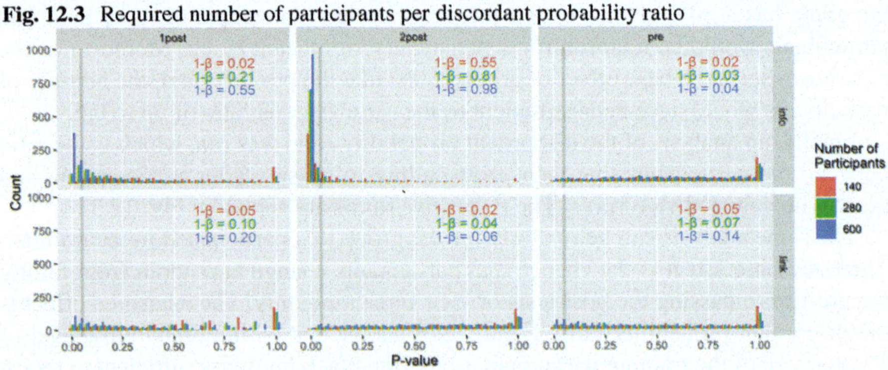

Fig. 12.4 Marginal analysis with resampling procedure

which hypothetical results the chi-square test would give if more participants had responded.

Figure 12.4 shows the results of this procedure. There are statistically significant results for at least two post-tests of whether or not the link was clicked with large statistical power, as the numbers for (1-β) in the plot demonstrates. The synthetic dataset for these cases used a sample size that was double to four times as large as the effective sample size in the experiment. Hence, with a larger sample size of respondents, a statistically significant relationship between participation in the serious game and passing the post-test of whether or not information was provided could have been observed.

12.4 Conclusion

This chapter presented the results of an experiment that tested the extent to which serious gaming could immunize participants against social engineering attacks. In a tabletop serious gaming approach, participants were confronted with the rationales and techniques that social engineers use for their malicious attacks. The interactive experiential learning style provides participants with the opportunity to acquaint themselves with knowledge about social engineering and build resilience against such attacks. The results suggest that participation in the game reduces the probability to fall for such an attack, but this probability also depends on the focal participant's level of self-confidence.

While the sample size in this study was small, discordant probability analysis suggests the effect of serious gaming on immunization is positive and significant. Hence, with a larger experimental setting of about 500 participants, statistically significant effects would probably be observable. Future research should therefore explore more serious gaming approaches in larger settings.

Somewhat ironically, a high level of confidence in one's own capabilities to spot social engineering attacks is a significant predictor of victimization. Future research should therefore further investigate how this typical human fallacy could be modeled by serious gaming techniques to make participants aware.

This experiment tested a particular social engineering technique (phishing) which is indicative of, but not exclusively congruent with social engineering as such. Future research should therefore complement this experiment with studies of other techniques to arrive at a more complete picture of how social engineering can be spotted and prevented.

References

1. Aladawy, D., Beckers, K., & Pape, S. (2018). PERSUADED: Fighting social engineering attacks with a serious game. In S. Furnell, H. Mouratidis, & G. Pernul (Eds.), *Trust, privacy and security in digital business* (pp. 103–118). Cham: Springer.
2. Beckers, K., & Pape, S. (2016). A serious game for eliciting social engineering security requirements. In *Proceedings of the 24th IEEE international requirements engineering conference (RE)*.

3. Bullée, J., Montoya, L., Pieters, W., Junger, M., & Hartel, P. (2017). On the anatomy of social engineering attacks - A literature-based dissection of successful attacks. *Journal of Investigative Psychology and Offender Profiling, 15*(1), 20–45.
4. Bullée, J., & Junger, M. (2020). Social engineering. In *The Palgrave handbook of international cybercrime and cyberdeviance* (pp. 849–875).
5. Cialdini, R. (2021). *Influence, new and expanded: The psychology of persuasion*. HarperCollins.
6. DoJ. (2020). Three individuals charged For alleged roles in Twitter hack. United States Department of Justice, July 31st, 2020, see https://www.justice.gov/usao-ndca/pr/three-individuals-charged-alleged-roles-twitter-hack
7. Fischer, H., Boone, W., & Neumann, K. (2014). *Quantitative research designs and approaches* (1st. Ed.). Routledge.
8. Ghafir, I., Saleem, J., Hammoudeh, M., Faour, H., Prenosil, V., Jaf, S., Jabbar, S., & Baker, T. (2018). Security threats to critical infrastructure: the human factor. *The Journal of Supercomputing, 74*, 4986–5002.
9. Green, B., Prince, D., Busby, J., & Hutchison, D. (2015). The impact of social engineering on industrial control system security. In *Proceedings of the first ACM workshop on cyber-physical systems-security and/or privacy* (pp. 23–29).
10. Maxfield, M., & Babbie, E. (2017). *Research methods for criminal justice and criminology* (8th Ed.). Wadsworth Publishing.
11. Mouton, F., Leenen, L., & Venter, H. (2016). Social engineering attack examples, templates and scenarios. *Computers & Security, 59*, 186–209.
12. Muhly, F., Leo, P., & Caneppele, S. (2022). A serious game for social engineering awareness creation. *Journal of Cybersecurity Education, Research and Practice 1*(4), article 5.
13. Muhly, F. (2023). Serious gaming as crime prevention? The effectiveness of a serious game and the role of personality traits in reducing the proneness towards social engineering fraud. Thèse de Doctorat, Université de Lausanne, Faculté de droit et des sciences criminelles. (UNIL/CHUV, ID Serval: serval: BIB A7ACAD9F0113)
14. Newbould, M., & Furnell, S. (2009). Playing safe: A prototype game for raising awareness of social engineering. In *Proceedings of the 7th Australian information security management conference*.
15. Olanrewaju, A. S., & Zakaria, N. (2015). Social engineering awareness game (SEAG): An empirical evaluation of using game towards improving information security awareness. In *Proceedings of the 5th international conference on computing and informatics (ICOCI) Istanbul*.
16. Popper, K. (1966). *The open society and its enemies* (5th ed.). Princeton NJ: Princeton University Press.
17. Robinson, J. (2008). *Researchers dupe banks with heists without holdups* (p. D5). Arizona Republic.
18. Rusch, J. (1999). The "social engineering" of internet fraud. In *Proceedings of the 1999 internet society conference*.

Fabian Muhly holds a PhD in Criminology from the University of Lausanne (Switzerland) and a MA in Economics from the University of Fribourg (Switzerland). His ideas and research have already been published in outlets such as Harvard Business Review and MIT Sloan Management Review. He is the co-founder of a cyber advisory start-up firm that consults on strategic aspects of cyber risks. He is also a member of EUROPOL's expert network in data protection and cybercrime and an affiliated lecturer for the International Master in Security, Intelligence and Strategic Studies at the University of Glasgow.

Chapter 13
Next Generation Cyber-Physical Architecture and Training

Siddhant Shrivastava and Aditya P. Mathur

13.1 Mixed Reality Architecture

Mixed reality (MR)—a technology that combines elements of both virtual and augmented reality—can create a more immersive and interactive user experience. MR improves the safety, security, and effectiveness of the defense of cyber-physical systems in general and industrial control systems in particular. First, it allows operators to remotely monitor and operate assets, so that the need for human intervention in potentially dangerous areas is reduced. For example, an oil and gas company could remotely control and monitor offshore drilling platforms, so that operators could safely assess and respond to potential hazards without physically traveling to the site. This not only improves safety but also reduces costs associated with travel and maintenance.

Second, operators can use MR technology to train proper procedures and emergency response protocols. They can practice handling emergency situations, such as a chemical spill, in a safe and controlled environment. This can significantly reduce the risk of human error and improve emergency response times in real-life situations. In addition, these systems can be used to train operators on new equipment or procedures, allowing them to quickly and efficiently adapt to changes in the infrastructure.

Third, MR empowers the user to detect and respond to cyber threats in real time. By providing operators with a simulated view of the plant, MR can identify and respond to anomalies or suspicious activity that may indicate a cyberattack. Since surveillance can be a time-consuming task, and because detecting the cause of any problems in complex industrial system is difficult, operators can administer their systems more efficiently.

One of the main advantages of mixed over virtual reality is that MR allows operators to interact with the physical environment, while it still provides them with

---

S. Shrivastava (✉) · A. P. Mathur
iTrust Center for Research in Cyber Security, Singapore University of Technology and Design, Singapore, Singapore
e-mail: shrivastava_siddhant@sutd.edu.sg

A. P. Mathur
e-mail: aditya_mathur@sutd.edu.sg

M. M. Keupp (ed.), *Cyberdefense*, International Series in Operations Research & Management Science 342,
https://doi.org/10.1007/978-3-031-30191-9_13

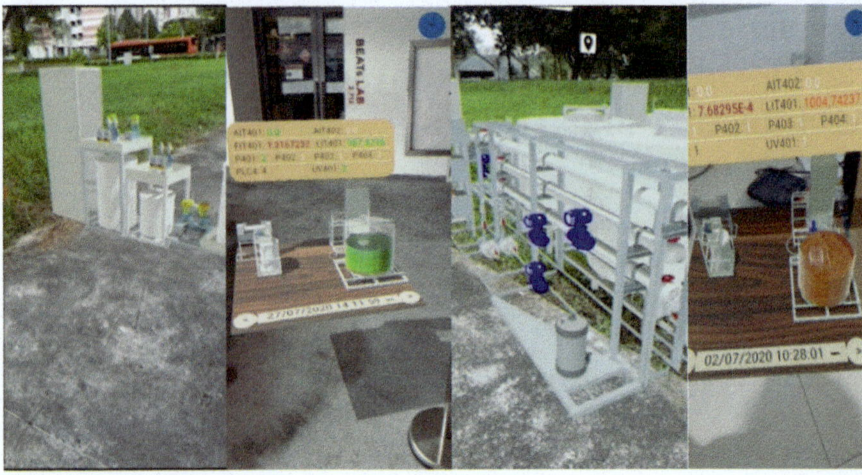

Fig. 13.1 Interaction of physical and virtual layer in PlantXR

virtual information. This can be especially beneficial in industrial control systems where operators need to physically manipulate equipment while they receive real-time data and instructions.

We exploited this property to design *PlantXR*, a virtual, three-dimensional world that lets operators visualize cyber-physical systems [12]. The system lets operators virtually overlay the physical environment with real-time data, so that they can identify problems and resolve them quickly. Figure 13.1 illustrates how the operator sees the virtual and physical layer simultaneously.

PlantXR can be used in plant design, simulation, training, monitoring, and forensic investigation. It intends to enhance the cyber-physical security and safety of industrial control systems by integrating both spatial and numerical information. PlantXR displays both seamlessly, providing operators with a more holistic view of the plant, and it lets them explore different scenarios in a safe and reproducible environment. Figure 13.2 shows how an operator can virtually walk the plant.

Users can access PlantXR by using an Oculus Rift headset, a handheld device, or a desktop computer. Operators can roam the plant and interact with virtually displayed information and control panels. For example, an operator can virtually blend in data streams while physically walking the plant's control systems and use MR to visually highlight any unusual activity or deviations from normal operating parameters. PlantXR is also connected to the physical plant in real time, so the plant can be operated remotely.

We implemented this prototype in the experimental water treatment facility *SWaT* which serves to simulate such plants. It replicates an industrial water processing

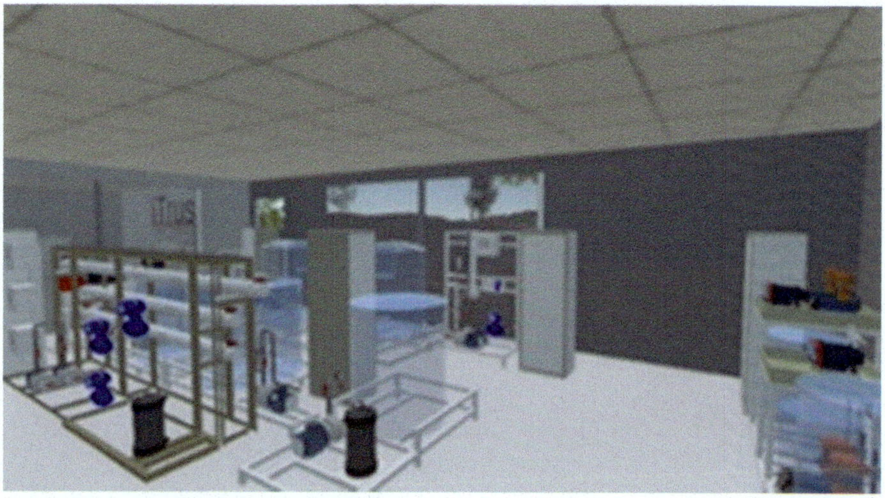

Fig. 13.2 Virtual operator walk

plant in which operators must monitor a large number of parameters, such as pH or chlorine levels, turbidity, reverse osmosis, or desalination.[1]

PlantXR can assist operators with detecting and responding to cyber threats before these cause significant damage. Furthermore, it can be used to conduct regular security audits. Figure 13.3 shows how interconnected and virtualized testbeds empower operators to explore cascading attacks that span multiple sections of the plant.

PlantXR demonstrates how operators can tap into the technological potential of MR to quickly identify and respond to potential hazards or cyber threats without the need to switch between different monitoring systems. For example, in an industrial plant, an operator could use MR to overlay real-time data on top of the physical plant, highlighting any unusual activity or deviations from normal operation. This can help detect and respond to cyber threats before they can cause significant damage.

However, MR also has some disadvantages. One of the main challenges is the cost and complexity of implementing MR systems. Developing and maintaining MR systems can be costly, and it requires specialized equipment and trained personnel. Additionally, the technology is still relatively new, and there is a lack of standardization in the industry, which can make it difficult for different systems to communicate and work together. Another disadvantage is the fact that MR technology relies on a high degree of accuracy and precision, which can be affected by environmental factors such as lighting and reflections. This can make it difficult to maintain a stable and consistent MR experience, which can impact the effectiveness of the system.

While we are aware of these problems, we suggest that international cyber-physical exercises are recognizing the role that mixed reality can play in future

[1] This facility is located with the iTrust Center for Research in Cyber Security at the Singapore University of Technology and Design. Its technical structure is explained in detail by [9, 12].

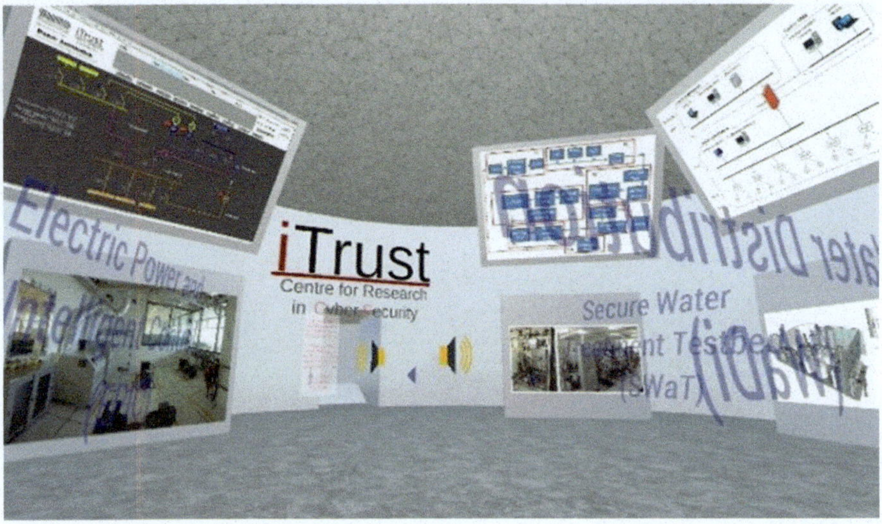

Fig. 13.3 Interconnectedness of testbeds in PlantXR

defense efforts. These cyber defence exercises comprise red, blue, green, and purple teaming. They can be instrumental in improving the preparedness of governments, industries, and academia to protect against and respond to cyber-physical attacks on critical infrastructures. Furthermore, these exercises can also train staff members to appropriately react to attacks [11, 12].

Red teaming is a simulation of an adversarial attack, where a team of experts acts as an attacker to test the security of an organization. The goal of red teaming is to identify vulnerabilities and weaknesses in the organization's systems, processes, and procedures, and to develop strategies to mitigate and respond to potential threats. For example, a government agency can use red teaming to simulate a cyberattack on a critical infrastructure such as a power grid, and to test the effectiveness of their incident response plans.

Blue teaming, also known as defensive teaming, involves simulating a cyber incident, and testing the organization's ability to detect and respond to the attack. The goal of blue teaming is to identify and address any gaps in the organization's incident response plans and procedures. For example, a power company can use blue teaming to test its ability to detect and respond to a cyberattack on their control systems.

Green teaming is a simulation of a cyber-physical incident, where a team of experts simulates both attackers and defenders to test the security of an organization. The goal of green teaming is to identify vulnerabilities and weaknesses in the organization's systems, processes, and procedures, and to develop strategies to mitigate and respond to potential threats. For example, a transportation company can use green teaming to simulate a cyberattack on a train control system and test the effectiveness of their incident response plans.

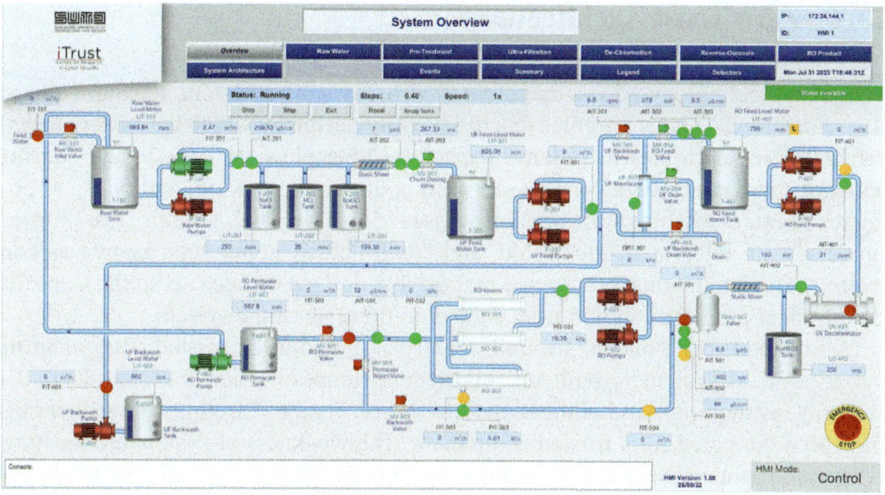

Fig. 13.4 Human-machine interface of digital twin water treatment plant

Purple teaming refers to the combination of Red and Blue teaming, where the Red team simulates an attack and the Blue team defends against it. This approach allows the organization to identify vulnerabilities, improve incident response, and also to train the staff on how to detect and respond to a cyberattack.

These exercises can be further enhanced by mixed reality technology. For example, by using virtual reality simulations, operators can practice how to handle emergency situations in a safe and controlled environment. Thus, they can reduce the risk of human error and improve emergency response times in real-life situations. Additionally, MR can also be used to conduct regular security audits and penetration testing, allowing organizations to identify and address vulnerabilities before they can be exploited by attackers. The 2022 NATO exercise *Locked Shields* already uses such intricate simulation and training infrastructures. It brings together international teams whose members must defend realistic simulations of cyber-physical incidents in real time [15].

Since 2010, it has been organized annually by the NATO Cooperative Cyber Defence Centre of Excellence. Over the recent years, the exercise has embraced the use of digital twins of a water treatment plant as an attack and defense target. Figure 13.4 shows the human-machine interface that we used for the digital twin of a water treatment plant in both Locked Shields and other exercises. The next logical step would be to virtualize the experience with MR, so that participants could interact on a more advanced technological level [2, 7].

13.2 Zero Trust Architectures

While MR technology allows operators to virtually walk a system, it cannot change its architecture. This fact implies that the security design by which the system is built critically co-determines its defense capacity. Cyber-physical systems use sensors, actuators, and controllers connected via computing, networking, and physical processes to interact with entities and processes in the physical domain. The physical processes are integrated, monitored, and controlled by computers, known as controllers. The intelligence programed in the cyber domain decides about the steps that the physical processes should take, subject to the state of the system.

All of these components are traditionally assumed to be trusted. But when the cyber-physical system is built on this trust assumption, then the confidentiality, integrity, availability, and authenticity can all be compromised once attackers can pass off a tampered for a trusted component. The weakness of system architectures which are based on trusted devices became clear during the 2015 attacks against the Ukrainian power system.

A professionally executed attack led to a blackout in several regions of Ukraine which affected approximately 225,000 households. The primary targets of the attack were Windows-based machines that were used in the plant network as HMIs and to manage power administration. The power circuit breakers for the regional substations were affected directly by remote access to the HMI. The breakers were remotely opened in a number of affected substations. The SCADA system was remotely controlled by a remote user with *administrator* privileges. The UPS was configured to remain switched off even in the case of a power cut. The call center service was disrupted due to a telephonic denial-of-service effort by the attackers on the power company's call center. That further delayed the time it took to estimate the scope of the attack, in terms of affected regions and people. The `BlackEnergy3` malware and a modified `Dropbear SSH` server were used for C&C operations. The `KillDisk` component of `BlackEnergy3` enabled the master boot record wipeout which made it impossible for systems to be restored without manual intervention.[2]

This attack highlighted the security flaws that exist in conventional industrial control systems. The attack consumed much fewer resources than other malware-based attacks since it exploited the legitimate features of the system, such as macros in Microsoft Office products, rather than any zero-day vulnerabilities. The VPNs lacked two-factor authentication. The firewall configuration made it possible for the attackers to remotely control the environment by using a Dropbear SSH client that connected to the affected computers. There were no active network security monitoring tools in place. We therefore believe that a cyber-physical system is not secure unless its elements are designed to interact in a trustless manner with each other. Thus, we advocate that a zero trust architecture can increase the effectiveness of the cyberdefense of industrial control systems.

[2] More detailed evidence of `BlackEnergy` operations against industrial control systems is available in ICS-ALERT-14-281-01.

Under a zero trust security architecture, all users, devices, and networks are not trusted by default but instead are identified and authenticated before any access is granted. While zero trust has been widely adopted in traditional IT environments, its application in cyber-physical systems and critical infrastructures has received less attention.[3] This can be achieved by implementing secure authentication methods such as multi-factor authentication and identity management. Additionally, operators can use network segmentation and micro-segmentation to subdivide any industrial control system into smaller, isolated networks that are more difficult for attackers to access. Finally, since unauthorized access is displayed, but not granted, operators can better audit their networks and respond quickly to mitigate intrusion attempts.

We believe that a zero trust architecture can be applied to industrial control systems. For example, any communication to and from a PLC would have to be authenticated, authorized, and validated. For operators of SCADA systems, applying zero trust implies that they are able to perform actions only when authorized and authenticated in multiple ways (e.g., by using multi-factor authentication). A zero trust design can therefore prevent different classes of cyber-physical attacks on cyber-physical systems, and particularly so on critical infrastructures: it forbids unauthorized access to control elements by designing systems with strong security controls, it prevents unauthorized users from gaining access to the system, and it prevents malware or other malicious software from infiltrating CIs by designing systems with robust security controls, such as firewalls, antivirus software, and intrusion detection systems, It impedes prevent denial-of-service attacks by designing systems with redundant components and backup systems to ensure that the system remains operational even if one component fails or is attacked. It thwarts unauthorized changes to control elements by designing systems with robust change management processes and controls, such as version control and rollback capabilities, to ensure that only authorized changes are made to the system. Finally, it negates any unauthorized exfiltration of data by designing systems with strong data protection controls, such as encryption and access controls.

However, implementing zero trust in cyber-physical systems can be challenging due to the complexity of these systems and the difficulty of verifying the trustworthiness of devices and users with currently available tooling. Despite these problems, recent academic work stresses the role zero trust architectures can play to effectively protect industrial control systems (e.g., [4, 8]), as do network security analysts (e.g., [3, 6]).

[3] For an introduction and discussion about the benefits and problems of a zero trust architecture, see Rose et al. [10] and Buck et al. [5].

13.3 Automated Defense

Finally, we advocate that automated protection systems (APS) can address the inadequacies of current anomaly detectors against ransomware attacks and modern time-sensitive attacks, but also the delay with which humans can respond to such attacks. Existing detection and analysis tools can alarm operators about detected threats, but operators may fail to respond adequately. Delays due to human error may cause service disruptions or damage to physical components. Many attacks also happen faster than operators can respond, so that the impact is felt before operators note that IT or OT components have been attacked.

In such situations, APS can rapidly detect and respond to anomalies without the need for human intervention [1, 12]. An automatic defense mechanism depends on a pervasive, orthogonal detection mechanism that is resilient to cyberattacks at multiple layers of the plant (network, computation, power). Such an APS should empower operators to maintain visibility into system operations during an attack, and guarantee that even if attackers can access plant controls, they cannot cause damage to plant components. It is important to note that such an APS is different from emergency plant control mechanisms which are designed to protect the facility and its personnel, and also from failsafe or hot standby mechanisms which ensure the continued operation of a facility once a failure or malfunction occurs (e.g., by activating backup generators or redundant equipment).

In the SWaT testbed described in Sect. 13.1, each of the six water processing stages is controlled by its own set of dual PLCs, one serving as a primary and the other as a backup in case of any failure of the primary. Each PLC obtains data from sensors associated with the corresponding stage and controls pumps and valves in its domain. Level sensors in each tank inform the PLCs when to turn a pump on or off. Several other sensors are available to check the physical and chemical properties of water flowing through the six stages. PLCs communicate with each other through a separate network. Communications among sensors, actuators, and PLCs can happen by either wired or wireless links, and manually operated switches control the status changes from wired to wireless and vice versa.

Simulating a popular cyber-physical attack on this infrastructure, we studied the extent to which an APS could be applied to and provide effective defense for an industrial control system [13, 14]. We followed a 'security by design' philosophy to design a defence system, trying to understand how an attacker would execute an attack on a given cyber-physical structure [1]. This APS offers visibility into operations when the plant is under attack, and it provides protection against rogue commands channeled to plant components. A prototype of this APS has been successfully tested in a cyber-physical exercise and is currently being extended for bidirectional plant control in a live-fire exercise in 2023 [12].

Acknowledgements This work is supported (in part) by the National Research Foundation, Singapore and the Cyber Security Agency of Singapore under its National Cybersecurity R&D Program (NRF2018NCRNSOE005-0001). Any opinions, findings and conclusions, or recommendations expressed in this material are those of the author(s) and do not reflect the views of National Research Foundation, Singapore or the Cyber Security Agency of Singapore.

References

1. Adepu, S., & Mathur, A. (2021). SafeCI: Avoiding process anomalies in critical infrastructure. *International Journal of Critical Infrastructure Protection, 34*, 100435.
2. Adepu, S., & Mathur, A. (2016). Introducing cyber security at the design stage of public infrastructures: A procedure and case study. In M. Cardin, S. Fong, D. Krob, P. Lui, Y. Tan (Eds.), *Complex Systems Design & Management Asia*. Advances in Intelligent Systems and Computing (Vol. 426, pp. 75–94). Cham: Springer.
3. Airgap Corp. (2021). Zero trust isolation: Solution brief. https://airgap.io/blog/zero-trust-network-isolation-for-industrial-control-systems.
4. Alagappan, A., Venkatachary, S. K., & Andrews, L. (2022). Augmenting zero trust network architecture to enhance security in virtual power plants. *Energy Reports, 8*, 1309–1320.
5. Buck, C., Olenberger, C., Schweizer, A., Völter, F., & Eymann, T. (2021). Never trust, always verify: A multivocal literature review on current knowledge and research gaps of zero-trust. *Computers & Security, 110*, 102436.
6. Delinea Corp. (2023). Zero trust for ICS/SCADA systems. https://delinea.com/blog/zero-trust-for-ics-scada-systems.
7. Goh, J., Adepu, S., Junejo, K. N., & Mathur, A. (2017). A dataset to support research in the design of secure water treatment systems. In G. Havarneanu, R. Setola, H. Nassopoulos, & S. Wolthusen (Eds.), *Critical information infrastructures security* (pp. 88–99). Berlin, Heidelberg: Springer LNCS.
8. Køien, G. M. (2021). Zero-trust principles for legacy components. *Wireless Personal Communications, 121*, 1169–1186.
9. Mathur, A., & Tippenhauer, N. (2016). SWaT: A water treatment testbed for research and training on ICS security. In *Proceedings of the 2016 International Workshop on Cyber-physical Systems for Smart Water Networks (CySWater)* (pp. 31–36).
10. Rose, S., Borchert, O., Mitchell, S., & Connelly, S. (2020). Zero trust architecture. NIST Special Publication 800-207, U.S. Department of Commerce: National Institute of Standards and Technology.
11. Seker, E., & Ozbenli, H. (2018). The concept of cyber defence exercises (cdx): Planning, execution, evaluation. In *Proceedings of the 2018 IEEE International Conference on Cyber Security and Protection of Digital Services (Cyber Security)* (pp. 1–9).
12. Shrivastava, S., Furtado, F., Goh, M., & Mathur, A. (2022). The design of cyber-physical exercises (CPXS). In *Proceedings of the 14th International Conference on Cyber Conflict: Keep Moving!(CyCon)* (pp. 347–365).
13. Shrivastava, S., Adepu, S., & Mathur, A. (2018). Design and assessment of an orthogonal defense mechanism for a water treatment facility. *Robotics and Autonomous Systems, 101*, 114–125.
14. Shrivastava, S., Kurniawan, O., & Sockalingam, N. (2022). Extended reality for enhanced learning beyond the classroom: Three pandemic-proof prototypes. *Proceedings of the International Conference on Best Innovative Teaching Strategies (ICON BITS), 2021*, 309–313.
15. Smeets, M. (2022). The role of military cyber exercises: A case study of locked shields. In *Proceedings of the 14th IEEE International Conference on Cyber Conflict: Keep Moving!(CyCon)* (pp. 9–25).

Siddhant Shrivastava researches and develops emerging technologies at the iTrust Centre for Research in Cybersecurity at the Singapore University of Technology and Design with a focus on securing ritical nfrastructures, conducting cyber-physical exercises, training, mentorship, and building defence systems. He has previously worked on space applications with the Indian Space Research Organization and the Mars Society, design with MIT Media Lab, robotics (Google Summer of Code) and finance (Goldman Sachs).

Aditya Mathur is the iTrust Center Director at Singapore University of Technology and Design. He manages a 50+ group of researchers in cyber security and has led the design and operationalization of three fully operational research testbeds for water treatment, water distribution, and power generation, transmission, and distribution. Aditya is a co-inventor of Distributed Attack Detection (DAD) that makes use of invariants derived from plant design for detecting anomalies in process behavior that may arise due to cyber or physical attacks.

Chapter 14
Improving the Effectiveness of Cyberdefense Measures

Sébastien Gillard and Cédric Aeschlimann

14.1 Introduction

Administrators, users, and artificial intelligence in a computer network can exchange indicators of compromise (IoCs) which inform about threats, vulnerabilities, or exploits. Thus, these experts can benefit from mutually shared experience and information to organize cyberdefense [12, 19].

Although users and machines generate IoCs when an attack occurs, the information they convey lacks order and completeness unless relations and dependencies between IoCs are detected. Information recombination and integration are therefore key to the creation of effective knowledge [2, 9]. Thus, the better defenders can combine different IoC into a more complete picture, explaining linkages and networks between them, the more accurately they can analyze the threat.

While some threat information sharing platforms may be able to auto link novel with extant content (e.g., by auto-completion), they scarcely consider all relevant information criteria [11]. At the same time, the manual recombination of such information by human agents is probably excessive in terms of both time, transaction cost, and the odds of errors.

We therefore propose an automated model that can provide defenders with this integrated information, so that their cyberdefense efforts become more effective. It automatically generates a network of all IoCs and identifies and clusters similarities. It considers all available features in the data structure to collocate new with extant IoCs according to relevance and centrality.

Supplementary Information The online version contains supplementary material available at https://doi.org/10.1007/978-3-031-30191-9_14.

S. Gillard (✉) · C. Aeschlimann
Department of Defense Economics, Military Academy at the Swiss Federal Institute of Technology Zurich, Birmensdorf, Switzerland
e-mail: sebastien.gillard@vtg.admin.ch

C. Aeschlimann
e-mail: cedric.aeschlimann@vtg.admin.ch

M. M. Keupp (ed.), *Cyberdefense*, International Series in Operations Research & Management Science 342,
https://doi.org/10.1007/978-3-031-30191-9_14

14.2 Model

We consider the setting of a platform where users can submit IoCs. Every single IoC has a number of features, i.e., specific fields that record string (e.g., plain text), boolean (e.g., "true" or "false"), or numeric information about threats. Let $\mathcal{C}$ define the finite set of available characters, i.e., all letters, numbers, and non-reserved characters that users can employ to report an IoC.[1] Let $\mathcal{X}$ denote the set of all strings of length N produced with characters in $\mathcal{C}$, where $N \in \mathbb{N}_{<\infty}$.

Each IoC conveys both text, boolean and numerical information, each of which corresponds to a peculiar function of the finite set of functions $\mathcal{F}$ which refers to these different types of information. A specific function f_γ then corresponds to one of these types which contains N characters, so the specific set is given by

$$c_\alpha = (c_{\alpha,1}, \ldots, c_{\alpha,i}, \ldots, c_{\alpha,N}), \quad \text{where } \alpha \in \mathcal{C} \text{ and } i < N \tag{14.1}$$

With Eq. (14.1), the string of characters can be expressed as

$$x_\beta = (c^\beta_{\alpha,1} \cdots c^\beta_{\alpha,i} \cdots c^\beta_{\alpha,N}), \quad \text{where } \beta \in \mathcal{X} \tag{14.2}$$

Applying the function f_γ to the string in Eq. (14.2) then yields

$$f_\gamma(x_\beta) = \{c^\beta_{\alpha,1} \cdots c^\beta_{\alpha,i} \cdots c^\beta_{\alpha,N}\}, \quad \text{where } \gamma \in \mathcal{F} \tag{14.3}$$

With Eq. (14.3), the full set $\mathcal{D}$ that comprises all IoCs which populate the platform can be described. Then, a matrix **P** can be derived that contains all information stored on the platform. By using cardinalities which describe the size of a finite set $\in \mathbb{N}_{<\infty}$, we can write $D = \text{Card}(\mathcal{D})$ and $F = \text{Card}(\mathcal{F})$ and obtain

$$P = (f_{k,l}(x_{k,l}))_{k \in [1,D], l \in [1,F]} = \begin{bmatrix} f_{1,1}(x_{1,1}) & \ldots & f_{1,l}(x_{1,l}) & \ldots & f_{1,F}(x_{1,F}) \\ \vdots & \ddots & \vdots & \ddots & \vdots \\ f_{k,1}(x_{k,1}) & \ldots & f_{k,l}(x_{k,l}) & \ldots & f_{k,F}(x_{k,F}) \\ \vdots & \ddots & \vdots & \ddots & \vdots \\ f_{D,1}(x_{D,1}) & \ldots & f_{D,l}(x_{D,l}) & \ldots & f_{D,F}(x_{D,F}) \end{bmatrix} \tag{14.4}$$

[1] For example, a code syntax could require strings to be opened and closed by the brackets "{" and "}", so that these reserved characters would have to be filtered.

14.2.1 Sequence Matching Procedure

We now introduce an algorithm that allows us to compare these strings and to identify the extent to which they are similar or related. Once these relations are known, cluster and network analysis can be applied to group and discover relations between them. Our algorithm is based on prior research in the field of natural language processing [7].

The algorithm attempts to find the longest substring which is common to two strings and does not contain unwanted artifacts. It was implemented with the Python `sklearn` and `scikit` libraries. In a first step, the strings of characters are cleaned from spaces and punctuation symbols, and upper are transformed to lower cases. The following example shows how the algorithm identifies matching substrings. Consider two strings of characters $x_1 = (c^1_{\alpha,1} \cdots c^1_{\alpha,i} \cdots c^1_{\alpha,n})$ and $x_2 = (c^2_{\alpha,1} \cdots c^2_{\alpha,j} \cdots c^2_{\alpha,m})$, where $n, m \in [0, N]$, $i \in [1, n]$ and $j \in [1, m]$. We extend the notation from Eq. (14.2) for these two strings as follows:

$$
\begin{aligned}
x_1 &= \left(\overbrace{c^{\star}_{\alpha,1} c^{\star}_{\alpha,2}}^{1} \, c^1_{\alpha,3} \, \overbrace{c^{\circ}_{\alpha,5} c^{\circ}_{\alpha,6}}^{2} \cdots c^1_{\alpha,i} \cdots c^1_{\alpha,n} \right) \\
x_2 &= \left(c^2_{\alpha,1} \, \underbrace{c^{\star}_{\alpha,1} c^{\star}_{\alpha,2}}_{1} \, c^2_{\alpha,4} c^2_{\alpha,5} \, \underbrace{c^{\circ}_{\alpha,5} c^{\circ}_{\alpha,6}}_{2} \cdots c^1_{\alpha,i} \cdots c^1_{\alpha,m} \right)
\end{aligned}
\tag{14.5}
$$

where the superscripts $\star$ and $\circ$ represent matching substrings. There are $\mathcal{M} = 2 \cdot 2 = 4$ matches.

The algorithm works the sequence according to which the strings are ordered, so that the comparison of x_1 with x_2 is not identical to the comparison of x_2 with x_1. It scans each string from left to right and attempts to identify every possible match between a character in a given string and all occurrences of this character in subsequent strings. If a match is found, another character is added to the left of the original string, and the search is performed again. This recursive procedure runs until the longest common substring has been found.

The similarity score $\varrho \in [0, 1]$ then captures the relatedness of two strings x_1 of length n and x_2 of length m between which $\mathcal{M}$ substring matches are found:

$$
\varrho = \frac{2 \cdot \mathcal{M}}{(n + m)}
\tag{14.6}
$$

where the factor of 2 in the numerator suggests that the obtained matches appear in the two strings, while the denominator gives the total number of characters across the two strings. We assume that $\varrho \geq 0.8$ suggests the strings are similar.

The algorithm computes these similarity scores for all IoCs in the matrix $\mathbf{P}$, so that it generates a score matrix $\mathcal{S}_l = (\varrho_{p,q})_{p,q \in [1,D]}$ of size $D \times D$ for the l-th field (i.e., column of the matrix **P**), where $l \in [1, F]$ and $\varrho_{p,q} \in [0, 1]$. Then, each selected column provides a corresponding score matrix. We will subsequently use these scores to inform the network analysis featured in Sect. 14.2.3.

14.2.2 Clustering Method

Cluster analysis is useful when one wants to identify features by which elements in a dataset are related [13]. Since the data we analyze has both features with different (text, boolean, numeric) values and requires manipulation such as cleaning, transformation, and labeling, we use a random forest classifier (RFC). This supervised learning method is advantageous when one wants to solve classification problems in big datasets [8]. It categorizes data in a forest of decision trees where each tree predicts a class. Moreover, analysts can define the relative importance of each classification variable (in our case, the columns of the matrix **P**) should have [5].

We set one of the columns in the matrix **P** as our target (explained) variable w whose variation is to be explained by the set of explanatory variables K which comprises all other columns. The subsequent discussion of our method does not depend on which column is selected as the explained variable.

The RFC partitions the matrix **P** into a training set A (67% of the initial dataset) and a test set B (33%) in which it also inserts randomness. Before it can run, all categorical must be transformed into ordinal variables, and both the number of trees T and their maximum depth δ must be specified. We use the training set A to generate T, while the test set B is used to evaluate the performance of the predictions.

Let $a_i \in A$ denominate training vectors from the training dataset, with $i \in [1, D]$. The vector $y = [1, \cdots, F]$ represents the features of the dataset. We designate the quantity of data at node k as Q_k which is composed by a number of samples q_k.

At each node, there is a possibility $\Theta = (\gamma, \zeta_k)$, where $\gamma \in y$ and ζ_k is a chosen threshold, that Q_k splits into two child sets:

$$Q_k^{\leftarrow}(\Theta) = \{(a, y) \mid a_\gamma \leq \zeta_k\} \tag{14.7}$$

$$Q_k^{\rightarrow}(\Theta) = Q_k \backslash Q_k^{\leftarrow}(\Theta) \tag{14.8}$$

With these subsets, the function that evaluates the splitting can be written as

$$G(Q_k, \Theta) = \frac{q_k^{\leftarrow}}{q_k}\Omega(Q_k^{\leftarrow}(\Theta)) + \frac{q_k^{\rightarrow}}{q_k}\Omega(Q_k^{\rightarrow}(\Theta)) \tag{14.9}$$

In Eq. (14.9), Ω_k is the Gini impurity:

$$\Omega(Q_k) = \sum_{\sigma=1}^{U} \nu_\sigma^k (1 - \nu_\sigma^k) \tag{14.10}$$

where ν_σ^k is the frequency of label σ at node k and U is the number of unique labels. To define the split, we seek the optimal parameter that minimizes $G(Q_k, \Theta)$:

$$\Theta^\star = \text{argmin}_\Theta G(Q_k, \Theta) \tag{14.11}$$

This algorithm is iterated until the maximum depth δ is reached or $q_k = 1$. Once the RFC has generated a tree, the significance of a node η_k with $k \in [1, D]$ can be expressed by using binary trees for two child nodes:

$$\eta_k = \lambda_k \Omega_j - \lambda_k^{\leftarrow} \Omega_k^{\leftarrow} - \lambda_k^{\rightarrow} \Omega_k^{\rightarrow} \tag{14.12}$$

where λ_k is the weighted number of samples reaching node k, Ω_k is the Gini impurity of node k, $\lambda_k^{\leftarrow}$ and $\lambda_k^{\rightarrow}$ are the weighted numbers of samples which reach the left or right child nodes from node k, and $\Omega_k^{\leftarrow}$ and $\Omega_k^{\rightarrow}$ are the Gini impurity values for the child nodes to the left or right of node k. With Eq. (14.12), we can now compute the importance $\mathcal{I}_l$ that each feature l has in the decision tree:

$$\mathcal{I}_l = \frac{\sum_{k=1}^{\theta_l} \eta_k}{\sum_{l=1}^{F} \sum_{k=1}^{\theta_l} \eta_k} \tag{14.13}$$

The numerator in Eq. (14.13) represents the number of node splits θ_l over the features l, while the denominator is the sum of all such node splits over all features. Finally, the importance $\mathcal{I}_l$ can be conditioned on values between 0 and 1:

$$\tilde{\mathcal{I}}_l = \frac{\mathcal{I}_l}{\sum_{l=1}^{F} \mathcal{I}_l} \tag{14.14}$$

Since Eq. (14.14) gives the result for one tree only, we compute the mean over all trees $\mathcal{T}$ the RFC produces:

$$\text{RF}_l = \frac{\sum_{\tau=1}^{\mathcal{T}} \tilde{\mathcal{I}}_{l,\tau}}{\mathcal{T}} \tag{14.15}$$

The results from Eq. (14.15) now allow us to determine which features explain most of the variation in the target variable w, so that we can rank them. Finally, we assess the accuracy of the classification by computing precision, recall, and F scores. Further, results can be classified in a confusion matrix to measure the accuracy of the prediction and to identify false positives and false negatives [14].

To define the precision of the classifier, we apply the classification with our test set B to obtain the associated predicted values for $\widehat{b}_j$. We then compare these to the real features $b_j \in B$. The precision score is then given by the ratio $\Gamma_P \in [0, 1]$ of correct predictions and all elements in the test set B.

The recall score $\Gamma_R \in [0, 1]$ gives the ratio of elements in a feature $\widehat{r}_\gamma$ that the classifier identified correctly and the total number of elements of this feature. It is computed as the average over all chosen features in the dataset. With both values Γ_P

and Γ_R, we can also compute the F-Score to measure the accuracy and performance of the algorithm:

$$\text{F-Score} = 2 \cdot \frac{\Gamma_P \cdot \Gamma_R}{\Gamma_P + \Gamma_R}. \tag{14.16}$$

14.2.3 Network Analysis

Networks can be conceived of as a set of nodes connected by edges. Even in large networks, each node is separated from every other node only by a short path, and cluster analysis can identify areas with similar relationships or content [3, 4, 17, 20]. We exploit these properties to model the extent to which IoCs are structurally related.

We model IoCs as nodes, and we compute a global similarity matrix $\mathcal{S}_G$ to define the edges that connect them. We first choose the features $\gamma^\star \in \mathcal{F}^\star$ which, according to Eq. (14.15), contribute most to explaining the variance of the target variable w.

If these features are sequences of characters, the sequence matching procedure is applied to compute similarity ratios $\varrho_{p,q}^{\gamma^\star}$ according to Eq. (14.6) for each possible pair of IoCs. If the features are numerical, boolean, or a strict sequence of characters, these similarity ratios are dichotomous, so $\varrho_{p,q}^{\gamma^\star} = 1$ if two pairwise compared IoCs are similar, and $\varrho_{p,q}^{\gamma^\star} = 0$ otherwise.

All similarity scores are recorded in the similarity matrix $\mathcal{S}_\star$, from which the global similarity matrix $\mathcal{S}_G$ can be written as

$$\mathcal{S}_G = \sum_{\gamma^\star=1}^{F^\star} \mathcal{S}_{\gamma^\star} = (\varrho_{p,q}^{G})_{p,q\in[1,D]} \tag{14.17}$$

where $F^\star = \text{Card}(\mathcal{F}^\star)$. The non-zero elements $(\varrho_{p,q}^{G})$ of $\mathcal{S}_G$ represent the weights of the edges. Since these edges are not yet directed and unidirectional, we order all IoCs from oldest to most recent and only keep those edges from older to more recent IoCs. This operation yields the following upper triangular matrix from which the directed and weighted network can be created:

$$\widehat{\mathcal{S}_G} = \begin{bmatrix} 0 \dots & \varrho_{1,q} & \dots & \varrho_{1,D} \\ \vdots \ddots & \vdots & \ddots & \vdots \\ 0 \dots & 0 & \dots & \varrho_{p,D} \\ \vdots \ddots & \vdots & \ddots & \vdots \\ 0 \dots & 0 & \dots & 0 \end{bmatrix} \tag{14.18}$$

Our model computes the distance between nodes relative to their similarity, so IoCs similarity is negatively associated with path length. In unweighted networks, distance is simply the minimal sum of edges required to travel from a given to a focal node. However, since the edges in our network are weighted according to their strength, we first inverse the weights and then apply Dijkstra's algorithm. The shortest path between two nodes in our network then is

$$d^{\omega}(i, j) = \min(\frac{1}{\omega_{ih}} + \cdots + \frac{1}{\omega_{hj}}) \tag{14.19}$$

where ω is the weighted adjacency matrix of a node, i is the focal node, j represents every other node, and h represents intervening nodes on the path between i and j [15].

When Eq. (14.19) is applied to every node in the network, a distance matrix **D** can be created which contains the weight of the shortest path between every pair of nodes. This matrix allows us to find IoCs which are closest and hence most similar to the focal node:

$$D = \begin{bmatrix} d^{\omega}(1, 1) & \ldots & d^{\omega}(1, j) \\ \vdots & \ddots & \vdots \\ d^{\omega}(i, 1) & \ldots & d^{\omega}(i, j) \end{bmatrix} \tag{14.20}$$

We also examine the centrality of a node in the network. Nodes with high betweenness centrality are more likely to be situated on the shortest path between two nodes, and thus they are more likely to be influential. With Eq. (14.19), we adapt the definition of betweenness centrality $C_B(i)$ originally introduced by Freeman (1978) for a weighted network:

$$C_B^{\omega}(i) = \frac{g_{jk}^{\omega}(i)}{g_{jk}^{\omega}} \tag{14.21}$$

where g_{jk}^{ω} is the number of weighted shortest paths between nodes j and k, and $g_{jk}^{\omega}(i)$ is the number of those weighted paths that pass through node i.

Finally, we compare the influence a node has in the network by computing PageRank centrality scores [16]. This measure awards a score to each node i based on its incoming edges which are weighted according to the score of the originating nodes:

$$PR(i) = \frac{1-d}{N} + d \sum_{j \in in(i)}^{N} \frac{PR(j)}{|out(j)|} \tag{14.22}$$

where N is the number of nodes in the network, d is a constant dampening factor, $in(i)$ are incoming links which connect to i, and $|out(j)|$ is the number of outgoing links from j. Hence, nodes with a large amount of incoming links are considered influential, and they share that influence with nodes to which they are connected. We exploit this property to discover those nodes whose influence stretches beyond their immediate neighbors. When these metrics are applied, we recommend to use statistical tests, in particular Spearman's ϱ, to analyze the congruence of the results across different indicators.

14.3 Worked Example

We illustrate the model with a random dataset we created. Note that this example of merely ten IoCs is purely illustrative and does not claim any statistical validity. Negligible elements were removed and all letters were changed to lower case prior to analysis. Table 14.1 details the dataset.

Table 14.1 Dataset for illustration

IoC #	IoC type	Boolean characteristic	Numerical characteristic	String characteristic	Timestamp
1	sha256	1	8781	loremipsum	1672527601
2	filename	1	8761	loremipsumdolor	1672614001
3	domain	0	2121	loremipsumamet	1672834152
4	hostname	1	1092	loremipsumsitamet	1674295238
5	hostname	0	2120	loremipsumxyz	1672587412
6	sha256	1	2128	loremipsumdoloramet	1672954682
7	sha256	0	9579	kwxyzqv	1674289160
8	sha256	0	9115	consecteturadipiscingelit	1673579514
9	domain	0	9136	consecteturadipiscingdolor	1673698521
10	filename	1	3973	kwxyz	1672894578
11	filename	0	1979	xyzq	1673483296
12	sha1	0	3987	seddoeiusmodadispingelit	1674568685

We chose *timestamp* as the explained variable and ran the random forest classifier. Figure 14.1 shows the result. It suggests that *IoC type* and *string characteristic* are the most relevant features that define relations between IoCs.[2]

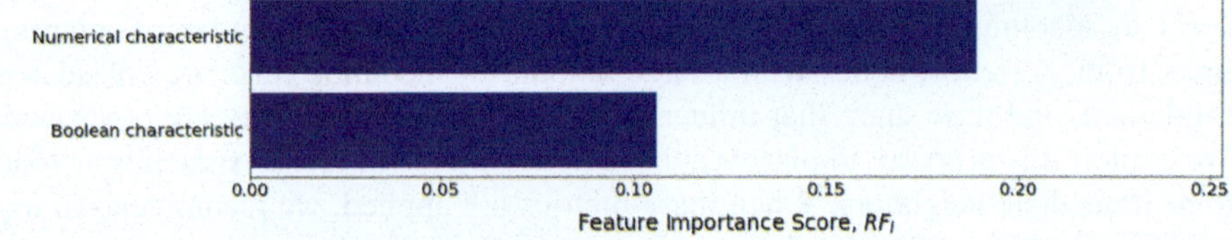

Fig. 14.1 Results for the feature importance score RF_I

[2] Note that we disregard the feature *IoC#* in the subsequent analysis since it is collinear to *timestamp*.

The feature *String characteristic* represents sequences of characters, so we applied the sequence matching procedure and obtained the similarity matrix $\mathcal{S}_{\text{String characteristic}}$:

$$\mathcal{S}_{\text{String characteristic}} = \begin{bmatrix} 1.00 & 0.87 & 0.80 & 0.83 & 0.00 & 0.69 & 0.00 & 0.29 & 0.17 & 0.00 & 0.74 & 0.12 \\ 0.87 & 1.00 & 0.71 & 0.74 & 0.33 & 0.62 & 0.35 & 0.26 & 0.15 & 0.30 & 0.67 & 0.11 \\ 0.80 & 0.71 & 1.00 & 0.69 & 0.00 & 0.88 & 0.00 & 0.30 & 0.49 & 0.00 & 0.62 & 0.21 \\ 0.83 & 0.74 & 0.69 & 1.00 & 0.00 & 0.85 & 0.00 & 0.36 & 0.15 & 0.00 & 0.90 & 0.16 \\ 0.00 & 0.33 & 0.00 & 0.00 & 1.00 & 0.00 & 0.67 & 0.00 & 0.00 & 0.83 & 0.00 & 0.00 \\ 0.87 & 1.00 & 0.71 & 0.74 & 0.33 & 0.62 & 0.35 & 0.26 & 0.15 & 0.30 & 0.67 & 0.11 \\ 0.69 & 0.62 & 0.88 & 0.85 & 0.00 & 1.00 & 0.00 & 0.32 & 0.44 & 0.00 & 0.78 & 0.23 \\ 0.00 & 0.35 & 0.00 & 0.00 & 0.67 & 0.00 & 1.00 & 0.00 & 0.00 & 0.73 & 0.00 & 0.00 \\ 0.29 & 0.26 & 0.30 & 0.21 & 0.00 & 0.18 & 0.00 & 1.00 & 0.86 & 0.00 & 0.24 & 0.61 \\ 0.17 & 0.15 & 0.49 & 0.15 & 0.00 & 0.44 & 0.00 & 0.86 & 1.00 & 0.00 & 0.14 & 0.48 \\ 0.00 & 0.30 & 0.00 & 0.00 & 0.83 & 0.00 & 0.73 & 0.00 & 0.00 & 1.00 & 0.00 & 0.00 \\ 0.74 & 0.67 & 0.62 & 0.90 & 0.00 & 0.78 & 0.00 & 0.33 & 0.14 & 0.00 & 1.00 & 0.15 \\ 0.18 & 0.16 & 0.21 & 0.16 & 0.00 & 0.23 & 0.00 & 0.61 & 0.48 & 0.00 & 0.24 & 1.00 \end{bmatrix}$$

Since the feature *IoC Type* is a strict sequence of characters, the sequence matching procedure need not be applied. If *IoC Type* is similar between two IoCs, then the corresponding matrix element in $\mathcal{S}_{\text{IoC Type}}$ takes the value 1, else it is zero. The comparison of all pairs of IoCs yields the following similarity matrix:

$$\mathcal{S}_{\text{IoC Type}} = \begin{bmatrix} 1.00 & 0.00 & 0.00 & 0.00 & 0.00 & 1.00 & 0.00 & 1.00 & 0.00 & 1.00 & 0.00 & 0.00 \\ 0.00 & 1.00 & 0.00 & 0.00 & 0.00 & 0.00 & 0.00 & 0.00 & 0.00 & 0.00 & 1.00 & 0.00 \\ 0.00 & 0.00 & 1.00 & 0.00 & 1.00 & 0.00 & 1.00 & 0.00 & 0.00 & 0.00 & 0.00 & 0.00 \\ 0.00 & 0.00 & 0.00 & 1.00 & 0.00 & 0.00 & 0.00 & 0.00 & 1.00 & 0.00 & 0.00 & 0.00 \\ 0.00 & 0.00 & 1.00 & 0.00 & 1.00 & 0.00 & 1.00 & 0.00 & 0.00 & 0.00 & 0.00 & 0.00 \\ 1.00 & 0.00 & 0.00 & 0.00 & 0.00 & 1.00 & 0.00 & 1.00 & 0.00 & 1.00 & 0.00 & 0.00 \\ 0.00 & 0.00 & 1.00 & 0.00 & 1.00 & 0.00 & 1.00 & 0.00 & 0.00 & 0.00 & 0.00 & 0.00 \\ 1.00 & 0.00 & 0.00 & 0.00 & 0.00 & 1.00 & 0.00 & 1.00 & 0.00 & 1.00 & 0.00 & 0.00 \\ 0.00 & 0.00 & 0.00 & 1.00 & 0.00 & 0.00 & 0.00 & 0.00 & 1.00 & 0.00 & 0.00 & 0.00 \\ 1.00 & 0.00 & 0.00 & 0.00 & 0.00 & 1.00 & 0.00 & 1.00 & 0.00 & 1.00 & 0.00 & 0.00 \\ 0.00 & 1.00 & 0.00 & 0.00 & 0.00 & 0.00 & 0.00 & 0.00 & 0.00 & 0.00 & 1.00 & 0.00 \\ 0.00 & 0.00 & 0.00 & 0.00 & 0.00 & 0.00 & 0.00 & 0.00 & 0.00 & 0.00 & 0.00 & 1.00 \end{bmatrix}$$

We then apply Eq. (14.17) to the two matrices $\mathcal{S}_{\text{String characteristic}}$ and $\mathcal{S}_{\text{IoC Type}}$ and order the IoCs, so that we can compute the 12×12 upper triangular matrix $\mathcal{S}_G$ according to Eq. (14.18):

$$\mathcal{S}_G = \begin{bmatrix} 0.00 & 0.87 & 0.80 & 0.83 & 0.00 & 1.69 & 0.00 & 1.29 & 0.17 & 1.00 & 0.74 & 0.12 \\ 0.00 & 0.00 & 0.71 & 0.74 & 0.33 & 0.62 & 0.35 & 0.26 & 0.15 & 0.30 & 1.67 & 0.11 \\ 0.00 & 0.00 & 0.00 & 0.69 & 1.00 & 0.88 & 1.00 & 0.30 & 0.49 & 0.00 & 0.62 & 0.21 \\ 0.00 & 0.00 & 0.00 & 0.00 & 0.00 & 0.85 & 0.00 & 0.36 & 1.15 & 0.00 & 0.90 & 0.16 \\ 0.00 & 0.00 & 0.00 & 0.00 & 0.00 & 0.00 & 1.67 & 0.00 & 0.00 & 0.83 & 0.00 & 0.00 \\ 0.00 & 0.00 & 0.00 & 0.00 & 0.00 & 0.00 & 0.00 & 1.32 & 0.44 & 1.00 & 0.78 & 0.23 \\ 0.00 & 0.00 & 0.00 & 0.00 & 0.00 & 0.00 & 0.00 & 0.00 & 0.00 & 0.73 & 0.00 & 0.00 \\ 0.00 & 0.00 & 0.00 & 0.00 & 0.00 & 0.00 & 0.00 & 0.00 & 0.86 & 1.00 & 0.24 & 0.61 \\ 0.00 & 0.00 & 0.00 & 0.00 & 0.00 & 0.00 & 0.00 & 0.00 & 0.00 & 0.00 & 0.14 & 0.48 \\ 0.00 & 0.00 & 0.00 & 0.00 & 0.00 & 0.00 & 0.00 & 0.00 & 0.00 & 0.00 & 0.00 & 0.00 \\ 0.00 & 0.00 & 0.00 & 0.00 & 0.00 & 0.00 & 0.00 & 0.00 & 0.00 & 0.00 & 0.00 & 0.15 \\ 0.00 & 0.00 & 0.00 & 0.00 & 0.00 & 0.00 & 0.00 & 0.00 & 0.00 & 0.00 & 0.00 & 0.00 \end{bmatrix}$$

With the matrix $\mathcal{S}_G$, we can create the network between the IoCs. The edges are directed according to the *timestamp* value associated with each IoC. Figure 14.2 shows the resulting network.

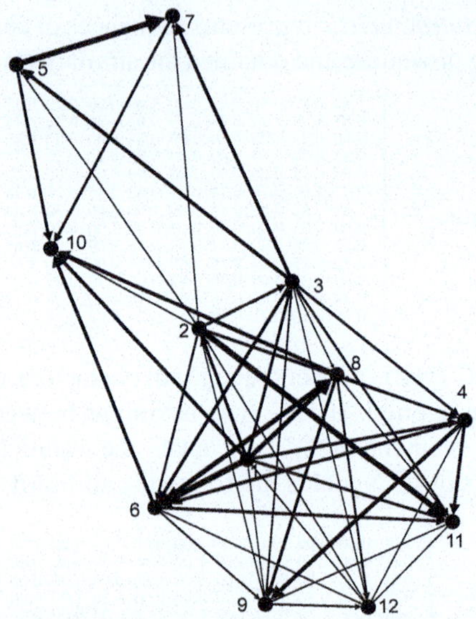

Fig. 14.2 Network generated from random dataset

Table 14.2 shows the weighted distance matrix for this network from which we can identify closely related nodes and obtain betweenness centrality and PageRank scores. For example, we find that node 6 is closest to node 1, with a minimum distance score of 0.40, and farthest from node 12, with a maximum distance score of 1.62.

Table 14.2 Weighted distance matrix

	1	2	3	4	5	6	7	8	9	10	11	12
1		0.78	0.85	0.82	1.49	0.40	1.52	0.53	1.31	0.68	0.92	1.64
2			0.95	0.92	1.63	1.09	1.63	1.30	1.50	1.46	0.41	2.41
3				0.98	0.68	0.77	0.68	1.28	1.38	1.45	1.09	2.39
4					1.66	0.80	1.66	1.31	0.59	1.47	0.75	2.00
5						1.45	0.41	1.49	2.06	0.82	1.77	2.60
6							1.45	0.51	1.30	0.68	0.87	1.62
7								1.61	2.06	0.93	1.77	2.72
8									0.79	0.68	1.44	1.11
9										1.47	1.34	1.41
10											1.55	1.79
11												2.49
12												

Table 14.3 gives the weighted betweenness centrality and PageRank scores. Whereas nodes 3 and 8 score highest on the former, node 1 is the most influential in the network.

Table 14.3 Score table

Node	weighted betweenness centrality	PageRank score
1	9	0.29
2	0	0.17
3	22	0.12
4	4	0.07
5	0	0.05
6	13	0.06
7	0	0.04
8	22	0.05
9	2	0.04
10	10	0.03
11	0	0.04
12	0	0.03

In our model, the prediction quality improves with every recursive step that brings new information to the network. We illustrate this effect with our example dataset by adding a new IoC as follows, then we examine how the scores and network topologies change. Table 14.4 provides the values for the novel IoC.

Table 14.4 Additional information from a novel IoC

IoC #	IoC type	Boolean characteristic	Numerical characteristic	String characteristic	Timestamp
13	domain	1	3127	xyloresed	1674721967

This novel IoC is now compared to all pairs of IoCs already in the network in order to compute the similarity scores. The resulting vector

$$(\varrho^G_{p,D})_{p\in[1,D]} = \left[0.53\ 0.45\ 0.50\ 1.52\ 0.29\ 0.43\ 0.31\ 0.24\ 1.17\ 0.25\ 0.46\ 0.18\right]$$

now becomes the 13-th column of the matrix S_G, and a new row with zeroes must be added to preserve its square property. Figure 14.3 shows the new network topology once the novel IoCs is added. The above operations are then repeated. Table 14.5 shows the new entries for the revised weighted distance matrix, and Table 14.6 gives the revised betweenness centrality and PageRank scores.

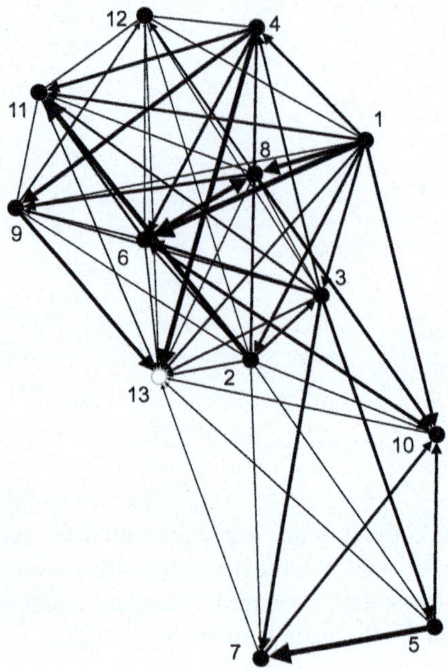

Fig. 14.3 Network topology after addition of 13th IoC

Table 14.5 Weighted distance table for novel IoC no. 13

Nodes	1	2	3	4	5	6	7	8	9	10	11	12	13
13	1.21	1.30	1.29	0.43	1.94	1.19	1.94	1.31	0.55	1.83	1.14	1.90	

Table 14.6 Revised score table after addition of 13th IoC

Node	weighted betweenness centrality	PageRank score
1	9	0.28
2	0	0.17
3	26	0.12
4	14	0.07
5	0	0.05
6	15	0.06
7	0	0.04
8	22	0.05
9	6	0.04
10	10	0.03
11	0	0.04
12	0	0.03
13	0	0.03

In this example, the addition of more information reduces the distance between the novel and the incumbent nodes, so that the results the algorithm renders become more accurate as more information is entered and matched. Hence, the model does not require the exhaustive set of all IoCs to run; it can work with smaller subsets which can then be gradually expanded as new information comes in. While no node alters its position in either centrality ranking once the novel information is entered, the scores are adjusted, which suggests that novel information helps to refine the predicted relatedness of nodes in the network.

14.4 Conclusion

We have offered a model that can spot and classify similarities and relatedness in a network of IoCs. The betweenness centrality scores allow analysts to identify IoCs which link together many other IoCs. Hence, they can identify specific incidents which are the root for subsequent anomalies. The PageRank scores inform them about the most influential IoC in the network, so they can recognize incidents which may have gone unnoticed but continue to exert influence on others. Finally, the distance from a focal to other IoCs lets them recognize the relative degree of similarity between incidents. Due to the recursive construction of our model, these analyses become more refined and more accurate the more IoCs are added to an extant network. There is hence a trade-off between precision and timeliness that analysts can exploit. For example, they can restrict the number of IoCs under scrutiny and first study those which are most related to their defensive goals. Defenders can use these insights to organize a defense that can not only respond faster once a threat is detected, but also more accurately. They can use the results our model provides to collocate related IoCs into comprehensive threat warnings which describe the relatedness between IoCs with a minimum of human error.

The model we propose is scalable and free, and the generalizable nature of its analytics implies it can accommodate a wide range of platforms and features. Still, the model could be extended in a number of ways. First, network theory offers a wide range of additional diagnostics—e.g., percolation centrality, assortativity, or spread—which have not employed in our short demonstration due to limited space [1]. Still, these would be useful to improve the assessment of the relative position and importance of particular nodes. Further, analysts could add IoCs authors to the analysis in order to obtain a bipartite network by which influential individuals who report many or influential IoCs could be identified. Future research may also explore how our model could predict the emergence of novel IoC based on the extant threat landscape, e.g., by adding a link prediction analysis procedure to the model.

References

1. Albert, R., & Barabási, A. L. (2002). Statistical mechanics of complex networks. *Reviews of Modern Physics, 74*(1), 47.
2. Balduzzi, D., & Tononi, G. (2008). Integrated information in discrete dynamical systems: Motivation and theoretical framework. *PLoS Computational Biology, 4*(6), e1000091.
3. Barabási, A. L., & Albert, R. (1999). Emergence of scaling in random networks. *Science, 286*(5439), 509–512.
4. Barabási, A. L., & Bonabeau, E. (2003). Scale-free networks. *Scientific American, 288*(5), 60–69.
5. Biau, G., & Scornet, E. (2016). A random forest guided tour. *TEST, 25*(2), 197–227.
6. Boccaletti, S., Latora, V., Moreno, Y., Chavez, M., & Hwang, D.-U. (2006). Complex networks: Structure and dynamics. *Physics Reports, 424*, 175–308.
7. Cambria, E., & White, B. (2014). Jumping NLP curves: A review of natural language processing research. *IEEE Computational Intelligence Magazine, 9*(2), 48–57.
8. Cutler, A., Cutler, D. R., & Stevens, J. R. (2012). Random forests. In C. Zhang & Y. Ma (Eds.), *Ensemble Machine Learning* (pp. 157–175). Boston, MA: Springer.
9. Engel, D., & Malone, T. W. (2018). Integrated information as a metric for group interaction. *PloS One, 13*(10), e0205335.
10. Freeman, L. C. (1978). Centrality in social networks: Conceptual clarification. *Social Networks, 1*(3), 215–239.
11. Gillard, S., Percia David, D., Mermoud, A., & Maillart, T. (2022). Efficient collective action for tackling time-critical cybersecurity threats. arXiv:2206.15055
12. Kokkonen, T., Hautamaki, J., Siltanen, J., & Hamalainen, T. (2016). Model for sharing the information of cyber security situation awareness between organizations. In *Proceedings of the IEEE 23rd International Conference on Telecommunications (ICT)* (pp. 1–5).
13. Maimon, O., & Rokach, L. (eds.). (2005). *Data mining and knowledge discovery handbook*. Springer Science & Business Media.
14. Miao, J., & Zhu, W. (2022). Precision-recall curve (PRC) classification trees. *Evolutionary Intelligence, 15*(3), 1545–1569.
15. Opsahl, T., Agneessens, F., & Skvoretz, J. (2010). Node centrality in weighted networks: Generalizing degree and shortest paths. *Social Networks, 32*(3), 245–251.
16. Page, L., Brin, S., Motwani, R., & Winograd, T. (1999). *The Pagerank citation ranking: Bringing order to the web*. Stanford InfoLab.

17. Schaeffer, S. (2007). Graph clustering. *Computer Science Review, 1*(1), 27–64.
18. Strogatz, S. (2001). Exploring complex networks. *Nature, 410*(6825), 268–276.
19. Sun, N., Zhang, J., Rimba, P., Gao, S., Zhang, L. Y., & Xiang, Y. (2019). Data-driven cybersecurity incident prediction: A survey. *IEEE Communications Surveys & Tutorials, 21*(2), 1744–1772.
20. Watts, D. J., & Strogatz, S. (1998). Collective dynamics of 'small-world' networks. *Nature, 393*(6684), 440–442.

Sébastien Gillard received an MSc in Physics from the University of Fribourg (Switzerland) in 2016. He specializes in computational physics and statistics, in particular, data analysis and applied statistical modeling and analytical and numerical resolution methods for differential equations. His current research interest is the application of insights from recommender systems to critical infrastructure defense, including the development of code that can power deep learning algorithms.

Cédric Aeschlimann is a researcher at the Department of Defense Economics at the Military Academy of the Swiss Federal Institute of Technology (ETH) Zurich. Before returning to academia, he worked for the Swiss Federal Department of Foreign Affairs and the United Nations Development Fund. His research topics focus on the application of social networks for policy-making. He holds an MA in public management from the University of Geneva.

Chapter 15
International Law and Cyber Defense Best Practices: The Way Forward

Sara Pangrazzi and Fabian Muhly

15.1 International Law and the Cyberspace

Back in 2010, the computer worm stuxnet which disabled the Iranian centrifuges that were supposed to enrich uranium, made legal scholars question the extent to which international law could be applied to the cyberspace, and if so, how it would have to be interpreted [6].

Traditionally, (public) international law is conceived of as an instrument by which statehood is applied in an international political context. It refers to all legally binding rules and principles (norms) that apply at the international level and concerns the responsibilities of nation-states and their behavior toward one another. Although there is not just one set of rules or approaches to international law, the totality of these norms regulates the behavior of nation-states by providing predictable, reciprocal patterns based on common rules, and thus contributes to creating peace and stability [19]. Usually, these norms bind states as a matter of customary international law, general principles of law or through bi- or multilaterally ratified treaties [18].

In this process, the United Nations (UN), multi- or bilateral treaty bodies, and international courts play an important role since they help shape these norms and provide arbitration and intervention mechanisms. The 'publicness' of these bodies

The original version of the chapter was revised: Chapter author corrections have been updated. The correction to this chapter is available at https://doi.org/10.1007/978-3-031-30191-9_16

S. Pangrazzi (✉)
Institute of International Law and Comparative Constitutional Law, University of Zurich, Zurich, Switzerland
e-mail: sara.pangrazzi@uzh.ch

F. Muhly
Department of Defense Economics, Military Academy at the Swiss Federal Institute of Technology Zurich, Birmensdorf, Switzerland
e-mail: fabian.muhly@milak.ethz.ch

M. M. Keupp (ed.), *Cyberdefense*, International Series in Operations Research & Management Science 342,
https://doi.org/10.1007/978-3-031-30191-9_15

appears as a supranational extension of statehood and is an important factor that contributes to the realizing of a global governance regime which helps states develop [19]. Particularly with respect to the cyberspace and its defense, such international norms are increasingly important since they can help reduce the risks to statehood, sovereignty, and prosperity that unprotected or undefended technology may imply [30, 34].

The broad (and mostly extraterritorial) dependence on the cyberspace does not only internationally interconnect states, but also pose important questions on how to approach security and defense in the digital realm [13]. The unrelenting stream of reports about both criminal and state-sponsored actors who attack others in the cyberspace for personal or political gains has led some scholars to question the relevance—or even the existence—of norms for the cyberspace. These positions paint the picture of a 'wild west' cybersphere, portraying it as an unregulated and dangerous field, where the application of norms is difficult if not impossible, and where attackers can hide in faraway jurisdictions. Moreover, nation-states which were not even attacked in the first place could nevertheless suffer damage from spillover effects or damaged cross-border infrastructures. These issues motivate some to posit that novel norms are required to secure the cyberspace (for more detailed discussions, see [7, 29, 41]).

Likewise, the international community of states has been quarreling for some time over the question if, in the context of international security, there are any applicable norms for the cyberspace at all [6, 40]. In September 2019, during the session at the United Nations' Open-Ended Working Group (OEWG) which was established by General Assembly resolution 73/27 to advance the discussion on responsible state behavior in cyberspace in the context of international security, some countries claimed that there was a need for a new and specifically tailored legal framework to fill the existing 'legal vacuum' [23, 43].

15.2 The Transformation Challenge

We believe that such views somewhat fail to understand the nature and applicability of extant norms. They are based on the assumption that the cyberspace is a new and inherently different 'field' or 'domain' of state conduct. According to these perspectives, international law could not be applied in cyberspace unless supported by sufficient evidence of domain-specific state practice and *opinio juris* [2]. However, international law governs *all* technology used by state and non-state actors, be it old or new, physical or digital (see more in dept and with further references on this argument: [2]). Hence, historically grown, extant norms and binding rules are generally applicable to the cyberspace, even if they were not conceived with a particular technological background in mind, or if they were written before contemporary information technology even existed. The fact that, to date, states have only hardly applied norms from international law to the cyberspace does not imply that these norms are irrelevant. There is hence no liability to specifically prove that a particular norm also applies to the cyberspace, and there is no overarching need to create 'novel' or 'domain-specific' norms [2, 17].

Furthermore, open disputes notwithstanding, a growing number of governments support the view that extant international law is applicable to the cyberspace. In this regard, throughout the last years, the mentioned UN-processes that were established to advance the discussion on state behavior in cyberspace in the context of international security have generated much improvement in terms of establishing a more transparent understanding of the application of international norms deriving from international law. Although nation-states do drive the development of international law, international organizations thus provide important fora to that end [6]. In this sense, at the 2013 and 2015 United Nations Group of Governmental Experts on Information Security (UN GGE), states agreed in the respective final reports that international law and the principles of the UN Charter do apply to states' activities in cyberspace [32]. Both reports were subsequently endorsed by the UN General Assembly [12]. NATO's Wales Summit declaration contains a likewise statement [25]. More recently, the Final Substantive Report of the OEWG reaffirmed that international law is applicable and essential to maintaining peace, security, and stability in the information and communications technology environment; this report was consensually adopted by *all* UN member states [2, 44]. Also, the UN GGE report that was adopted in May 2021 [33] reaffirms the general agreement that international law also applies to the activities states pursue in cyberspace, as well as to the digital infrastructure within their territory and under their jurisdiction. This seems particularly noteworthy as the UN GGE failed to produce a consensus report since their last one in 2015. Therefore, should states decide to engage in law-making processes through the establishment of new rules by treaties or new customary international law, they are not building on a legal vacuum, but rather are bound by and build upon existing frameworks [2].

It is true that the development of a common understanding and consensus on how to apply (or develop) international norms proceeds at a rather moderate pace. As the example of nuclear disarmament and control treaties shows, states take time to learn how to respond to disruptive technological change, and how to establish rules or institutions which can address it [30]. It took the international community about twenty years to reach first cooperative agreements in the nuclear era [28]. Today, about thirteen years after the stuxnet incident, the discourse surrounding responsible state behavior in cyberspace is still ongoing, but the frequency of academic contributions and reports by international gremia increases steadily [6]. Among others, the two Tallinn Manuals published in 2013 and 2017 and official state positions have contributed to substantive transparency and precision of some of the open normative questions concerning the cyberspace and international security [35, 36]. Furthermore, there are national laws and regional or international treaties that address cybersecurity issues, all of which can be also relevant to questions on effective cyber defense and resilience. In addition, industry-specific, cross-industry, and topic-oriented standards, some of which even qualify as soft law, can also play important (and more agile) guiding roles [47].

However, while information technology develops rapidly, governmental, legal, and societal efforts develop at a much more moderate pace. Although skeptical views tend to criticize this, the stability that is eventually obtained through a proactive but thoughtful process should not be underestimated. As is the case with the shaping of international norms, they are typically proposed and heralded by a group of states until they are eventually adopted by a wider community [11]. This—if lengthy—multilateral way by which these norms are developed raises the cost of non-compliant behavior [29] while keeping the involved parties 'on board'. Thereby, the multilateralization of such a process is an important factor that helps to strenghten the normative value of the underlying norms [30]. These developments are often accompanied by processes coordinated by international institutions such as the United Nations, the Council of Europe, the OECD, the WTO, and other bi- or multilateral fora. In principle, these processes are no different for the cyber defense context: For example, such a multilateralization process did and does take place with the OEWG. The OEWG, for the first time, constitutes an inclusive platform for dialogue among *all* states on the developments in the field of cyber and international security. Thereby, *every* UN-member state world-wide can access and engage in the discussions—which most of them actually do (see the broad participation of states in the final report 2021 [44]).

The OEWG process provides member states with an active platform to discuss how norms should be interpreted and applied [44]. Thus, the normative and multilateral value grows with the number of states subscribing to this consensus. Globally agreed norms provide transparency and expectations about behavior that can hold other states accountable and thus motivate predictable action. A deliberate pace of development is the price to be paid for this consensus. Once it exists, the norms in question can legitimize official actions and help states gain multilateral support when they decide that a norm has been violated [30]. Therefore, norms are not rendered irrelevant even if they are violated, and their compliance can be encouraged the more states have subscribed to a consensus that the norm in question should be applied and upheld. Convergence about the applicability of extant norms to the cyberspace is reached slowly and incrementally but can be considered effective in the long term. Therefore, the current process in relation to the clarification of cyber norms does not structurally differ from prior examples in legal history [6, 30].

However, as noted before, international state policy and defense in the cyberspace is not confronted with a 'legal vacuum' even if no domain-specific norms exist. With international law, an international regulatory framework *already exists* from which guidelines for application can be deducted. The issue at hand is not necessarily one of creating novel norms, but rather of understanding their scope and potential for application to the cyberspace. The challenge is therefore one of *transformation*: A process by which extant international norms are translated into national standards and legislation. For example, with respect to cybercrime, international frameworks such as the Budapest Convention (Council of Europe, ETS 185) exist, but, in principle, each state must transform and translate its provisions to the specific national contexts [4, 8].

The responsibility for this implementation process is not with international bodies, but ultimately with nation-states themselves. What [16] meant with a technical view to system security—'the challenge to defend infrastructure against intentional attacks is an architectural one'—certainly also applies to nation-states who must translate international norms into their legal landscapes.

In this sense, as extant international law applies to the cyber context, it can be deducted that there are international obligations that require states to secure certain national (critical) infrastructure or technological domains in order to not cause damage that is or may be relevant to public national and international security [2]. It therefore follows that meeting said obligations would require nation-states to contribute to an effective defense of such infrastructure. Thereby, the present understanding of 'cyber defense' primarily refers to an effective *protection* of digital infrastructure against cyberattacks. In order to be able to effectively protect digital infrastructure from being infected, this involves taking steps to prevent malicious cyber actions before actual (and large scale) harm occurs. States who want to achieve effective cyber defense should therefore focus on endeavours that support and enhance the resilience of infrastructures and networks [14]. In this regard, any resilience-based national defense requires, in the first place, a decent and clear understanding of national cyber landscapes. States should know about critical infrastructures and businesses, and also constantly assess vulnerable points, dependencies, and measures that can mitigate the consequences of large-scale cyber incidents [13].

However, achieving such progress is difficult since states must not only reflect about how they may apply, comply with, and implement existing and useful frameworks to that end, but also about the individual economic and technological capabilities at their disposal [6]. Furthermore, since a comprehensive and effective cyber defense that covers the complete attack surface of a state is highly complex, decentralized, and thus difficult to organize, a preventive and holistic approach toward cyber defense is key. We suggest that states could focus on four areas that are not only essential but also most promising to help transform and implement an effective cyber defense.

15.3 The Implementation Agenda

First, many obstacles stand in the way of effective security information sharing, as many chapters in this volume have noted and detailed. The sharing of relevant security information can be key to fastly and effectively detect and defend against cyberattacks as quite often various organizations can be affected by the same threat actor or by the same (large-scale) cyber campaign. States should therefore facilitate and encourage the (voluntary) sharing and reporting of relevant information to national govCERTS or other relevant incident response and security teams and networks. Note that this need not necessarily just entail mandatory security breach reporting as it already exists in several states or regional agreements (see for instance the reporting obligations according to the General Data Protection Regulation in the European Union [46] or in the more recently passed US Cyber Incident Reporting for Critical Infrastructure Act of 2022 (CIRCIA)). The important point is to create an environment that both significantly reduces the transaction cost of sharing and establishes trust between participants, so that ultimately every party benefits from such a collaboration. For example, in Switzerland, the National Cyber Security Center and its govCERT have been created with this goal in mind (among others). It understands cybersecurity as a joint task of society, the business community and the state, with shared (but different) responsibilities [26]. To that end, awareness raising and the building of trust are central aspects that accompany any such intersectoral interplay. Additionally, states can inform and sensitize about *why* information sharing can be crucial for cybersecurity and motivate individuals and organizations to contribute to relevant information sharing, or could even support open communities such as useful public information sharing platforms like the Open Source Threat Intelligence and Sharing Platform MISP (that is co-funded by the European Union). The access to a large amount of security threat information through such communities or national govCERTS allows for the aggregation of information in order to understand (and possibly predict) a bigger picture of technically accumulating risks. And if the added value of such cooperation and security information sharing is visible and comprehensible for every participant, this can contribute to a constructive cooperative environment (that could ultimately increase the security and defense of several IT systems).

Second, states should facilitate bi- and multilateral cooperative agreements as well as agreements between a nation-state and its private industry to harness civilian competence for national cyber defense. For example, NATO's Cooperative Cyber Defense Centre of Excellence [5] facilitates the exchange of security and defense information across NATO allies. As is the case with security information sharing, such cooperations will only prove fruitful if the transaction cost of entering and managing them remains low, and if productive outcomes of successful collaborative action are rewarded. Reciprocal conditions are necessary for an effective cooperation, but where this is not the case, national governments could step in and balance, coordinate, or encourage cooperation.

Public-private cooperation is an often discussed concept that appears to be very promising in the cyber (defense) context. As an often cited example, the private IT industry in Israel cooperates intensively with the government to develop and apply cyber defense technology, both within and across sectors, since the state and its national legislation provide them with incentives to do so [38]. Switzerland, for its part, has an established approach to public-private partnerships, which is primarily based on voluntary participation [3]. Nevertheless, the public-private cooperation landscape in the cyber domain is increasingly evolving too. And since many critical infrastructures are not only decentralized in terms of their IT posture but also privately run, the private sector takes an important role and initiative itself. For example, the sectoral network of the Swiss Bankers Association—note the banking sector is typically considered to have an advanced cyber security posture and network—incentivizes its members to cooperate on best practices and to jointly exploit expertise in cyber security and the defense of IT systems. Although this industry association primarily focuses on the banking sector, it stresses the fact that cooperation on cyber defense issues generates a public good which also protects the economy as a whole.

It therefore recommends cooperation to a wider public and states that future success depends on a close collaboration between the authorities and the private sector. In this sense, states can help create an environment that develops useful public-private partnerships which facilitate reciprocity and inter-industry exchange of information.

For example, in the United States, the Cyber Testing for Resilient Industrial Control Systems (CyTRICS), which is affiliated with the US Department of Energy, connects national laboratories and stakeholders from private industry to leverage analytic and defense capabilities in the energy sector [45]. It is based on the premise that human society and urban life in particular depend on critical infrastructures which often consist of and are controlled by physical components which are operative for decades before they are replaced. CyTRICS focuses on high-priority critical infrastructure and motivates vendors to supply bills of materials used to construct these infrastructures in order to identify specific vulnerabilities, and to share these with state authorities. This mapping is important, since the vendor can resolve information asymmetry between operators and state agencies at little cost; moreover, while vulnerabilities may be known for a specific component in isolation, they often are not mapped to all systems that use this particular component.

Additionally, CyTRICS can identify novel vulnerabilities by an intricate testing process that involves vendors and lets them immediately patch any weaknesses. Further, it involves key stakeholders, such as technology developers, manufacturers, asset owners and operators, and interagency partners in this process, in order to identify high-priority operational technology components, perform expert testing, share information about vulnerabilities in the digital supply chain, and inform about improvements in component design and manufacturing. Components with high impact, prevalence, and relevance to national security are prioritized for testing and analysis.

Thus, once a company joins this network, it is provided with a visible (and marketable) performance indicator and written certificates about the safety of its technology and the measures it took to guarantee it, so that the firm can improve its reputation in the marketplace. In return, it must cooperate and disclose relevant cyber security information in order to enjoy these benefits. This ends up in a win-win(-win) situation to both the state (1. win) and the participating energy sector entities (2. win), which ultimately even increases overall cyber security of very critical IT systems for the broader public (3. win).

Third, effective cyber defense does not only involve technical, but also human factors. Whenever the members of a human society interact digitally, vulnerabilities are spread across the state, and those who interact—be it as an individual or as a member of a bigger (critical) infrastructure—may become targets that can be relevant for critical state functions [13]. Any cyber defense or national cyber security measures are therefore intricately linked to society in general. Therefore, national cyber defense could be understood as a 'societal defense problem', since the resources a state must deploy to defend the attack surface of the whole society (and its critical infrastructures and services) are largely located outside the military and even government itself' (see more in depth on the concept of a "societal defense problem" in relation to national cyber defense: [13]). Governments and their militaries consequently not only benefit from, but highly depend on human and societal factors even when it comes to the security and defense of core state functions [9]. As a result, coordinated efforts across society are required, so that information and education campaigns are paramount.

Since there is a global skill shortage of about 3.5 million cybersecurity specialists [22], education becomes a key field where states could stimulate the development of cyber defense knowledge and capabilities. Hence, states should facilitate education and awareness programs which convey relevant knowledge and skills not only to prospective specialists, but also to the general public. Such programs could begin as early as during secondary education. National boards of education could revise their teaching curricula—e.g., by including serious games [24]—to equip as broadly a cohort as possible with relevant knowledge about the cyberspace and its protection. The same arguments also apply to tertiary education, and there are first initiatives to coordinate education and awareness programs on a supranational level. For example, COLTRANE is a cybersecurity awareness education community across Europe and a strategic partnership under the ERASMUS+ program that tries to modernize and standardize cybersecurity education across Europe [21]. States could take this pan-European cooperation in the education sector as an example to reflect how similar programs could be created on the national level.

Fourth and finally, an effective prevention and defense against cyberattacks goes hand in hand with robust law enforcement mechanisms. While the underlying legal regime of cybercrime as a matter of criminal justice needs to be distinguished from the context of national and international security, the very general goal of *preventing* such attacks in practice is largely the same. Therefore, states should continue to jointly develop standards and find ways to facilitate the prosecution of cyber incidents, even across territorial borders [39]. Since cybercrime can also compromise the homeland security of a state once crucial supply chains, hospitals, or energy providers are attacked, effective law enforcement mechanisms which thwart such crimes may also improve a state's national defense posture.

However, while cyber attacks (also by cyber criminals) mostly have a transnational component, law enforcement is often impeded by jurisdictional boundaries between states. Moreover, law enforcement is not only partitioned between different sub-domains of legal studies (e.g., criminal law, data protection law, public law) but also by disciplinary boundaries. Legal scholars thus should learn and be more comfortable in collaborating with technical specialists. The postmodern world will have to further strengthen and enhance an interdisciplinary and holistic way of approaching complex digital realities and of building bridges between domains. And in order to address the transnational dimension, supranational law enforcement mechanisms are required. The Budapest Convention on cybercrime is an ideal example for an international instrument that was created with this agenda in mind. As of April 2023, 68 countries have ratified the convention. It sets both guiding international norms and requires all signatories to adapt and harmonize national laws to comply with its principles [27, 37, 48]. Also, EUROPOL, Europe's joint law enforcement agency, has benefitted from legislation that allows law enforcement agencies to coordinate across borders [10].

15.4 Conclusion

In principle, international norms and evolving best practices can enhance and encourage an effective prevention of and defense against cyberattacks. Moreover, states are not acting in a legal vacuum when it comes to their international obligations toward another state. Precisely because a state is required to fulfill its obligations under international law, it will have to find ways to improve its national (cyber) security posture that—in the face of unrelenting transnational cyberattacks—may become relevant for national and international security. Ultimately, any effective defense of (critical) cyber infastructure, even in the military context, will significantly come down to core (and socially broad) cyber hygiene.

Thus, while states continue to explore their best ways to transform and implement security in their national contexts, they can deploy a range of tools that could entail security improvement efforts for bigger (internationally interconnected) critical sectors to security and awareness improvements for individual digital devices that are used by the broader civil society [1]. However, states can not only create legislation but also help create a favorable environment in which different actors can practically contribute to realize effective cyber defense. For example, economic mechanisms that facilitate self-governance and public-private cooperation between different stakeholders and technology leaders. The role of government is not necessarily restricted to top-down instructions which needs to consist in strictly directing or monitoring individual action; rather, it can also stimulate awareness, use market-based incentives and institutions that motivate, support, enable, or engage individuals who create and contribute to overall (and more "bottom-up") cyber defense. Since all of these stakeholders are digitally interconnected, the effectiveness of overall cyber defense largely depends on the interplay and contribution of every stakeholder. Hence, these collaborative environments will inherently have to be built on broad (and not least also social) trust and partnerships in order to be efficient.

While each state will build upon its own national norms and governmental landscape, international law seems to unite all such endeavors by setting commonly defined goals and directions. Although cyber technologies that are maliciously exploited can negatively affect both states and their civilizations, these technologies have ultimately been built by and for human beings in order to satisfy social, political, cultural, and economic needs. Even if the global impact of said technologies implies new layers of complexity and new ways to create and implement security, the legal side that addresses the human conduct responsible for this security remains very much grounded in the "real" world [2]. After all, cyber issues and the question of effective defense will remain integral to the existing geopolitical context, and state policy is and will be as relevant to the cyberspace as it is to the physical world [15].

References

1. Achten, N. (2021). *Governance approaches to the security of digital products*. Swiss Federal Institute of Technology Zurich: Geneva Dialogue of responsible behavior in cyberspace.
2. Akande, D., Coco, A., & de Souza, Dias T. (2022). Drawing the cyber baseline: The applicability of existing international law to the governance of information and communication technologies. *International Law Studies, 99*, 4–36.
3. Baezner, M., & Cordey, S. (2019). National cybersecurity strategies in comparison–Challenges for Switzerland. Center for Security Studies (CSS), ETH Zurich, March 2019.
4. Bande, L. (2018). Legislating against cyber crime in southern African development community: Balancing international standards with country-specific specificities. *International Journal of Cyber Criminology, 12*(1), 9–26.
5. Bernal, A., Monterrubio, S., Fuente, J., Crespo, R., & Verdu, E. (2021). Methodology for computer security incident response teams into IoT strategy. *KSII Transactions on Internet and Information Systems (TIIS), 15*(5), 1909–1928.
6. Broeders, D., de Busser, E., Cristiano, F., & Tropina, T. (2022). Revisiting past cyber operations in light of new cyber norms and interpretations of international law: Inching towards lines in the sand? *Journal of Cyber Policy, 7*(1), 97–135.
7. Buchan, R. (2016). Cyberspace, non-state actors and the obligation to prevent transboundary harm. *Journal of Conflict and Security Law, 21*(3), 429–453.
8. Clough, J. (2014). A world of difference: The budapest convention on cybercrime and the challenges of harmonisation. *Monash University Law Review, 40*(3), 698–736.
9. Dunn-Cavelty, M., & Suter, M. (2009). Public-Private Partnerships are no silver bullet: An expanded governance model for Critical Infrastructure Protection. *International Journal of Critical Infrastructure Protection*, 2(4), 179–187.
10. Europol. (2022). Cybercrime. https://www.europol.europa.eu/crime-areas-and-statistics/crime-areas/cybercrime.
11. Finnemore, M., & Sikkink, K. (1998). International norm dynamics and political change. *International Organization, 52*(4), 887–917.
12. GA Res. 70/237 (December 30, 2015).
13. Griffith, M. K. (2020). *The mice that roar: What small countries can teach great powers about national cyber-defense*. Berkeley: University of California.
14. Inversini, R. (2020). Cyber peace: And how it can be achieved. In M. Christen, B. Gordijn, M. Loi (Eds.), *The ethics of cybersecurity (The international library of ethics, law and technology)* (Vol. 21, pp. 259–276). Cham: Springer.
15. Keohane, R. O., & Nye, J. S. (1998). Power and interdependence in the information age. *Foreign Affairs, 77*, September/October 1998.
16. Keupp, M. M. (2020). *The security of critical infrastructures* (pp. 1–14). Cham: Springer Nature.
17. Koh, H. (2012). International law in cyberspace. *Harvard International Law Journal, 54*, December 2012. https://harvardilj.org/wp-content/uploads/sites/15/2012/12/Koh-Speech-to-Publish1.pdf
18. Kunz, J. L. (1953). General international law and the law of international organizations. *American Journal of International Law, 47*(3), 456–462.
19. Koskenniemi, M. (2017). International Law as "Global Governance". In *Searching for Contemporary Legal Thought*, Chap. 5 (pp. 199–218). Cambridge University Press.
20. Kulesza, J. (2016). Applying the due diligence principle–cybersecurity and national security issues. In *Due Diligence in International Law (Queen Mary Studies in International Law)*, Brill Nijhoff (Vol. 26, pp. 276–302).
21. Langner, G., Andriessen, J., Quirchmayr, G., Furnell, S., Scarano, V., & Tokola, T. J. (2021). The need for a collaborative approach to cyber security education. In *Proceedings of the 2021 IEEE European Symposium on Security and Privacy (Euro S&P)* (pp. 719–721).
22. Morgan, S. (2021). Cybersecurity jobs report: 3.5 million openings in 2025. Cybercrime Magazine, November 9, 2021.

23. Moynihan, H. (2019). The application of international law to cyberspace: Sovereignty and non-intervention. Just Security, December 13, 2019.
24. Muhly, F., Leo, P., & Caneppele, S. (2021). A serious game for social engineering awareness creation. *Journal of Cybersecurity Education, Research and Practice, 1*, 5.
25. NATO. (2014). Wales Summit declaration. North Atlantic Treaty Organization, September 5, 2014. https://www.nato.int/cps/en/natohq/official_texts_112964.htm.
26. National Cyber Security Centre NCSC, Principles, https://www.ncsc.admin.ch/ncsc/en/home/strategie/grundsaetze.html (last modification 13.04.2023).
27. Nguyen, C., & Golman, W. (2021). Diffusion of the Budapest Convention on cybercrime and the development of cybercrime legislation in Pacific Island countries: 'Law on the books' versus 'law in action'. *Computer Law & Security Review, 40*, 105521.
28. Nye, J. S. (2018). How will new cybersecurity norms develop? *Project Syndicate International Security*, 8 March 2018.
29. Nye, J. S. (2022). The end of cyber-anarchy? How to build a new digital order. *Foreign Affairs, 101*, December 14, 2021.
30. Nye, J. S. (2016). Deterrence and dissuasion in cyberspace. *International Security, 41*(3), 44–71.
31. OECD. (2022). Thinking out of the Competition Box: Enforcement Co-operation in Other Policy Areas, OECD Competition Policy Roundtable Background Note.
32. Report of the Group of Governmental Experts in the Field of Information and Telecommunications in the Context of International Security, UN Doc. A/68/98, June 24, 2013; Report of the Group of Governmental Experts on Developments in the Field of Information and Telecommunications in the Context of International Security, A/70/174, July 22, 2015.
33. Report of the Group of Governmental Experts on Advancing Responsible State Behaviour in Cyberspace in the Context of International Security, UN Doc. A/76/135 (July 14, 2021).
34. Saxena, A. (2022). The near future of international law in cyberspace: Contentions and realities. *Digital Frontiers*, January 15, 2022. https://www.orfonline.org/expert-speak/the-near-future-of-international-law-in-cyberspace-contentions-and-realities/.
35. Schmitt, M. N. (Ed.). (2013). *Tallinn Manual on the international law applicable to cyber warfare*. Cambridge University Press.
36. Schmitt, M. N. (Ed.). (2017). *Tallinn manual 2.0 on the international law applicable to cyber operations*. Cambridge University Press.
37. Seger, A. (2011). The Budapest Convention 10 years on: Lessons learnt. ISP C, 167.
38. Tabansky, L. (2020). Israel defense forces and national cyber defense. *Connections, 19*(1), 45–62.
39. Tennis, M. M. (2020). A United Nations convention on cybercrime. *Capital University Law Review, 48*, 189–235.
40. Tikk-Ringas, E. (2012). *Developments in the field of information and telecommunication in the context of international security: Work of the UN First Committee 1998–2012*. Geneva: ICT4Peace Publishing.
41. Tsagourias, N. (2018). Law, borders and the territorialisation of cyberspace. *Indonesian Journal of International Law, 18*(4).
42. United Nations. (1948). Universal declaration of human rights. *General Assembly Resolution, 217*A III, Article 26(2).
43. United Nations. (2019). Open-Ended Working Group on developments in the field of information and telecommunications in the context of international security (9th meeting). Video recording, September 13, 2019. https://media.un.org/en/asset/k1x/k1xubugkf4.
44. United Nations. (2021). Final substantive report of the Open-Ended Working Group on developments in the field of information and telecommunications in the context of international security, U.N. Doc. A/AC.290/2021/CRP.2, March 10, 2021.
45. United States Department of Energy. (2022). CyTRICS: Vulnerability analysis tailored for critical infrastructure. Idaho National Lab, Idaho Falls ID, Report INL/CON-22-69227-Rev000. https://cytrics.inl.gov/.

46. Voss, W. G. (2016). European union data privacy law reform: General data protection regulation, privacy shield, and the right to delisting. *The Business Lawyer, 72*(1), 221–234.
47. Weber, R. H., & Yildiz, O. (2022). *Cybersicherheit und Cyber-Resilienz in den Finanzmärkten*, EIZ Publishing. https://eizpublishing.ch/wp-content/uploads/2022/04/Cybersicherheit-und-Cyber-Resilienz-in-den-Finanzmaerkten-Digital-V1_01-20220404.pdf.
48. Wicki-Birchler, D. (2020). The Budapest Convention and the general data protection regulation: Acting in concert to curb cybercrime? *International Cybersecurity Law Review, 1*(1), 63–72.

Sara Pangrazzi recently finished her PhD at the Institute of International Law and Comparative Constitutional Law at the University of Zurich (Switzerland). In her doctoral research she analyses the applicability of international law to cyberattacks. She holds a Bachelor and Master of Law degree from the University of Zurich. She was also a visiting fellow of the Hague Program for Cyber Norms, a visiting scholar at the Lauterpacht Centre for International Law at the University of Cambridge, and an associated researcher at the Digital Society Initiative of the University of Zurich.

Fabian Muhly holds a PhD in Criminology from the University of Lausanne (Switzerland) and a MA in Economics from the University of Fribourg (Switzerland). He is the co-founder of a cyber advisory start-up firm that consults on strategic aspects of cyber risks. He is also a member of EUROPOL's expert network in data protection and cybercrime and an affiliated lecturer for the International Master in Security, Intelligence and Strategic Studies at the University of Glasgow.

Correction to: International Law and Cyber Defense Best Practices: The Way Forward

Sara Pangrazzi and Fabian Muhly

Correction to:
Chapter 15 in: M. M. Keupp (ed.), *Cyberdefense*, International Series in Operations Research & Management Science 342, https://doi.org/10.1007/978-3-031-30191-9_15

The original version of the chapter was inadvertently published without incorporation of the final corrections, which have now been updated. The erratum chapter 15 has been updated with the changes.

The updated version of this chapter can be found at
https://doi.org/10.1007/978-3-031-30191-9_15

M. M. Keupp (ed.), *Cyberdefense*, International Series in Operations Research & Management Science 342, https://doi.org/10.1007/978-3-031-30191-9_16

The manufacturer's authorised representative in the EU is Springer Nature Customer Service Centre GmbH, Europaplatz 3, 69115 Heidelberg, Germany. If you have any concerns regarding our products, please contact ProductSafety@springernature.com

Printed and bound by CPI Group (UK) Ltd, Croydon, CR0 4YY
28/09/2026
02224077-0003